TUDOR BATH

Other books by John Wroughton:

The Routledge Companion to the Stuart Age, 1603-1714 (2006)

Stuart Bath: Life in the Forgotten City, 1603-1714 (2004)

450 Years: King Edward's School, Bath, 1552-2002 (2002)

Mr Colston's Hospital: The History of Colston's School, Bristol, (2002)

An Unhappy Civil War: the Experiences of Ordinary People in the West (1999)

The Stuart Age, 1603-1714 (1997)

A Community at War: the Civil War in Bath and North Somerset (1992)

King Edward's School at Bath, 1552-1982 (1982)

English Historical Facts, 1603-1688 (with Chris Cook, 1980)

Seventeenth Century Britain (1980)

Documents on World History (2 vols., with Denys Cook, 1976)

Bath in the Age of Reform (1972)

Documents on British Political History (3 vols., 1971)

Smuggling (with John Paxton, 1971)

Plots, Traitors and Spies (1970)

Cromwell and the Roundheads (1969)

TUDOR BATH

LIFE AND STRIFE IN THE 'LITTLE CITY'

1485-1603

JOHN WROUGHTON

It is but a little city, yet one of the most ancientest in England

(William Smith, *The Particular Description of England*, 1588)

THE LANSDOWN PRESS

First published in 2006 by
The Lansdown Press
41 The Empire   Grand Parade
Bath BA2 4DF

ISBN   0 9520249-6-9   (paperback edition)
ISBN   0 9520249-7-7   (cased edition)

Typeset in 11 / 13 Times New Roman
Typesetting, design and origination by
The Lansdown Press, Bath

Printed in Great Britain by
The Cromwell Press, Trowbridge, Wiltshire

Contents

Preface

As I worked on my book, *Stuart Bath: Life in the Forgotten City, 1603-1714*, I was soon struck by the realisation that the problems and controversies, which were emerging, could only be understood properly by tracing them back to their roots in the previous century. It quickly became apparent, however, that Tudor Bath - shrouded as it was by an impenetrable mist - was even more of a forgotten city than its successor. This book has therefore been written to fill that gap as a companion volume to *Stuart Bath* and is to be read alongside it.

Although many aspects of social life remained unchanged throughout the two hundred years (including security, public health, water supply and local government), I have tried to avoid repetition - hence the need to consult both volumes in order to gain the fullest picture. I have equally endeavoured to find a totally new set of illustrations for this book - although this task becomes more and more difficult the further back in history we go. Indeed, there are very few prints or drawings which relate specifically to Bath. Therefore, in order to illustrate aspects of life in the city (particularly religious activity), I have sometimes drawn on material from other areas so that the reader can visualise what was happening locally.

Documentary evidence, too, is much more limited - the Bath chamberlain's accounts, for instance, do not start until 1568, while existing council minute books are only available from the seventeenth century. On the other hand, the churchwardens' accounts of St Michael's Church Without, which have miraculously survived for the entire period, provide rich and colourful material on life in that parish.

Modern spellings have been adopted throughout in the numerous quotations from contemporary sources. The cost of items taken from documentary material has been left in its original 'old money' form. It should be remembered, therefore, that before decimalisation there were twelve old pence to the shilling - today worth five new pence - and twenty shillings to the pound. It should also be noted that the annual Bath chamberlain's accounts (which are used extensively throughout) initially covered a period from June to May in the following year - but later (by the end of the century) from October to the following September. As it is not normally possible therefore to pin-point whether an entry refers to one year or the next, the earlier date is always taken.

John Wroughton
August 2006

Acknowledgments

The author wishes to thank the following people who have contributed in various ways to the production of this book:

those who have provided original illustrations, including Elizabeth Fitzpatrick for two excellent pictures; the late Stephen Beck, a distinguished illustrator of historical books, for a number of imaginative and authentic line drawings; and Shane Feeney for his colourful impression of Queen Elizabeth's visit to the city in 1574, which has formed a superb basis for Martin Latham's striking cover design;

the staff of the British Library and the National Archives in London; the Bodleian Library in Oxford; the County Record Office in Taunton; and the City Record Office in Bath - for their courtesy and helpfulness in my research of documentary material;

the staff of the British Library; the Mary Evans Picture Library; the National Portrait Gallery Archive; the Pepys Library, Magdalene College, Cambridge; the Guildhall Library, London; the Bath Record Office; and the Folger Shakespeare Library, Washington, for their patient assistance and expertise in my search for contemporary illustrations;

individuals who have provided help over particular illustrations, including Dom Aiden Bellenger, Prior of Downside Abbey; Alan Morley; Michael Blandford at the Bishop's Palace in Wells; Pat Beck for permission to use Stephen's drawings; Kenneth Hylson-Smith; and the Rector of Bath Abbey;

other individuals, who have helped in various ways, including Elizabeth Holland, whose detailed knowledge of the people and buildings of the period has been invaluable; Allan Keevil for his expert knowledge on the Barton; Frank Thorn for offering meaning to a number of Latin terms in connection with the visit of Queen Elizabeth; and Rodney Morant not only for his painstaking correction of the typescript, but also for supplying a new translation of one crucial Latin document - though I would stress that any errors are mine and not theirs.

The copyright source of each illustration is acknowledged within the text.

John Wroughton

CHAPTER 1

1485: The Birth of the Tudor City

Nothing is more elegant and magnificent. Amongst [Bath's] charms are shady groves, flowery meadows,
pleasant streams, transparent fountains;..for the very hills themselves by which the city is surrounded
seem to smile and to diffuse a delight...so that the whole region round about may be rightly named a sort
of paradise, to which nothing in the whole world is equal in respect of beauty and delight.
Thomas Chaundler, *Libellus de Laudibus Civitatum* (1452)

The Medieval City

In 1485, when Henry VII claimed the throne of England, Bath was a small but very
prosperous clothing centre, nestling in a low-lying bowl surrounded by beautiful hills.
Like most medieval cities, the majority of its houses were protected by ancient walls
(built in this case on substantial Roman foundations) - although from the twelfth
century a small overspill population had existed outside the North and South Gates.
These gates provided the two main entrances to the city, while the West Gate gave
access to the meadows outside and the small East Gate (a postern which remained open
after the nightly curfew) led down to the river, the ford and the mill. The Ham Gate, on
the other hand, was chiefly used by the monks to gain direct access from the priory to
their grazing land on the meadow outside (namely, the Ham and the Ambury).

    Under repeated pressure from successive kings, the citizens of Bath had tried hard
to maintain these **defences** in good repair throughout the medieval period. The first
major repair took place in 1138, when - according to the chronicle, *Gesta Stephani* -
King Stephen visited the city during a time of civil turmoil. Bath itself (a royal
garrison) was apparently being threatened by the 'freebooters and robbers' who were
holding Bristol. Bearing in mind that the city had already been plundered and badly
burnt during the 1088 rebellion against William Rufus, Stephen ordered its defences

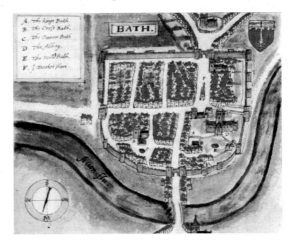

William Smith's map of Bath, 1588, from his
Particular Description of England. *This earliest*
known depiction of the city reveals its strong
fortifications and the state of the old Priory
precinct in the south-east corner following the
demolition of its cloisters (see Chapter 2).
Also notice at the bottom the church in
Widcombe, which had been at the centre of
controversy at the very time when Smith was
drawing his map (see Chapter 4). By
permission of the British Library
(Add.Mss.2596. f39)

to be strengthened by increasing the height of the walls and building earthworks outside.

Once the danger had passed, however, neglect quickly set in - as witnessed by the detailed survey of the state of the country, which Edward I ordered on his accession in 1273. The local inquiry revealed, among other things, that stones had been plundered wholesale from the city walls. Although thirteen offenders were identified by name, it transpired that the most surprising plunderers of the stone were the prior (for building an almshouse), the miller of Monks' Mill (for repairing the mill pool) and the master of St John's Hospital (for extending his house!).

As the threat of a French invasion slowly receded, so the walls were used more and more as a quarry by builders. However, in 1369, Edward III - realising that war against France again seemed imminent - ordered a survey of all fortifications throughout the land. The subsequent report on Bath made sorry reading - the walls and towers 'in divers places' were so far 'destroyed and broken' that they were 'threatened with imminent ruin'; while the ditch around the wall was not only 'obstructed by trees and herbs' growing in it, but was also used as a dung heap for the disposal of human waste 'and other filthy things thrown therein'. [This sort of pollution, which created a foul-smelling atmosphere, was to remain a serious problem in Bath until the seventeenth century, when such sewage was spread over the common instead.] The mayor was consequently ordered to repair the walls and scour the ditch by raising a tax to cover the cost and conscripting local men to carry out the work.

The enclosed area, containing just twenty-five acres, was surrounded by fields, meadows and orchards which ran right up to the very foot of the walls. The city was also protected in part by a large loop of the river Avon, which could be crossed by a **twelfth-century bridge** below the South Gate. The bridge had its own gate for protection together with a small oratory chapel, dedicated to St Lawrence, where travellers could offer prayers and thanks for safety on their journey. In the late thirteenth century, Robert Cherin had been granted a tenement and meadow for his own use in return for controlling the gate on the bridge in time of war.

Access to the city was in fact extremely difficult. The roads were in a permanent state of disrepair, which made the task of negotiating the hills around Bath

Although this restored section of the old medieval city wall in Upper Borough Walls is the only visible reminder of what these defences were like, recent research by the Bath Archaeological Trust has revealed that large sections of the wall still remain intact below pavement level in the cellars of more recent buildings.

(Author's photograph)

almost impossible during wet weather. William Hull, a local citizen felt so strongly about this in 1409 that he actually bequeathed money in his will 'for the repair of the causeway beyond Bath Bridge'. The river, too, which in theory gave local farmers and clothiers access to the profitable markets in Bristol, was often badly silted up or choked by man-made obstacles such as weirs and fishponds. Indeed, the situation had become so bad by 1372 that the king ordered the churchwardens of urban parishes and landowners in those parts of the countryside through which the river passed to clear away all such barriers to trade.

It is estimated that **the population** of Bath during the period 1066-1485 varied between eleven and thirteen hundred residents - a total which had been affected partly by the devastation of the city during the 1088 rebellion and partly by the consequences of the Black Death, which swept the country in 1349. Even by the middle of the seventeenth century, the total population did not exceed two thousand. Nevertheless, local citizens did have one very considerable advantage in terms of good health, which greatly increased their chances of survival - namely a supply of clean, fresh water. As early as the thirteenth century (and possibly even earlier), water had been piped down into the city from springs on

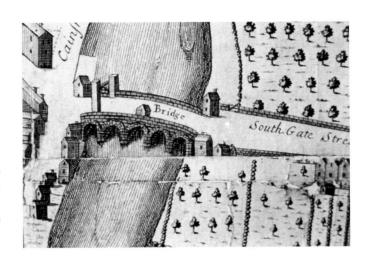

A view of Bath Bridge taken from Joseph Gilmore's map of Bath, 1694. It shows the gate, which guarded the entrance to this twelfth-century bridge and the small oratory chapel, which stood in the middle. (Author's collection)

Beechen Cliff and Beacon Hill to serve drinking conduits - or fountains - inside both the city itself and the precinct of the Priory (and, later, the homes of wealthier citizens). In 1261, for instance, Prior Walter de Anno had repaired St James's conduit (which stood by the South Gate) and agreed with the mayor to establish St Peter's conduit in the High Street.

The Struggle for Power

Throughout the whole period between 1091 and 1485, life in the city of Bath was dominated by a combination of **the diocesan bishop and the local prior**. On his accession to the English throne in 1066, William the Conqueror had immediately assumed ownership and landlord rights of the city and its suburbs. However, his successor - William Rufus - not only installed his own physician, John of Tours (or Villula) as Bishop of Wells, but also decided to grant him the city of Bath together with its Benedictine Priory as the new headquarters of the diocese. John, therefore, now styled himself the 'Bishop of Bath' and, as titular Abbot of Bath in addition, proceeded to take up residence there for much of the year. [As the bishop, of course, was not a Benedictine monk, it was the prior who actually organised and controlled the monastery on a day-to-day basis - hence the fact that it became known as Bath Priory rather than

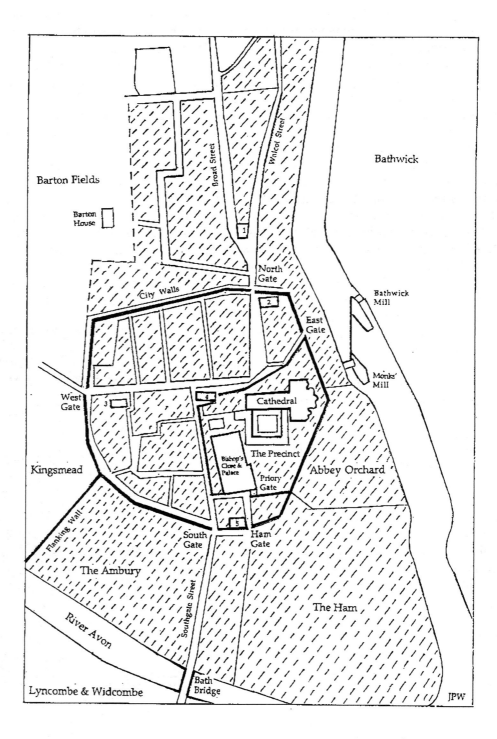

Map of the Bath Hundred. This administrative area (shaded) represented the actual bounds of the city until enlargement took place under the terms of a new charter in 1590 (see Chapter 6). Notice the walled enclosure of the Priory precinct in the the south-east corner and observe how John of Tours diverted its northern wall in order to enlarge its total area (see page 11-12). Also notice the meadows and the Barton Fields, where monks and citizens alike grazed their cattle (see below); and the location of the five parish churches (1 = St Michael's Without; 2 = St Mary's by the North Gate; 3 = St Michael's Within; 4 = St Mary de Stall's; 5 = St James's). (Map by the author)

Bath Abbey.] In spite of the fact that a later bishop (Bishop Savarac) returned the city to the king in 1192 in exchange for the wealthy abbey at Glastonbury, Bath was eventually regained by Bishop Robert Burnell in 1278 in a new deal.

As the effective landlord for most of this period, the bishop was therefore able to enjoy the profits raised by law suits, the 'fines' imposed when land was leased or ownership transferred and the considerable rents levied on property. The official limit to his jurisdiction was set by the boundary of the Bath Hundred, an administrative area with its own Hundred Court and consisting of the walled city itself together with the suburbs to both north and south (see map opposite).

Surrounding the Bath Hundred lay the *forinsecum* or Foreign Hundred (later known as the Bathforum Hundred), which contained eighteen of our modern parishes. This area stretched from Langridge in the north to Freshford in the south and from Kelston in the west to Bathford in the east. It also included the Barton in Walcot, an area of rich agricultural land, which was leased from the king by Bath Priory. Indeed, in 1204, King John granted the Priory not only the Barton but also the whole of the Foreign Hundred for an annual rent of twenty pounds.

The bishop and prior together, therefore, exercised a major influence over the running of the city's affairs and the lives of its inhabitants. Many townsfolk, for instance, rented strips of land on the open fields in the Barton from the Priory, grazed their animals on its common or became its employees in the production of cloth. It was the bishop - not the citizens - who had been authorised by the king to hold fairs within the city and to run the twice-weekly market in the High Street.

Furthermore, the citizens required the approval of the bishop before undertaking any major changes to city life - such as the renaming of Souter Street (which meant Shoemakers' Street) to Cheap Street in 1398; just as the installation and repair of drinking fountains was tackled largely on the initiative of the prior. After all, as the lives of citizens and monks were closely intertwined, any changes made independently by local people would inevitably have impacted on those who lived in the Priory.

Nevertheless, in spite of the seemingly unassailable position of the bishop and prior, by the end of the twelfth century a sustained challenge to their monopoly of power was already being mounted by affluent cloth merchants and traders, who were becoming increasingly frustrated by their own lack of status and influence within the city. A wonderful opportunity suddenly presented itself in 1189, when a cash-strapped Richard I was

The Charter, granted at Dover in 1189 by Richard I. (By courtesy of the Bath Record Office, Bath & North-East Somerset Council)

about to set sail from Dover on his Third Crusade. A group of citizens therefore rushed down to the port and persuaded the king (for a large payment, no doubt) to grant them a charter. This conveyed to 'the citizens of Bath, who are its Merchant Guild', the right to trade freely, wherever they travelled, without payment of tolls. The charter was significant because, for the first time, **the Merchant Guild** gained recognition not only as an established body of merchants, but also as the representative body of the citizens of Bath. Furthermore, the church had been excluded from the negotiations.

Gradually, over the next three centuries, the Merchant Guild extended its powers, strengthened its status and enlarged its identity. By the early thirteenth century, guildsmen were beginning to act as official witnesses of property deals alongside those provided by the Hundred Court. At the same time, they established a proper organisation for the guild's affairs with the appointment of a scrivener (clerk) and cofferer (treasurer). After this dramatic transformation of a body of citizens into an efficiently-run Merchant Guild, it was then but a short step to the adoption of a further new identity - namely that of 'the Commonalty of Bath' (which, from 1590, was re-styled the Corporation of Bath).

Progress was rapid. A 'Mayor of Bath' first appeared in documentary sources as early as 1230; a seal of the 'Citizens of Bath' was being used by 1249; powers were granted by royal authority enabling 'the commonalty' to appoint the city coroner (1312), collect the king's taxes (1341) and recruit armed men for the king's army (1346); two members of parliament were returned to represent the city (1332); and, in a further extension of power granted by royal charter in 1447, they were instructed - as justices of the peace - to control trade, wages, employment, beggars, the abuse of coinage and lawlessness.

This gradual growth in responsibility and status had partly been made possible through the absence of the bishop from the city between 1192 and 1278 (i.e. after the re-surrender of Bath to the king - see above); and partly through the fact that, from the fourteenth century, later bishops preferred to live in Wells. [As early as 1176, the pope had decreed that both Bath and Wells should be regarded as seats of the bishop with equal status, thus cancelling the earlier decision of John of Tours to concentrate solely on Bath. Then, in 1245, a subsequent pope had confirmed that the title should in fact be 'Bishop of Bath and Wells'].

Sensing weakness, the citizens seized every opportunity to confront both prior and bishop over rights. In 1272, for instance, a jury of local citizens reported the prior to the king for illegally quarrying stone from the city wall for building work in the Priory; while in 1408, local people challenged the longstanding tradition that the Priory should ring its bells before those of the parish churches were sounded at both dawn (to herald to start of the working day) and dusk (to mark the curfew when gates would be closed).

From 1355 (or possibly earlier), the Merchant Guild (alias the Mayor and Commonalty) had established its headquarters in a building, appropriately named the Guildhall, which stood in a narrow lane situated between the High Street and the East Gate. Its own seal, which was used to authenticate documents, clearly displayed this building standing proudly behind the city wall (see illustration). From 1249, the guild also possessed its own chapel, dedicated to St Catherine, within the Church of St Mary de Stall. It was there that the guild admitted its own members and prayed for the souls of those who had died.

By 1485, therefore, it had successfully established itself as the corporate body chiefly responsible for controlling the affairs of the city. Although the Priory still exercised influence (it remained a major landowner), it was by then in a perilously weak condition. Buildings were visibly crumbling in a state of disrepair, while the number of monks had dwindled to a mere twenty from a peak of forty at the start of the thirteenth century.

The Local Economy

By 1485, Bath was a busy **market town** providing ample opportunity for local producers and manufacturers to display and sell their goods. Even as early as the thirteenth century, leases were being granted for 'shops' within the walled area (usually with a cellar below, a kitchen behind and living accommodation above). The shop fronted the street with wooden shutters, hinged at the bottom so that they could be pulled down to form a display counter. Alongside the shops was also a large number of stalls, many of

This fourteenth-century seal of the Merchant Guild or 'The Citizens of the City of Bath' depicts the Guildhall surrounded by the city walls. (By courtesy of the Bath Record Office, Bath & North-East Somerset Council)

which were actually clustered along 'Stall' Street. Trading inside the city from shops and stalls, however, was restricted to **the 'freemen'**, who had normally gained this privileged status by serving a seven-year apprenticeship with a master who was already a freeman.

There was, therefore, a sharp distinction between a 'citizen', who was a freeman, and an ordinary inhabitant. It is likely that, out of a population of between 1100 and 1300 people, there would be no more than one hundred freemen. These affluent traders and merchants were the very men who made up 'the Commonalty of Bath' - the body which had gradually gained control of civic affairs (see above). It is worth mentioning, however, that - by the fifteenth century - a dominant inner group was beginning to emerge even from within that body - a group of active individuals which, in 1590, was to be transformed officially into the 'Bath Corporation', consisting of a mayor, aldermen and common councillors (see Chapter 6).

Nevertheless, in spite of this rigid restriction on trade, outsiders were allowed to enter the city to sell or barter their produce from baskets or stalls at **the twice-weekly market**. This was chiefly held in the High Street on Wednesdays and Saturdays, although there is evidence to suggest that stalls often spread into neighbouring streets. This market, which had been held 'since time immemorial', was confirmed in 1371 by Edward III in a charter granted to the bishop (who therefore enjoyed the fees paid by stall holders).

Annual fairs provided another opportunity for traders who lived outside the city, including the Candlemas Fair on 2nd February and the Lammas Fair on 1st August. The main fair, however, was the Cherry Fair, which ran for ten days during the Feast of

St Peter and St Paul in June. This had also been granted to the bishop by Edward I in 1284. However, as Allan Keevil has shown, two later fairs were assigned to the prior in 1304: one in Lyncombe held in May in the area now known as the Bear Flat; and the other - the Lansdown Fair - held in August on a site near the present Blathwayt Arms.

Most people who lived in and around Bath in 1485 were involved, one way or the other, in **the production of food**. This was undertaken by growing fruit and vegetables in their gardens, keeping chickens and pigs around their homes (often leaving them to wander around the streets in search of scraps), grazing animals on the common land or cultivating strips on the open fields. Indeed, the land which made up the Barton estate in Walcot was regarded in effect as Bath's own farmland to be enjoyed by monks and townsfolk alike. The property, all of which had been granted to the Priory by King John in 1204, was extensive and consisted of a good mixture of arable, woodland and pasture.

Although some areas had already been enclosed by 1485, there were still two large open fields in the Barton (the East Field of around 250 acres and the West Field of 200 acres) - one of which, in rotation, was left to recover in a fallow state each year. These open fields benefited local people in two ways, as Allan Keevil has indicated. On the one hand, the inhabitants of Walcot (a parish which then lay just outside the city bounds) were the customary tenants of the lord of the manor (i.e. the prior). As part of their tenement, they held small strips of land on the open fields - equally divided between the two - on which they grew crops chiefly for their own use.

On the other hand, the 'citizens' of Bath itself (i.e. the freemen) enjoyed a special privilege of their own in relation to this estate. An agreement made with the prior in 1260 gave them the right to graze their cattle - along with those of the prior - in Kingsmead meadow from 1st August each year. In return, the prior would receive one penny 'for each head of cattle having a tooth' and one halfpenny for each toothless animal. Then, when the prior transferred his cattle after harvest to graze on the stubble in either the East or West Field (whichever was being cultivated that year), they were to do likewise - for a slightly reduced payment. The cattle remained on the stubble until 25th October (when the autumn ploughing commenced), after which they returned to Kingsmead until 30th November. The freemen also had similar rights to put their cattle

This wonderful drawing shows two country women bringing their goods to market with handkerchiefs over their mouths to protect them from dust; a water-carrier just about to fill his large container with fresh water at the fountain or conduit (similar to those found in Bath); and two women selling live pike from a tank. One of the women is slitting open a fish before placing the guts on her hand - a process, which (according to Thomas Platter in 1595) was undertaken 'to show whether the pike was sufficiently fat'. (By courtesy of Guildhall Library, Corporation of London)

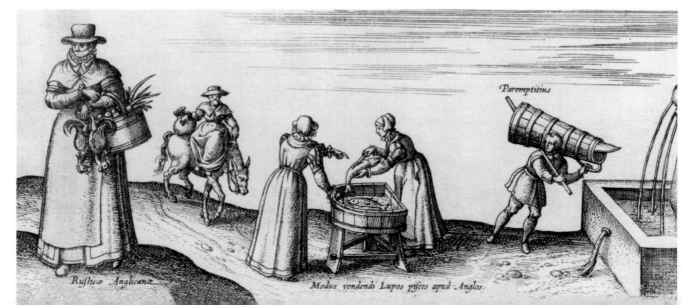

Eastcheap Butchers' Market, London, taken from Hugh Alley's Caveat for the City of London, *1598. A similar market developed in Bath, where animals were brought 'on the hoof' before being slaughtered in the vicinity of the shops (a practice which was later forbidden as constituting a health hazard). Notice the carcasses and large joints hanging on display - and the woman and her maid, who are totally unconcerned about the animals bearing down on them (an indication that this was an everyday experience for people living in towns). (By permission of the Folger Shakespeare Library)*

into the enclosed arable fields of the estate - but not until three weeks after the prior had done so with his.

For their own part, the monks of the Priory were largely self sufficient in food, growing fruit and vegetables in Abbey Orchard by the river; grazing their cattle on Kingsmead Meadow; growing crops on the Barton estate; pasturing their sheep either on the surrounding downs in summer or on the lower slopes in winter; cultivating vines in Lyncombe, Widcombe and Walcot; and farming fish in two specially-built fishponds, one of which was probably situated in the ditch outside the city walls and the other in Lyncombe Vale.

Although agriculture was of course vital to the local economy, it was the **manufacture of cloth** which largely accounted for the city's prosperity in the fourteenth and fifteenth centuries. The Priory led the way by establishing its own operation. In addition to the large quantity of raw wool produced by their own flocks of sheep (the 'Ewe Flock' and the 'Hogg Flock', each of which consisted of over three hundred animals), the monks regularly bought a considerable number of bales of wool from west country merchants. They then employed a large team of spinners and weavers to produce the cloth, which was finished in the Priory's own mill (Monks' Mill) by the river. This served as both a grist mill for corn and a fulling mill for cloth. The fulling process involved the scouring and pounding of the wet cloth to make it shrink and thicken (or felt) before it was stretched out to dry on large 'tenter' racks in the fields.

By 1485, there were also two fulling mills at Twerton on the other side of the river - an indication that the monks by no means monopolised the entire cloth trade.

This contemporary woodcut shows a tenant farmer sowing seed by hand on a strip on the open field, while another in breaking up the soil with a horse-drawn harrow. (Author's collection)

Indeed, within Bath itself, a number of prominent citizens had already made their fortunes as cloth merchants. The 1379 poll tax returns for the city - a personal tax which was payable by every adult with married couples paying the single rate - indicated that, out of the 328 individuals listed, there were eleven spinners, three weavers and six fullers. However, these numbers would have been greatly increased by married women or young people under the age of twenty-one (many of whom were apprenticed or undertook spinning in the family home).

As Peter Davenport has shown, other townsfolk were heavily involved in **small-scale manufacture**, construction work and various service industries. Evidence has revealed, for instance, that horn and bone objects were produced locally, while the churchwardens' accounts of St Michael's outside the North Gate show feverish activity by teams of masons, carpenters, thatchers, tilers and plasterers in building or repairing houses in the Walcot Street/Broad Street area. The 1379 poll tax returns indicate that there were forty-one artificers (or craftsmen of various trades) and 118 labourers.

The growing affluence of Bath is perhaps indicated by the presence of several skilled workers serving the luxury end of the market, including one goldsmith, eight tailors and eight shoemakers. Indeed, a small leather industry - based on a tannery in Southgate Street - was supported by two skinners and one tanner. The family's daily needs were catered for by six brewers, three butchers and twenty-three domestic servants. Later, the chamberlain's accounts in the 1580s continue to refer to such people as Moreford the maltster, Green the pewterer and Panter, the limeburner. Lime, of course, was an essential ingredient for the mortar used in building construction (although burning lime, brewing malt and tanning leather all contributed to the pollution of Bath's humid

The monks owned two specially-constructed fish ponds, which helped to make them self-sufficient in this vital ingredient of their diet. Woodcut by permission of the British Library (Roxburghe Ballads, RAX.Rox.I. 297)

atmosphere).

Although the old Roman **hot water baths** (centred on the King's Bath) were still being used in 1485, it was not until the sixteenth century that 'health tourism' was actively encouraged through a large-scale programme of refurbishment and expansion (see Chapter 6). However, the healing qualities of the natural spring were already well known by the twelfth century - as witnessed in the book *Gesta Stephani*, which was published in 1138. In it the author marvels at 'the streamlets of water' which were thrown up 'from the very bowels of the earth' into the beautifully constructed baths 'in the middle of the city, warm and wholesome and charming to the eye'. As a result, 'sick persons from all over England resort there to bathe in these healing waters - and the fit also to see these wonderful burstings out of warm water and to bathe in them'. Later still in 1480, William Caxton was to sing the praises of 'the hot baths which wash away pus, sores and scabs'.

Although it is true that the King's Bath (which, along with the others, was the responsibility of the prior) had been improved in the twelfth century by adding twenty-four arched semi-circular recesses to the old Roman structure, there is little evidence of a tourist boom. The 1379 poll tax returns made no mention of bath attendants and listed only two ostlers (or stable keepers at local inns). Visitors, therefore, were probably few and far between. Nevertheless, the baths were certainly used by the monks themselves. It is thought that two additional baths (referred to as the Abbot's Bath and the Prior's Bath) were actually constructed within the walls of the Abbey precinct and served by water drawn from the King's Bath. Furthermore, the Cross Bath and the Hot Bath in the south-west corner of the city also received a degree of refurbishment during this period.

It is interesting to note that, during the years 1066 to 1485, **people's names** underwent something of a transformation, as shown by those recorded as witnesses on property deeds. Until the early fourteenth century, names often reflected the occupations of the individuals concerned - such as Gilbert Cissor (tailor), Adam Fullo (fuller), John de Venur (hunter), Reiner the Goldsmith, Richard the Miller and Walter de Lavender (washerman). Other names referred to the person's place of origin or residence - such as Robert de Hampton, Richard de Ford, Swan de Weston, John de Iford and John de Southstoke. During the fourteenth century, however, an increasing number of more modern names began to appear, including William Rouse, Richard Ford, John Savage and William Hull.

Streets and Houses

By 1485, **the monastery precinct** occupied the whole of the south-eastern sector of the city. Although its buildings had latterly developed ominous signs of outward decay, they had originally been both striking and imposing. After the devastation of Bath by rebel forces in 1088, the new bishop - John of Tours (1088-1112) - had seized his opportunity to re-plan and re-develop the city. Crucial to his design was the enlargement of the area occupied by the monastery. Therefore, although he retained much of the old Saxon street grid within the walls, he immediately set about the task of building a new street (Stall Street) to replace an earlier road, which had run more to the east; and, at the same time, constructing a new South Gate to give a direct through route to the meadow and bridge beyond. There is further evidence that he also diverted the former line of Souter (or Cheap) Street, which would previously have run in a straight line to a gate in the eastern wall (see map on page 4).

By these changes, Bishop John had created a much larger space for the monastery precinct, which was now enclosed with a stone wall. Over the next seventy-five or so years, he and his successors - particularly Bishop Robert of Lewes (1136-66) - built an impressive new cathedral church (measuring 350 feet long by 90 feet broad), complete with cloisters, refectory, monks' dormitory, chapter house, infirmary and lodgings for the prior. They went on to construct, within the precinct, a fine Bishop's Palace set in its own close with the Bishop's Chapel alongside. The latter was in fact a conversion of the nave of the old church of St James - a decision which necessitated the construction of a replacement parish church in 1279 (with the same name) on a site by the new South Gate. The monastery precinct also contained the church of St Mary de Stall and the King's Bath (named after Henry I), which was duly refurbished (see above).

In view of the displacement caused by these changes - some residents' houses would almost certainly have been demolished during the construction of the new road scheme - it is thought likely that Bishop John now began to encourage the development of the suburbs both north and south of the city walls. Indeed, the earliest maps of Bath give a clear hint that a certain degree of planning had taken place in Walcot Street and Southgate Street with the setting out of long, narrow plots of land (see map in Chapter 3). This enabled householders to enjoy the benefit of large gardens behind their homes, which naturally fronted onto the street.

In 1485, most of the houses in Bath would have been timber-framed with wattle-and-daub infilling and thatched roofs. Only the wealthy could have afforded houses built entirely in stone, although some homes did in fact have stone foundations and lower walls with timber framing above. According to the 1379 poll tax returns, some parts of the city were more densely populated than others. Out of the 328 individuals listed, no fewer than 176 were concentrated in the centre of town in Stall Street (77), Westgate Street (18), Souter or Cheap Street (39) and Northgate Street (42). There was a further concentration of 112 taxpayers in the less affluent area outside the North Gate -

The Priory owned two large flocks of sheep, which were grazed on the downs surrounding the city in summer. They usually employed local people to act as shepherds. Woodcut dated 1579 from J.R. Green: A Short History of the English People *(1907 edtn.) by permission of the Guildhall Library, Corporation of London.*

including Broad Street (47) and Walcot Street (65) - whereas just 18 of them were based in Southgate Street. The situation had not greatly changed by the time John Speed drew his map of the city in 1610.

The Religious Life of the People

It is extremely difficult in the twenty-first century to get under the skin of those living in late medieval England - and, in particular, to understand the extent to which religion dominated their lives. People dwelling in Bath in 1485 would - in common with those living elsewhere in the country - find themselves engulfed at every turn by the church in all its forms. We have already seen how many of them were dependent on the Benedictine monks of Bath Priory for their very livelihood in both farming and cloth production. Of even greater importance, however, was the way in which their local parish church provided a focus for their social, emotional and spiritual needs throughout the entire year, binding the community together through a wealth of activities.

The Christian calendar consisted of a long sequence of major festivals together with additional feast days to celebrate the lives of particular saints. The most important of these included Christmas Day, Candlemas, Lent, Palm Sunday, Maundy Thursday, Good Friday, Easter Day, Rogationtide, Ascension Day, Whitsuntide, Corpus Christi, All Saints' Day and All Souls' Day. Each of the main church services associated with these festivals was based on elaborate ritual, often accompanied by colourful processions around the parish (see below). Furthermore, the religious celebration itself was frequently followed by days of feasting and merrymaking for the whole community - such as those associated with the twelve days of Christmas, Collop Monday, Shrove Tuesday, Easter Monday, the May Games, Midsummer Day and Michaelmas (see Chapter 6).

Quite apart from these services and ceremonies, the Christian calendar also imposed many restrictions on the lives of all individuals, as Eamon Duffy has illustrated. Marriage, for instance, was banned during the four weeks of Advent and the six weeks of Lent. Fasting from meat and dairy products was also obligatory for everyone on around seventy days in the year, including Lent itself, the anniversaries of the apostles and other major festivals in the church calendar. Furthermore, in addition to these fast days, there were between forty and fifty feast or holy days throughout the year (some with a particular local connection). On these days people were required not only to attend three church services (as they did on Sundays), but also to abstain from all but vital work. In consequence, these 'holy days' became 'holidays' - a tradition which people always applauded, but employers increasingly resented. Many of these were therefore swept away by Henry VIII in 1536 after his breach with Rome.

Although church attendance was compulsory, most people in 1485 would in any case have felt drawn into a close dependence on religious activity within the parish. For men and women from all ranks of society were fearful at the idea of death and terrified at the thought of damnation. They therefore saw their active involvement in church ritual, sacrificial giving and service to the parish as part of their **quest for salvation**. In late medieval England, death after all was a frequent visitor to every street. Quite apart from a much lower life expectancy and a much higher infant mortality rate, memories of the Black Death in 1348-49 still haunted every community - a monumental catastrophe which, in just over a year, swept away almost half the population of the country.

This contemporary woodcut provides a reminder that death was a frequent visitor to the streets of Bath, striking with devastating effect during times of severe epidemic. By permission of the British Library (Roxburghe Ballads, RAX.Rox.II. 103)

In the diocese of Bath and Wells, it was reported that an average of two priests a week were dying of the disease, while no fewer than nine parishes around the city of Bath lost their priests during the epidemic. To people believing - as they did - in the doctrine of purgatory (the place where the souls of the departed were purged of their sins before passage into heaven), it was of crucial importance to do what they could to relieve the suffering of their deceased relatives and speed that passage. This was achieved partly through prayer and partly through the lighting of candles at the altars of the saints, who would then intercede with God on behalf of the dead.

Wealthier individuals often made provision for this in their wills. In 1409, William Hull left ten shillings to the rector of St James's Church in Bath 'to celebrate a trental of masses for my own soul and the souls of my wives, Agnes and Edith' - plus a further ten shillings to the prior 'to celebrate my soul'. Furthermore, he set aside one hundred shillings for the appointment of a suitable chaplain to celebrate regularly his own soul and the souls of his wives 'at the altar of the Blessed Virgin Mary' inside St James's Church. Similarly, William Phylyps (clothier) granted the mayor 'three tenements, a barn and a chamber', together with their rents, on two conditions - that the mayor should personally be present at his funeral and mass; and that money should be released each year for an 'obit' [i.e a mass said in memory of an individual] for the souls of himself and his wife.

This 'cult of the dead', which offered a strong link with dead ancestors, was an important element in medieval life. As Darren Oldridge has shown, there was a strongly-held conviction that 'the ties between this life and the next were not severed completely at death', thus enabling communication between the living and the deceased to continue. Indeed, most people believed in the existence of 'revenants', who returned from the grave either to complete unfinished business or to warn relatives of the terrors which awaited sinners in hell. Sometimes, too, Satan would send his demons to possess these revived corpses in order to terrorise the living. It is hardly surprising, therefore, that this invisible world of the spirits aroused in medieval man feelings of both fear and fascination.

People living in Bath in 1485 were well provided for in their spiritual quest. Quite apart from the Priory Cathedral, there were **five parish churches** (a large number in fact for a population of no more than thirteen hundred souls) - St Mary de Stall's, St Michael's Within (i.e. inside the city walls) by the West Gate, St Michael's Without beyond the North Gate, St Mary's just inside the North Gate and St James's by the South Gate (see note at the end of the chapter). In addition, there were a number of other religious foundations, including St Werburgh's Chapel at the top of Broad Street (founded in 1170); the oratory of St Lawrence on the bridge; the Hospital of St Mary

Magdalen for poor lepers on Holloway; the Hospital of St John the Baptist, founded in 1174, for six to eight poor people; and the Hospital of St Catherine in Binbury Lane, founded in 1444 as an almshouse for eight people.

These establishments were, of course, all part of the universal Roman Catholic faith. Clear indications of the traditions and ritual involved in worship are revealed in the churchwardens' accounts for St Michael's Without from 1349 to 1485. There was a high altar draped in silk cloth and five other altars (with lights always burning) dedicated to the Blessed Virgin Mary, the Holy Trinity, St Catherine, St Egidius (the patron saint of lepers and cripples) and St Christopher. There was an open hearse in the chancel, fitted with numerous candelabra, where the coffins of eminent citizens rested during the singing of the requiem mass; a silver gilt cross; six copes of cloth of gold and silk; nine silver rosaries; leather-bound missals; a candelabra of fifteen lights - and many other lavish decorations, many of which had been bequeathed to the church by faithful worshippers.

The Ritual Year at St Michael's Church

Historians who attempt to recreate life in a sixteenth-century parish face the problem of an acute lack of documentary sources - particularly those which feature eyewitness accounts or personal observations such as diaries, letters or the reports of official investigations. In consequence, researchers are for the most part forced to rely on the somewhat stark entries contained in the accounts of the city chamberlain (which, in the case of Bath, do not start until 1568) and the parish churchwardens' accounts. Fortunately, those for St Michael's Church Without, (available from 1349) at least enable the historian to ascertain - from payments recorded - that the main feasts in the Christian calendar were indeed being faithfully observed at the start of the Tudor period in 1485. Frustratingly however, rich descriptions of what actually took place are lacking.

Nevertheless, Ronald Hutton has demonstrated in his masterly work on the ritual year that it is possible to build up a vivid picture of typical, normal practice out of details gleaned from parish records throughout Britain. It is highly likely therefore that the celebrations at St Michael's followed the pattern outlined below (a description which relies heavily on Hutton's findings). In each case, sample quotations have been extracted from St Michael's churchwardens' accounts to illustrate the theme.

The medieval church of St Michael Without, which was demolished in 1731. Depicted here in a lithograph of 1835 by Joseph Holloway. (Author's collection)

Christmas Day

1460   To Simon the waxmaker for one journal against the feast of the nativity of our Lord...3d
1461   For half a pound of wax candles against the Nativity...3d
         For one lamp before the cross there...1d

Excited parishioners would gather in the little church before dawn for the first mass of Christmas Day in a joyful celebration of the birth of Our Lord. They would have prepared themselves for over four weeks by fasting on a diet of mostly fish and soup. Once the mass had ended, the story of the descent of Jesus (as told in St Matthew's gospel) would be intoned by a singer up in the rood loft. *[The nave - where the congregation sat or stood - was divided from the chancel - where the high altar was situated - by the carved, wooden rood screen on which was fixed the 'rood', consisting of a cross and an image of Christ. Above the screen was the rood loft, also carved in wood, reached by a staircase.]* The large candle, manufactured by Simon the waxmaker, would almost certainly have illuminated the singer in the rood loft, while 'the lamp before the cross' would have lighted up the image of Christ on the rood screen. After the service, the congregation would hurry home to enjoy their first decent meal for weeks, signalling the start of a twelve-day festival (see Chapter 6).

Candlemas

1457   For one wax light at the feast of the blessed Virgin Mary...6d
1459   For oil bought for the feast of the purification of the blessed Virgin Mary...3.5d

This feast, on 2nd February, celebrated the Purification of the Blessed Virgin Mary - the day on which, according to tradition, the mother of Jesus made an offering in the temple at Jerusalem to purify herself forty days after the birth of her son. It also celebrated the words of Simeon, who greeted Jesus as the long-expected Messiah. The old man's words of prophesy - 'a light to lighten the Gentiles' - formed the basis for the ceremony of the candles, which took place during the service.

Each member of the congregation of St Michael's would be expected to provide his or her own candle, which would then be carried up to the altar and presented to the priest together with one penny in parochial dues. The candle would duly be sprinkled with holy water with the assurance that, once it had been lit, 'the devil may flee away in prayer and trembling'. Before the mass itself had ended, the people would process around the church with great joy, carrying their sanctified candles in a combined effort to drive away evil spirits. After the service had ended, the candles would be taken home and greatly cherished throughout the ensuing year, often being lit during moments of stress or difficulty (such as sickness, death or violent thunderstorms).

The expensive 'wax light', purchased by the churchwardens at St Michael's in 1457, would almost certainly have been placed on the side altar dedicated to the Blessed Virgin Mary.

The rood screen and rood loft in the Church of St Peter and St Paul in Eye, Suffolk, dating from 1480, gives a hint of what once existed in St Michael's Church, Bath. At the base of the screen are original figures of saints, bishops and kings painted in panels. The two figures which flank Christ above the loft (which was restored in 1925) are those of the Virgin Mary and St John. The remains of a stair turret, which led to the old rood loft, are still evident in the church of St Thomas à Becket at Widcombe. (Photograph by permission of Simon Knott and www.suffolkchurches.co.uk))

Lent

1463   *For a small cord to draw up a veil before the crucifix* [etc]...*4s 6d*

1508   *Half a bushel of green beans and making the same into pottage...8d*

In the Christian calendar, Lent was a time of personal preparation and self-denial before the great festival of Easter. It was marked by a period of fasting from Ash Wednesday until Easter Day, during which (in 1485, at least) the eating of meat, cheese and eggs was banned. Fish (in particular salted herring) therefore became the basis for a monotonous family diet - a situation which particularly tested the patience of the young. One fifteenth-century schoolboy described his own frustration in his school book: 'Thou will not believe how very I am off fish and how much I desire that flesh were come in again'.

The service on Ash Wednesday contained two important rituals, which were calculated to remind the people of the reality of both death and damnation. At St Michael's, therefore, the priest would first bless some specially-prepared ashes as he sprinkled them with holy water, before pressing a little of the substance onto the forehead of each member of the congregation - a solemn reminder of the words spoken by God to the man in the book of Genesis: 'Thou art dust and to dust thou shalt return'.

The second ritual was intended to emphasis a vital truth in the gospel story that salvation was only possible through the sacrifice of Christ on the cross and his subsequent resurrection - events celebrated in the festival of Easter, which lay ahead. The period of Lent, therefore, represented a period of darkness when sinful man faced up to the certainty of eternal damnation. At St Michael's - as in churches throughout the country - all the altars and images of saints would therefore be hidden from view by covering them with silk or linen cloths. At the same time, a beautiful large cloth would be hung across the rood, by means of a cord and pulley system, to conceal the crucifix and the image of Christ - while the 'Lenten Veil' would be raised to hide the high altar. Thus all the symbols of comfort and salvation would now have been obscured.

The cord, bought in 1463 to draw up a veil before the crucifix, is just a small surviving clue as to what actually happened in St Michael's Church, while the purchase of 'green beans' to make soup for the poor people of the parish in 1508 is a reminder of the fast. 'Pottage' became the staple diet of the less affluent during Lent (and often at other times, too).

Holy Week

1459   *For wax bought for* **the Paschal** *light and for making the same...5s 7d*

1460   *For* **the Judas** *candle...4d*

1462   *For wax burning before* **the sepulchre** *containing two pounds...11d*

1532   *4d paid to* **the guards** *or watchmen of the lights in the sepulchre this year*

On Palm Sunday, an excited congregation at St Michael's would arrive at church carrying evergreen branches of yew, box or willow (representing the palms strewn before the path of Christ on his entry into Jerusalem). These would then be carried in procession around the churchyard, where anthems were sung. Inside the church itself, at the beginning of the mass, the cloth covering the rood would be drawn aside for the duration of the service to offer a glimpse of the image of Christ and, with it, the coming hope of salvation. Each individual would then make his or her own small cross out of the branches - crosses which would be blessed by the priest and treasured for their special powers throughout the following year. During mass on the Wednesday of Holy Week, the Lenten Veil (which concealed the high altar) would finally be removed during the gospel reading of the account of the tearing of the veil in the temple from top to bottom.

During the mass on Maundy Thursday, three 'hosts' *[the consecrated bread, representing the body of Christ]* would be consecrated for use during the Easter celebrations. Then all the altars in the church would be ritually stripped of their coverings and washed with a mixture of water and wine (representing the stripping of Christ for death on the cross and the water and blood which gushed from his side).

During the service on Good Friday (in what became known as the ceremony of 'creeping to the cross'), the clergy and congregation would creep forward on hands and knees with bare feet to kiss a veiled crucifix, which had been brought into the church. Later, the ceremony of the Easter Sepulchre would take place. To symbolise the burial of Christ after his crucifixion, the priest would carry one of the prepared hosts in a special casket to the north side of the chancel where - together with the veiled crucifix - it would be placed inside a miniature **'sepulchre'**, which symbolised Christ's tomb. This would take the form either of a temporary wooden structure or an elegantly carved, permanent niche which had been set in the wall. There, covered with a fine cloth and surrounded by lighted candles, it would be **guarded** day and night by members of the congregation until Easter Sunday in recollection of the soldiers who watched over Christ's tomb.

Meanwhile, on the Saturday, the ceremony of **the 'Paschal'** or Easter Candle would be enacted. Every candle inside the church would first be extinguished before the priest created a new flame by striking flint. The Paschal Candle, which would by that stage be the largest candle on view, would then be lit. The high cost of the candle purchased by the churchwardens in 1459 suggests that it could have weighed anything up to twenty pounds - quite normal in other parts of the country. To provide the semblance of even greater height, the candle would then be fixed to a wooden rod -

The fourteenth-century Easter Sepulchre at St Andrew's Church in Heckington, Lincolnshire - reputed to be one the three finest in the country. Carved in stone to house the 'host' between Good Friday and Easter Sunday, it depicts the angels and the women who flank Christ's tomb together with the sleeping soldiers below and the risen Christ above. The sepulchre in St Michael's Church, though far less elaborate, would undoubtedly have just as much significance to local parishioners. (Author's photograph by permission of the vicar)

known as a **'Judas'** - which would have been painted in the form of a candle. In St Michael's Church, the entire device was finally set up in the centre of a candelabrum of fifteen lights, suspended from the rood loft. The 1477 accounts, for instance, mention 'Judas on the rood loft'.

Easter Day provided the climax to what would have been at the time a most joyous week with active involvement by the entire parish in the dramatic representation of the death and resurrection of Christ. Arriving at the church before dawn, the congregation would first have witnessed the ceremony of the opening of the sepulchre, symbolising the discovery of the empty tomb. The priest would then have carried the casket containing the host to the high altar which, together with the side altars and the images of Christ and the saints, would now be uncovered for the first time since Ash Wednesday. Christ had risen and people would be able to take comfort again in the assurance of salvation.

Rogation and the Feast of the Ascension

1460	*For carrying the banners, cross and torch on rogation days...5d*
1461	*For drink on the day of the Ascension...4d*
1462	*For small candles bought against the feast of the Ascension of our Lord...2.5d*

On the three days prior to Ascension Day (which fell on the sixth Thursday after Easter), all the parishioners of St Michael's church would have assembled for the Rogationtide processions led by the clergy. These had two purposes - first, to walk around the neighbouring open fields, where many residents cultivated strips of land, in order to bless the growing crops; and secondly, to perambulate around the parish boundaries to ensure that the fixed markings were still in place and that encroachment by others had not occurred. The boundary stones were ceremonially thrashed with willow wands - partly to ensure that the exact location of the boundaries was firmly imprinted on the memories of the parishioners for future reference.

These gatherings were also designed to strengthen a sense of parish unity and to heal divisions between neighbours by driving out of the community those evil spirits which had caused such dissension. At St Michael's, the people carried up to four banners (in 1467, the parish owned two made of silk and two of painted cloth), a cross and a burning torch (in 1463, the churchwardens paid 4s 8d 'for a torch weighing 24 pounds bought of John the waxmaker).

The processions - with church bells ringing in the background - would halt from time to time en route for prayers and the singing of hymns. At the mass on Ascension Day itself, the Paschal Candle, which had been lit during the services on all holy days since Easter, would finally be extinguished as an indication that Christ had ascended into heaven. It was customary to reward those members of the congregation, who had carried banners or torches, with liquid refreshment - hence the payment for 'drink' in 1461. At St Thomas à Becket Church in Widcombe there is a visible reminder of the importance and frequency of such parochial processions - namely, two arched doorways (now blocked up, on the north and south sides of the tower), which would have been used by parishioners as the processions left the church.

Pentecost

1459   Paid for carrying the banners in Pentecost week...1d
1461   For candles against the feast of Pentecost...1d
1506   For smoke farthings at the feast of Pentecost...2 .5d

On the seventh Sunday after Easter (and ten days after Ascension Day), the congregation of St Michael's would assemble to celebrate the Feast of Pentecost on what became known as Whit Sunday. Processions with church banners were again the order of the day as people rejoiced at the coming of the Holy Spirit. It was traditional on that day for congregations throughout the land to process to the cathedral or monastery which they regarded as their church's parent body. There symbolic offerings, known as 'smoke farthings' or 'Pentecostals' would be made - hence the above entry from the churchwardens' accounts. Although Wells Cathedral was frequently cited by Bath residents in wills of the period as 'the mother church', it is more likely that the parishioners of St Michael's processed to the local Benedictine Priory - for it was the prior who held the advowson *[the right to appoint the clergy]* of their church.

Corpus Christi

1461   For carrying the cross, banner and torch at the feast of Corpus Christi...3d
1468   For a cord for the canopy...1d
1482   For potation for le players, *in remembrance of their plays on divers occasions...8d*
*   For skins for the same play...20d*
*   To William Bayle for staining divers utensils ordered for the said play...3s 0d*

This was one of the most colourful celebrations of the whole church calendar, dating from 1318 and held on the second Thursday after Pentecost. It was essentially an open-air procession to highlight the importance of the eucharist and to emphasise the real presence of Christ in the 'host', which had been consecrated by the priest

This contemporary line drawing illustrates a Corpus Christi procession from the church after the celebration of a Catholic mass. Note two people at the front with their rosary beads. From The Acts and Monuments of John Foxe, *ed. George Townsend (1843-49 edtn.)*

[i.e. the doctrine of transubstantiation, which taught the miraculous transformation of the consecrated bread into the actual body of Christ]. The procession was always a grand civic affair, which would have involved the mayor and corporation together with the local trade guilds. In many instances, the guildsmen would not only have organised the whole festivity but would also carry the banners and torches. The clergy from all the churches would lead the procession, bearing on their shoulders the host which would have been placed in a special casket under a canopy - hence the purchase of a cord 'for the canopy' in 1468.

Although the inhabitants of Bath would have knelt in solemn silence as the procession passed by, the joyousness of the occasion was marked by the ringing of church bells throughout the city and the lavish decoration of church interiors with colourful flowers and greenery. Even as late as 1569, the city chamberlain paid 6s 2d for bread, ale and cheese 'upon Corpus Christi evening' for the councillors to celebrate in the Guildhall - which was itself festooned with 'green'.

After the procession, it was traditional in many towns to perform a play with a religious theme on a temporary stage outside one of the churches. The 1482 accounts for St Michael's, therefore, make reference to the cost of props and costumes - not to mention the refreshment of beer, bread and cheese provided for 'le players'. [Although the accounts were written in medieval Latin, the scribes were often unsure of the correct word - hence their frequent lapse into English or even French! In 1473, for instance, one entry read: 'John Smythe pro emandacione de la locke in the tower...1d'.]

Feast of St Michael the Archangel

1368	*Wax bought to make two lights against the feast of St Michael...2s 6d*
1377	*3lbs of wax bought to be placed at the foot of St Michael...1s 10d*
1461	*For candle bearer against the day of the dedication of the church...3d*

A special celebration was held on 29th September each year in St Michael's parish to mark the dedication of the church to its patron saint, St Michael the Archangel.

Although we have no details of what form the celebration took, there are at least some clues in the churchwardens' accounts. It would seem that, at the beginning of the mass on that day, two specially-made candles of considerable size (judging by the large amount of money spent on them in 1368) were carried by an appointed candle bearer (who was duly

A picture by Van Bons, dating from 1580, showing preparations in progress for a mystery play by a group of travelling players - similar to those who visited St Michael's Church in 1482. The parishioners gather round to watch with interest. (By courtesy of the Mary Evans Picture Library)

rewarded for the task) in a procession to the statue or picture of St Michael, where they were lit. This was undoubtedly an important and meaningful occasion for the congregation, who felt a special relationship with this particular saint and trusted him to intercede with God on their behalf.

All Saints' Day

1462	*For a candle bought on the day of All Saints...1d*
1414	*For the night of All Saints for candles...0.5d*

All Saints' Day - along with All Souls' Day - fell right at the beginning of November and formed part of Hallowtide, the Festival of the Dead. The main service, which featured a candle-lit procession, was in the evening when prayers were said on behalf of those who had died in an attempt to improve their condition in purgatory - just as the ringing of the church bells until midnight sought to bring reassurance to their souls.

*****

It can be seen, therefore, that the events of ritual year totally dominated the lives of local people. There is little doubt that, in the main, they greatly looked forward to the festivals and the atmosphere generated. After all, such occasions provided this deeply religious congregation - surrounded as it always was by the ravages of death - with spiritual satisfaction and the reassurance of eternal life. Furthermore, they also created an enjoyable focus for social gatherings and the generation of both neighbourliness and community spirit. It should be remembered that most members of St Michael's Church in 1485 lived otherwise drab lives in distinctly modest homes and seldom travelled beyond the parish boundary.

Only very occasionally were they excited by sensational events within their midst - such as the murder committed inside St Michael's in the middle of the fifteenth century. In consequence, the bishop had made a special visitation to reconcile and bless the church 'lately polluted by the shedding of blood'. Under normal circumstances, however, it was the colourful processions and subsequent merriment which not only brought a welcome degree of entertainment, but also a much-needed opportunity for emotional release. Largely illiterate, the parishioners relished the portrayal of the gospel story in visual form as the year unfolded through striking ceremonies and dramatic ritual - ritual in which they themselves played a full and active part.

SOURCES USED IN CHAPTER 1

Printed Material:
Buchanan, Brenda: 'The Avon Navigation and the Inland Port of Bath' (in *Bath History*, vol. 6, 1996)
Cunliffe, Barry: *The City of Bath* (1986)
Davenport, Peter: *Medieval Bath Uncovered* (2002)
Devenish, William H: *A Guide to St Thomas à Becket* (1919)
Duffy, Eamon: *The Stripping of the Altars: Traditional Religion in England, 1400-1580* (2005 edtn.)
Fawcett, Trevor & Bird, Stephen: *Bath: A History and Guide* (1994)
Green, Emanuel: 'A Bath Poll Tax, 2, Richard II' (in *Proceedings of the Bath Natural History & Antiquarian Field Club*, vol. 6, no. 3, 1889)
Green, Emanuel: 'The Earliest Map of Bath' (in *Proceedings of the Bath Natural History & Antiquarian Field Club*, vol. 6, no. 1, 1889)
Holland, Elizabeth: 'The Earliest Bath Guildhall' (in *Bath History*, vol. 2, 1988)
Hutton, Ronald: *The Stations of the Sun: A History of the Ritual Year in Britain* (1996)
Hylson-Smith, Kenneth: *Bath Abbey: a History* (2003)
James, P.R: *The Charters of Bath*, vol. 2, (1942)
Jenner, Michael: *The Architectural Heritage of Britain and Ireland* (1993)
Keevil, A.J: 'The Barton of Bath' (in *Bath History*, vol. 6, 1996)
King, A.J. & Watts, B.H: *The Municipal Records of Bath, 1189-1604* (1885)
Oldridge, Darren: *Strange Histories* (2005)
Pearson, Prebendary: 'Churchwardens' Accounts, St Michael's, Bath: Introduction' (in *Proceedings of the Somerset Archaeological and Natural History Society*, vol. 23, 1877). For edited transcripts of the accounts see also vol. 26, 1880.
Rubin, Miri: *The Hollow Crown: A History of Britain in the Late Middle Ages* (2005)
Shickle, C.W: *Ancient Deeds Belonging to the Corporation of Bath, 13th to 16th Centuries* (1921)
Shickle, C.W: *The Royal Seals and Charters of the Bath Corporation* (1908)
Shickle, C.W: *The Early Water Supply of Bath* (1917)

Documentary Material:

Bath Record Office:	Bath Chamberlain's Accounts, 1579-1603
Somerset Record Office:	St Michael's Bath Churchwardens' Accounts, 1349-1575
National Archives:	Acts of the Privy Council, March 1591 (complaint by the freemen)

Note: Although the prior held the advowsons (i.e. the right to appoint the clergy) of the five churches in Bath in 1485, all but one of the clergy so appointed enjoyed the status of 'rector' (i.e. they were entitled to receive all the tithes, both great and small, from their parishioners - usually paid in kind). The one exception was the priest in charge at St Mary de Stall, who was styled 'vicar'. The reason for this was that in 1263 Bishop Button had granted the rectories of both the church of St Mary de Stall and the chapel at Widcombe to the prior - on condition that the prior as rector appointed a vicar (or 'substitute') to be responsible for both parishes.

In 1322, Bishop Drockensford clarified the issue, after a dispute, when he allocated the greater tithes of the rectory (consisting of corn, hay, lamb and wool - and worth two-thirds of the total value) to the prior and the lesser tithes (milk, swine, eggs, flax, apples, beer etc) to support the vicar - on condition that the latter found a resident chaplain to take services at Widcombe.

After the dissolution of Bath Priory in 1539, all its property was seized by the king, including the rectories of St Mary de Stall and Widcombe. In 1545, therefore, Henry VIII - to raise money - leased the rectory of Widcombe to Richard Chapman, clothier. Meanwhile the church of St Thomas à Becket in Widcombe continued to be supplied with a chaplain by the vicar of St Mary de Stall's until the amalgamation of Bath churches in 1583 (see Chapter 4).

CHAPTER 2

1539: Decline of the Priory and the Economy

There were in [living memory] three clothiers at one time, thus named - Style, Kent and Chapman - by whom the town of Bath then flourished. Since the death of them, it hath somewhat decayed...

This John [of Tours] pulled down the old church of St Peter at Bath and erected a new, much fairer, and was buried in the middle of the presbytery thereof, whose image I saw lying there a nine years since; at which time all the church that he made lay to waste and was unroofed - and weeds grew about this John of Tours' sepulchre.

Source: Lucy T Smith (ed.): *The Itinerary of John Leland, 1535-1543* (1907 edtn.)

John Leland, a scholarly schoolmaster, was commissioned by Henry VIII in 1533 to investigate the contents of monastic libraries so that their priceless collections 'might be brought out of deadly darkness into lively light'. This task took him on an extensive tour of the country, during which he developed a deep fascination for the towns and buildings he observed along the way. His thoughts were written down in what became known as his *Itinerary*. He certainly visited Bath on two occasions - probably in 1533 and again in 1542. These extracts highlight the decline of two vital aspects of life in the city - namely, the cloth industry and the Priory.

John Leland (?1506-1552). An engraving by Thomas Charles Wageman from a painting by Hans Holbein the Younger. (By courtesy of the National Portrait Gallery, London)

The Benedictine Priory

(i) Daily Life in the Priory

If religion in the fifteenth century dominated the lives of individuals in the parish of St Michael's *without*, then the Benedictine Priory made a major impact on everyday affairs within the city of Bath. Not only did it physically occupy over one quarter of the land inside the city walls, it also controlled - for much of the late medieval period - the city's affairs and the livelihood of its residents (see Chapter 1). By 1485, therefore, the Priory's twenty-two monks - dressed in their characteristic black robes - had become well-known figures to Bath residents and very much part of the local community.

Although the chief task of the monks was to live a life of prayer, worship and service, the priory had also emerged as a centre of scholarship. The monks delighted not only in making use of their long-established library of valuable books, but also in working in the peaceful atmosphere of the cloisters on the task of illuminating beautiful manuscripts. Furthermore, they provided relief for the poor, medicine for the sick and education for the sons of local citizens, not all of whom went on to join the Benedictine order (see Chapter 3).

Many of the more senior monks had special responsibilities. The prior, who was the head of the community and appointed for life, was assisted by **the sub prior**, who drew up the daily programme of tasks, dealt with matters of discipline and ensured that the doors were locked at night. **The sacrist**, who was responsible for the church interior, looked after the bread and wine, robes, altar cloth, chalices and candles - not to mention the ringing of the bell and the cleaning of the floor. **The precentor** (or cantor) was in charge of the music, the training of novices and the issue of books, ink and parchment.

The cellarer, with overall responsibility for food and drink, not only visited the market to purchase any items required over and above those produced by the monks themselves, but also stood at the hatch in the refectory to ensure that nothing went to waste. While **the kitchener** was in sole charge of the cooks and the production of meals, **the refectorian**'s task was to organise fresh rushes for the floor; supply napkins, cups and spoons for use during the meal; and set out the water and towels required for the washing of hands in the 'lavatorium', just outside the dining room door. Hygiene of this sort was important at at time when forks were unknown and food was largely eaten with the fingers. After the monks had filed into the refectory and the abbot had said grace, the meal was taken in absolute silence while a religious text was read from the pulpit. If, therefore, they required a neighbour to pass ingredients along the table, they could only communicate by means of their well-practised sign language

The infirmarian took care of any sick or infirm monks in the Priory's hospital, while **the janitor** or porter (who was sometimes a layman) controlled the main gate, checking the requirements of visitors. The work of two other officials illustrates the belief of the Benedictines in the importance of service in the outside world. **The guest master** (or hosteller) was responsible for offering overnight accommodation and sustenance to any pilgrims visiting the Priory's collection of relics or travellers passing through the city;

A Benedictine monk wearing a hood and cowl over the habit. (From Sir William Dugdale's Monasticon, *1655)*

whereas **the almoner** undertook the vital work of providing relief for the poor. As Mike Chapman and Elizabeth Holland have shown, part of his duty was to receive needy travellers on their arrival in the area just inside the West Gate. In the thirteenth century, several properties were held by him at the far end of Westgate Street (presumably in connection with his work among impoverished visitors to the city).

The Priory was, in fact, extremely generous in helping the poor and distressed. Kenneth Hylson-Smith has demonstrated, for example, that up to a hundred impoverished local people were frequently fed on important religious anniversaries throughout the year. Furthermore, when a monk died, the cellarer continued to issue that monk's daily ration of food for the ensuing twelve months - for distribution amongst needy individuals; while, on the anniversary of the monk's death, the

Two contemporary pictures taken from Abbot Gasquet: English Monastic Life *(1904), showing the community of Westminster in the choirstalls (below) and the Chapter House (above).*

local poor were treated to a gift of bread and ale. It was also traditional on Maundy Thursday for the cellarer to issue a special invitation to the exact number of poor people as there were monks in the priory. Each monk then proceeded to wash the feet of his guest (as Christ had washed the feet of his disciples), before serving him with a meal which included the rare luxury of meat.

Much of each day, of course, was spent in prayer and worship with a round of **nine services** in all, commencing with matins at midnight. The monks slept fully dressed, except for their cowls and fur-lined shoes, so that they could move quickly to the church via the night stairs (which led straight down from their dormitory). In between these services, there was ordinary work to be undertaken - a daily meeting in the chapter house for practical matters to be discussed, after the reading of a chapter from the Rule of St Benedict; private study in the cloisters; manual labour among crops and animals in the neighbouring fields; fishing in the fishponds; or supervision of production in their highly-profitable woollen cloth industry. [It is worth noticing that the importance of weaving to the Priory's fortunes from the fourteenth century onwards was reflected in the fact that a shuttle was incorporated into its official arms.]

After the church itself, it was **the cloister** that really dominated the monk's daily life. Not only did it

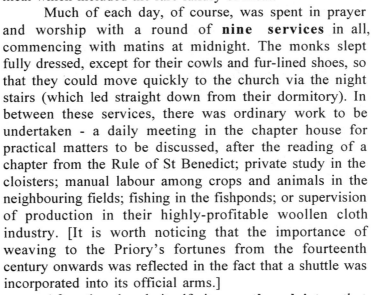

Three photographs showing the cloisters of the former Benedictine monastery at Gloucester Cathedral, built with this magnificent fan vaulting in the fourteenth and early fifteenth centuries. The west section (bottom) was where the novices and children were taught. Individual carrels or cubicles (top left) provided monks with the opportunity of studying quietly or illuminating manuscripts at their own desks. The lavatorium (top right), supplied with water from the Fullbrook stream, was where the monks would wash their hands before entering the refectory. The lavatorium in Bath Priory would also enjoy the luxury of running water, thanks to the city's network of pipes - see Chapter 1. (Author's photographs)

provide a gathering place before meals in the refectory, services in the church and meetings in the chapter house, it also offered - on the north side - a sunny spot where the monk could study at his desk. While the west side gave space for the schoolroom, where novices and children from outside were taught, the east side was taken up by the Priory's administration officials.

    Life - at least in theory - was hard; food simple; conditions spartan; sleep broken; and discipline strict. Monks who had erred were made to confess their sins in public at the daily meeting, where punishments - including flogging, meals taken in isolation or a diet of bread and water - were also decided. Sadly, however, this lifestyle based on dedicated self-sacrifice was - by 1539 - not always evident in practice.

(ii) The Decline of the Priory

When Bishop Oliver King conducted a visitation of Bath Priory in 1499, he found to his horror a state of lax discipline, idleness, dilapidated buildings and a group of monks who were all too eager to succumb to the temptations of the flesh. Women, for instance, were often to be found within the precincts of the Priory 'at unseemly hours'; while feasting occurred outside the restricted zone of the refectory. In point of fact, this decline in standards was no sudden occurrence, but was rather the end result of **an accumulation of neglect** stretching back over two centuries. This was partly reflected in the gradual slump in size suffered by the community over the years with just twenty-two monks on the roll in 1499, compared with forty in 1206. There were many contributing factors to this situation.

    The fact that the bishop, who was the titular abbot of the Priory, was largely absent from the city throughout the fourteenth and fifteenth centuries (see Chapter 1) meant that effective control was often lacking. In consequence, there were frequent reports of extravagance and immorality, which largely went unchecked under a succession of weak priors. In 1346, for instance, the prior himself - John de Iford - was actually found guilty of adultery; while in 1445, Dom Robert Veyse was charged with both adultery and living 'an evil life'. Bishop Beckington, who had arrested Veyse by royal writ, despatched the culprit back to Bath for punishment (namely, strict imprisonment on a perpetual diet of bread and water) - only for Prior Southbroke to ignore the order and permit Veyse's escape.

    Secondly, the cathedral church was enormous in size, highly expensive to maintain and ridiculously unsuited to such a small number of monks. The result was - given the wanton extravagance of a succession of priors - that the buildings fell into a state of total disrepair through both lack of resources and lack of will. Prior Crist, for example, had run up a debt of over £700 by the mid-fourteenth century. Indeed, such was the state of the fabric that the bishop twice (in 1310 and 1324) ordered churches within the diocese to make contributions towards a programme of minor, but urgent repairs at Bath. However, as Peter Davenport has shown, no substantial work took place thereafter for almost one hundred years.

    This serious situation was greatly exacerbated by the totally irresponsible behaviour of **Prior John Dunster** in the 1470s. Setting himself the ambition of rebuilding the refectory - even though the church itself was suffering from structural decay of a terminal nature - he raised over £666 through loans and the sale of corodies. The purchase of a corody gave the recipient various long-term benefits (often for life) - for instance, the right to receive free board and lodging at the Priory, the security of a pension or various other special allowances (see page 43). Although the detail varied from case to case, the accumulated on-going cost of this practice proved to be highly damaging to the Priory's future financial commitments.

When Dunster's successor, **Prior John Cantlow**, arrived in 1482, he found that the place 'was in great poverty for many causes', resulting in 'the sudden ruin of the most of the church'. Indeed, a large part of the building had already collapsed! Such was the size of the community's deficit that it was actually excused payment by the crown of the tax known as 'the tenth' for a period of eleven years from 1485 [for an explanation of this tax see below]. Cantlow was also furious at Dunster's outrageous conduct on leaving the Priory in 1482. He had apparently purloined a large quantity of silverware belonging to the institution - including a number of valuable items from the prior's own chapel - with the aim of presenting them (as an impressive gesture) to the community of St Augustine's, Canterbury, where he had just been appointed abbot.

Prior John Cantlow's contemporary portrait in stained glass, which is set in the east window of St Catherine's church in Batheaston. From W.H. Devenish: A Guide to St Thomas à Becket, Widcombe *(1919)*

It has to be said, however, that Prior Cantlow himself did little to salvage the parlous state of the Priory's finances. He, too, was ambitious to achieve personal glory - not to mention a large measure of personal comfort! A substantial section of the Prior's lodgings (later known as Abbey House), on the west side of the cloisters, was rebuilt at great cost. Furthermore, he launched himself on three costly construction projects outside Bath with major alterations or rebuilding work being undertaken at the Hospital of St Mary Magdalene on Holloway, St Thomas à Becket's Church in Widcombe and St Catherine's Church in Batheaston.

In view of all these circumstances, **Bishop Oliver King** resolved - following his visitation in 1499 - that the time had now come for decisive action. On the death of Prior Cantlow in that year, he immediately vetoed the monks' preferred choice as successor and appointed his own man instead - namely, William Bird. Finding however that the cathedral church was 'ruined to the foundations', King quickly came to the reluctant conclusion that it was now beyond repair and that any attempt to rebuild it would be far outside the means of the Priory itself - even 'within a hundred years'.

According to Sir John Harington (writing a century later), it was at this point that King - while agonising over what course of action to take - had a dream. In it he saw angels ascending and descending a ladder to heaven, alongside which was an olive tree with a crown resting on top. He also heard a voice saying: 'Let an Olive establish the Crown and let a King restore the Church'. The bishop, who had worked closely as adviser to Henry VII as secretary of state, interpreted this as a call from God to spearhead the rebuilding of the cathedral church. As a result of this experience, he now firmly resolved to set himself at the forefront of a fundraising campaign - or, in his own words 'to put our helping hands to the work, without sparing our labour or expenditure', thus ensuring 'a speedy dispatch or completing of the said work'.

He immediately wrote to Prior Bird in 1500 to sting him into vigorous action, setting out a series of injunctions aimed at a root-and-branch reform of the institution:

With sorrow we have found - among other things - that our cathedral church of Bath, by the negligence of several of the priors, has not been repaired or restored, nay has gone utterly to destruction; and that they themselves have frittered themselves away in pleasures. And we deplore with paternal sorrow that the present prior - to whom we do not ascribe the fault of his predecessors - is remiss and not zealous for the repair or re-building of the said church...

Therefore, with the intention of preventing the above defects of the monks, their pleasures and slothfulness, and the ruin of the church arising from over-indulgence in pensions, in clothing, food and drink - and also not to risk the loss of the goodwill of the faithful in giving alms, if we leave the said prior and convent unreformed - we decree that these present injunctions are to be faithfully observed by the same.

This stone carving of an olive tree with a crown resting in it, which stands on the west front of Bath Abbey, provides a permanent reminder of Oliver King's dream. His bishop's mitre is set above the tree. (Author's photograph)

The bishop had in fact made a revealing discovery in the Priory's accounts, which he had carefully examined - namely, that their annual income from property and other sources amounted to the not inconsiderable sum of £480. On the strength of this knowledge, he now proceeded to set a most stringent budget for future years. The strictest economies were therefore imposed in the injunctions he now relayed to Prior Bird. Monks in future would only be permitted to eat their meals in the refectory, where portions would be tightly controlled by the cellarer. The days of feasting outside were at an end. Meat, for instance, would be reserved exclusively for those who were physically weak. Their clothing was to be made of inexpensive and coarse material and each monk was required to produce an inventory of all the items he possessed, returning all non-essential goods to the common store. Then, after careful consideration, Bishop King calculated that a sum of £180 a year out of the revenue would be sufficient to support the general running of the Priory, leaving £300 a year to be set aside as a contribution to the building of a new church.

(iii) Rise of the New Church

Prior William Bird rose to the challenge set before him by Bishop King and set about the task of reforming the Priory while, at the same time, supervising the construction of the new church. King had wisely decided to plan a much smaller building in keeping with the reduced size of the Benedictine community, which now averaged just twenty-two monks. Bearing in mind that it was deemed essential to build alongside the existing cloisters, the final solution saw the entire replacement contained within the boundaries of the nave of the old Norman cathedral. Nevertheless, the bishop was determined that the style of the new church should be elegant, modern and impressive - much in keeping with the splendid work undertaken by Henry VII in London, which he had witnessed at first hand during his time as adviser to the crown. It is hardly surprising, therefore, that he turned to the brothers, Robert and William Vertue, the king's master masons, to undertake the work in Bath.

In spite of all his other duties, Bishop King continued as a regular and enthusiastic visitor to the site until his death in 1503, by which time the construction was well under way. Building as far as possible on the foundations of the Norman cathedral and using as much of the old stone as could be salvaged, the workmen initially concentrated on the east end. Although the original intention had been to cap the whole church - built in perpendicular style - with a flat wooden roof, the Vertue brothers succeeded in persuading King, just before his death, that it would be far more sensible to have a stone roof with impressive fan vaulting of the kind they were installing in Henry VII's chapel at Westminster Abbey. 'There shall be none so goodly neither in England nor France', they assured him.

Meanwhile, Prior Bird remained totally committed to the project, even contributing much of his own private fortune. By 1518, the stonework and vaulting had largely been completed in the chancel and choir, although it was not until 1525 that the area was finally ready for services to take place. [Throughout this interim period, the monks had continued to worship in what remained of the former church.] Sadly, Bird died just before the official opening took place - but not before a most beautiful chantry chapel (the Bird Chapel) had been completed in his honour (see photograph in Chapter 3). The work of William Vertue, it contained the most exquisite, fine stone carvings. It was, therefore, Bird's successor - **Prior William Holloway** - who presided at the opening service, when he was carried shoulder high into the chancel to the strains of music played on the newly-fitted organ. By then, the whole area was looking resplendent, the striking east window having been glazed with the best glass imported specially imported from France.

Prior Holloway continued to press ahead with plans for completion. Although it had originally been intended to continue the fan vaulting over the nave (the stumps to take the necessary flying buttresses are clearly visible on John Speed's later map - but not the buttresses themselves), the plan was eventually abandoned and a wooden roof constructed instead. By the time of the Priory's dissolution in 1539, much of the outer stone work had been completed, including the tower, the transepts and the great west front with its imposing representation of Oliver King's dream. Certainly, when Dr Richard Layton visited the Priory in 1535 (see below), he observed that 'the buildings were in good repair'.

(iv) Dissolution of the Priory

By 1530, a growing sense of nationalism in England had stirred many members of parliament into a strong dislike of interference by foreigners in domestic affairs - while, at the same time, a growing sense of anti-clericalism had led others to express disgust at the perceived wealth, laziness and immorality of the monastic orders. When, therefore, Henry VIII found himself in headlong collision with the pope over his desire to divorce Catherine of Aragon and marry the protestant, Anne Boleyn, he was not lacking in support.

With the wholehearted backing of his new Archbishop of Canterbury, Thomas Cranmer, he defied the pope's authority on both matters and - through the Act of

Supremacy, passed by parliament in 1534 - duly became 'Supreme Head on earth of the Church of England'. Having broken with Rome and gained his new bride, Henry now cast his covetous eyes on the monasteries, which were temptingly rich. He quickly set about the task of establishing a case against them by appointing five commissioners to conduct a general **visitation of monasteries** throughout the land. The men chosen were lawyers, whose clear aim was to gain an outright conviction of guilt - not a gradual reform of weakness.

It was therefore in the summer of 1535 that commissioner **Dr Richard Layton** visited Bath. Later appointed Dean of York, he had already boasted that he would know an acquaintance living 'within ten or twelve miles' of each monastery visited, who would brief him in advance - 'so that no knavery can be hid from us in that country'. Eventually, he was able to enter his findings in the *Valor Ecclesiaticus* or 'Black Book of Monasteries'. This not only gave details of each commissioner's personal impressions, but also an account of the assets of each institution. Layton's report on Bath Priory presented, at first sight, a balanced assessment. He concluded, for instance, that Prior Holloway was 'a right virtuous man - and, I suppose, no better of his coat; a man simple and not of the greatest wit'.

The monks, on the other hand, were 'worse than I have any found yet, both in buggery and adultery - some of them having ten women, some eight and the rest so fewer'. Furthermore, although the buildings were 'well repaired', the Priory was £400 in debt. In view of the fact that Dr Layton clearly understood the king's desire to uncover unsavoury evidence against the monasteries, it is highly likely that the report on Bath Priory was biassed in the extreme and the faults exaggerated - particularly in relation to the immorality of the monks. Layton was also keen to provide Thomas Cromwell, the king's vicar-general who had been charged with the task of organising the dissolution, with evidence of the presence of any holy relics which prompted superstition among the people. He therefore forwarded a number of examples located at Bath:

Henry VIII (1491-1547). Portrait by an unknown artist. (By courtesy of the National Portrait Gallery, London

I send you the chains of St Peter, which women put about them at the time of their delivery. It is counted a great relic because St Peter is supposed to be the patron of the church. It is a very mockery and a great abuse that the prior should carry it on Lammas Day [1st August - see Chapter 6] in a basin of silver in procession and every monk kiss it after the gospel with great solemnity - though they have no writing to show how they came by it. I send you also a great comb called St Mary Magdalen's comb, and St Dorothy's and St Margaret's combs. They cannot tell how they came by them.

EARL OF ESSEX.

(left) Thomas Cromwell, 1st Earl of Essex (?1485-1540). A portrait after Hans Holbein the Younger. (By courtesy of the National Portrait Gallery, London)

On the purely factual side, however, Dr Layton was able to reveal the exact **value of the Priory's assets**. In 1535, when the survey was taken, it owned estates and other properties in Walcot, Weston, North Stoke, Ford, Batheaston, South Stoke, Stanton Prior, Lyncombe, Widcombe, Chelworth, Compton Dando, Charlcombe, Yelverton, Ashwick, Monkton Combe, Combe Down and Priston - plus further lands in Gloucestershire, Wiltshire and Bristol. Nearer home, it also possessed a number of properties within the city of Bath. Marta Inskip has shown that, according to the prior's rental roll of 1504, there were 82 such properties listed in the following locations: Southgate Street 9, Stall Street 23, Westgate Street 13, Cheap Street 9, Northgate Street 15 and, in the area outside the North Gate 13. It should also be mentioned, however, that the actual number of ex-Priory properties granted as an endowment to King Edward's School in 1552 was 101. All-in-all, Dr Layton calculated that the Priory's net annual income from its possessions amounted to £617 2s 3d.

As a result of this valuation, Bath Priory was not included in the first wave of suppression in 1536, which affected all such institutions with an annual income of under £200 - allegedly dissolved because of their 'manifest sin, vicious, carnal and abominable living'. Nevertheless, Prior William Holloway quickly realised that it was only a matter of time before his community suffered the same fate. Determined therefore to salvage what he could out of a desperate situation, he now embarked on a cunning strategy to gain as much support and sympathy as possible. He had already sent the king, via Dr Layton, a thinly-disguised bribe in the form of a quantity of 'Irish hawks' to pander to the king's love of falconry.

He then turned his attention to Thomas Cromwell. Two bribes were therefore despatched - the first, 'an old book, *Opera Anselmi*' (which had been discovered in the Priory's library); and the second, a yearly pension of five pounds, drawn from the income of their estates at Ford. His two-fold aim in all this was, first, to secure an immediate release for himself and his monks from the injunction imposed by Dr Layton, forbidding them to leave the Priory precincts; and secondly, to ensure the best 'redundancy package' possible by way of pensions. Finally, the prior set about the task of winning powerful local allies in 1536 by leasing out many of the Priory's local farms at favourable rents and by granting corodies and other favours. This helped to create a powerful, vested interest of support, which the king would be reluctant to cross (see panel).

It the event, it all proved to be exactly as Prior Holloway had predicted. On 27th January 1539, Dr Tregonwell and Dr Petre arrived in Bath to organise what turned out to be the voluntary **surrender of the Priory**. There was no resistance by the monks - and no street protest by local people. The surrender document - which entailed the confiscation of all their estates by the king - was duly signed on 29th June by all twenty-one members of the community, including the prior. Partly as a result of their co-operation and partly, perhaps, as a result of the bribes, the terms of surrender were extremely favourable. Prior Holloway was granted an annual pension of £80, plus a tenement in Stall Street worth a yearly rent of ten shillings; and John Pitt, the sub prior, received a pension of £9, while the rest of the monks were allocated pensions ranging from £8 to £4 13s 4d.

Prior Holloway, in fact, did even better out of the settlement. Among the powerful local friends he had cultivated was Sir Thomas Arundel of Wardour Castle, a devout man, who had been appointed crown bailiff and receiver of surrendered monasteries in the area. Arundel agreed to permit Holloway to continue his occupancy of the Prior's Lodgings - a promise which was honoured also by Matthew Colthurst, who bought the lodgings in 1544 (see below). Holloway, therefore, remained there for the next eight years, during which time he was able to indulge his passion for alchemy, his search for the philosopher's stone and his quest for the elixir of life. In particular, he revelled in experiments based on the hot waters of Bath, which had been piped into the Priory.

There was, however, no happy ending to his life. Clearly heartbroken by the closure of the Priory and the church, which he had worked so hard to complete, he suffered a serious nervous breakdown following the theft of all his chemicals and medicines. According to his great friend, Thomas Charnock (the alchemist, with whom he had closely worked on experiments), these had been hidden within the Priory for security. 'He had our stores, our medicine, our elixir - all of which, when the abbey was suppressed, he hid in a wall'. Finding that these precious materials had been taken (an action which clearly destroyed his one remaining purpose in life), he finally lost his sanity and later his sight. He apparently ended his days wandering aimlessly around the country, guided by a young boy.

Nevertheless, events were to prove that Holloway had been right to cooperate with the king's commissioners and not to resist the confiscations. Exactly five months after the formal surrender of Bath Priory, the Abbot of Glastonbury was tried and executed - together with two other monks - 'for robbing Glastonbury Church'. In a report written to the king, Lord Russell described how the abbot had 'embezzled plate and ornaments' sufficient to set up 'a new abbey', hiding them 'in walls, vaults and other secret places'. After he had been found guilty at a trial in Wells, he was - according to custom - dragged along the streets on a hurdle to his place of execution in Glastonbury, where he was hanged, drawn and quartered. Then, as a warning to others, his legs and arms were dispatched to Bath, Wells, Ilchester and Bridgwater and set on poles for public display. His head was fixed 'on the abbey gate at Glastonbury'. Terror was an essential weapon of control for sixteenth-century monarchs.

(Below) *A contemporary print of 1555, which illustrates the ruthlessness with which the dissolution of the monasteries was put into execution. Six monks from Charterhouse in Finsbury are being dragged through the streets on a sledge to their execution on the scaffold, which can be seen in the distance. (By courtesy of the Guildhall Library, Corporation of London).*

Meanwhile, **Sir Thomas Arundel** had appointed Thomas Llewelyn - the prior's former steward at Bath - to carry on with his duty of collecting rents from the priory estates, but now of course on behalf of the king. The remaining problem facing Arundel and Llewelyn was what to do with the newly-built church and its adjacent buildings. It was eventually decided to offer the entire site to the mayor and corporation of Bath at the remarkably cheap price of 500 marks [around £750] - an offer which was apparently rejected by the corporation of Bath for fear of being charged later with fraudulently cheating the king of its true market value. Furthermore, the dean and chapter of Wells Cathedral also refused to buy the church. In view of the absence of potential bidders, therefore, Llewelyn decided to strip the property of its saleable assets in order to raise sufficient cash for the payment of the former monks' pensions.

Four hundred and eighty tons of lead were consequently removed from the roofs of the church and its cloisters and put up for sale (a fact which ensured that the wooden roof of the nave - now exposed to the elements - eventually decayed). Eight of the bells in the tower were sold to Francis Edwards, the Welsh brazier, for just over £98; all the glass and iron bars from the windows to Anthony Payne for £30; the masonry from the walls of the dormitory to Robert Cokes for £10 and that from the cloisters to Henry Bewshyn of Barton Grange for £8; and the contents and building materials of the refectory to Sir Walter Denys for £10. Within the space of just three years, therefore, the monastic buildings had virtually been razed to the ground. The shell of the church itself was left to deteriorate in a neglected state until interest in its future was at last awakened some thirty years later.

The badly-plundered site of the Priory was eventually sold (16th March 1543) to **Humphrey Colles**. The crown granted him not only the monastery precinct (including adjacent land lying to the north, east and west of the church), but also a number of plots in both the Barton and the manor of Lyncombe, together with the meadows known as the Ham and the Ambury to the south of the city. Two days later, he sold on this acquisition to **Matthew Colthurst** of Hinton Charterhouse. A young barrister, who was one of the crown surveyors of monastery estates in Somerset, Colthurst was also seeking nomination at the time as member of parliament for Bath.

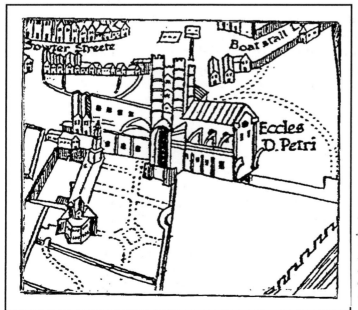

With this in mind, he was keen to find a house in the city. He immediately saw enormous potential in the Prior's Lodgings as a family dwelling - the only monastic building to have survived the recent destruction (largely thanks to the intervention of Thomas Llewelyn - see above).

This section of John Speed's map, probably drawn in the late sixteenth century, shows the former Priory Cathedral in its ruined state before the restoration had taken place. The nave is clearly lacking a roof, the north transept is completely missing and the old cloisters have been demolished. (Author's collection)

It is probable that historians have been mistaken in the past in dismissing Colles as a mere property speculator intent on making quick money from the sale of monastic estates. Based in Pitminster in Somerset, he was already a much-respected, major landowner in his own right and was eventually honoured by being appointed sheriff of Somerset in 1558. As Katharine Symons has pointed out, Colles and Colthurst knew each other extremely well, having worked closely as crown surveyors of monastery lands. In view of the fact that they were both interested in increasing their own land holding, it is not impossible that on occasions they acted for each other when desirable property came onto the market.

But whatever the background to the sale, Colthurst (who was indeed elected member of parliament for Bath in 1545) set about converting the Lodgings into a private house (later called Abbey House), once ex-Prior Holloway had left in 1547. On his death in July 1559, Colthurst's whole estate passed to his son, Edmund, who also lived in Hinton Charterhouse. Ten years later, in a most generous gesture, Edmund announced his intention to donate - free of charge - the former priory church, its churchyard and the adjacent land to the mayor and corporation of Bath. This sudden twist to the story was to spark off a series of events leading to the revival of the church (see Chapter 4).

*****

There is no evidence to suggest that the monks of Bath Priory had been unpopular with local people or that members of the council had led street demonstrations against their alleged immorality and corruption. Indeed, after they had been pensioned off, most of them were quietly absorbed into the community. Nicholas Jobbyn, for instance, not only became vicar of St Mary de Stall's Church and chaplain to the corporation, but also emerged as a major benefactor to the newly-established grammar school in 1552; while two other former monks were appointed to local churches - William Clements as rector of St Mary's by the North Gate; and Richard Gibbs as chaplain of St Thomas à Becket's in Widcombe.

There is, however, little doubt that the dissolution of the Priory changed the face of the city in a most dramatic and visible manner. Almost overnight, a large segment of the space within the city walls had virtually become redundant; and many individuals, who had worked for the Priory in various capacities, now found themselves facing the future with great uncertainty. Nevertheless, it is equally true to say that the dissolution was an event of mammoth significance, which sparked off a great revival in the city's fortunes.

As we have already seen in Chapter 1, the 'commonalty of Bath' (later to be styled 'the corporation') had been growing in strength and importance since 1189. Now, having shaken off the shackles of Priory dominance, it grasped its opportunity - as the century progressed - to increase its own power, seize vast tracts of land and establish tight control over all major areas of city life, including the church, the hot water baths, the school and the market. By doing all this, it gradually transformed the economy of Bath through the creation of a modern health resort to replace the declining cloth industry on which the medieval city had relied.

Nor can there be any doubt that - throughout it all - the hard-nosed businessmen, who made up the membership of the corporation, displayed a determination, zeal and commitment to do their very best for the city and its future. It is equally true, however, that these opportunists employed unscrupulous tactics, which at times bordered on the criminal (see Chapters 3 and 4).

Decline in the Economy

The prosperity of Bath in the fourteenth and fifteenth centuries had largely been based on the cloth industry. As we have already seen in Chapter 1, the whole operation of spinning, weaving and finishing the cloth had been controlled in the main by the Priory - although a number of prominent citizens had also made their fortunes as cloth merchants. Even the churchwardens of St Michael's Church Without kept a small flock of sheep to boost church income. Their accounts therefore give details of the sale of wool (twelve pence 'for 3lbs of wool of certain church sheep' in 1505); the cost of feeding the sheep in winter (thirteen pence in 1504); and the cost of pasture in summer (normally two shillings).

The local cloth industry undoubtedly enjoyed **a golden period** during the early sixteenth century, thanks to the work of three famous clothiers - Thomas Chapman, John Kent and Thomas Style (along with his son, Robert). Quite apart from their involvement in the cloth trade, these men also played an influential role in the life of the city as aldermen - and, in the case of Robert Style, as mayor. Thomas Chapman was incredibly wealthy and a major landowner. In his will, he left his wife and sons five houses (one of which contained two looms for weaving); and his three fulling mills in Weston, Twerton and Widcombe, together with all his equipment and stock. Thomas Style owned a large farm and some fulling mills in Bathwick, all of which eventually were inherited by his son, Robert, who also occupied a shop in Bath. (See the tax assessments on pages 41-42 to gain an idea of the enormous wealth of these people.)

As Joe Bettey has pointed out, the dissolution of Bath Priory in 1539 witnessed 'a ruthless scramble for monastic land'. Several of the clothiers, fullers and weavers, who had money to invest, took advantage of this opportunity, often employing unscrupulous methods in the process. William Chapman, for instance - who was a member of the wealthy clothier family - had apparently tricked William Felior, a broadloom weaver, into surrendering the lease, which he had been granted by the Priory for land in Widcombe. Chapman had allegedly promised him that, in return for the lease, he would always provide Felior with enough work to keep him busy on one loom. Felior had accepted, believing that this would give him far greater security for his wife and family than working on the land. Chapman, however, had reneged on his promise, denying before

A contemporary woodcut of two shepherds at work on the downs. (By permission of the British Library: Roxburghe Ballads, RAX.Rox. I.381)

the Court of Chancery in 1537 (to which Felior had complained) that he had ever made such a deal.

By the time of this complaint, however, the local cloth trade was already in a **state of decline**. When John Leland visited the city (probably in 1542), he remarked that the trade which had flourished so vigorously in the time of Style, Kent and Chapman had 'somewhat decayed' since their deaths. Bearing in mind the considerable number of people whose livelihoods had become dependent on it, the consequences of decline were considerable. An Act of Parliament in 1540 'for re-edifying towns' declared that houses had fallen down in Bath and 'do lie as desolate and vacant grounds, many replenished with uncleanness and filth'. Poverty, through lack of employment, inevitably brought with it signs of gradual decay.

There were several reasons for this decline of Bath as a major centre for cloth production at a time when the export of woollen cloth was continuing to expand. Of great significance was the growth of **large-scale capitalist clothiers**, who shifted the production of cloth away from the controls of guild-dominated towns, such as Bath, to the countryside outside. There they were free to develop the 'putting-out system', which involved a considerable number of families working in their own homes with materials provided by the capitalist. As D.C. Coleman has described, children carded the wool; women spun it into yarn; and men wove the fabric - after which the cloth was returned to the clothier for fulling and finishing.

Locally, therefore, we see the growth of production throughout the century in such villages as Twerton, Bathwick, Widcombe, Beckington, Lullington and Freshford - all of which were able to draw on the Avon and its tributaries for power to drive the fulling mills and clear water for scouring the cloths after fulling. The best local example of the new breed of capitalist clothier was John Ashe from Freshford, who employed up to two thousand workers along the Avon valley from the beginning of the seventeenth century, dispatching his finished cloths in weekly convoys to London for export to the continent. By 1603, production in Bath itself was largely confined to small independent clothiers, spinners and weavers, who traded their materials in the weekly cloth market outside the North Gate.

The other problem facing the traditional Bath clothier was that of **competition** from areas such as East Anglia, where operators had benefited from new techniques brought over by Dutch and Flemish immigrants. Whereas the industry in North Somerset had always specialised in the manufacture of a fine, heavy broadcloth (measuring some five feet in width) - cloth

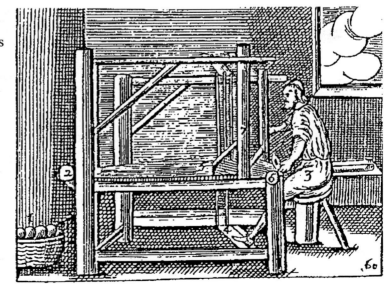

A contemporary woodcut showing a broad loom weaver at work. Many such looms were to be found in Bath within the area of Walcot Street and Broad Street. From J.A. Comenius, Orbis Sensualum Pictus, *1672 edtn. by permission of the British Library (1607.2351)*

which was exported undyed to Germany and Holland - the East Anglian producers were beginning to manufacture the new 'Spanish medley', which was a much lighter, smoother cloth in an attractive range of colours. This quickly appealed to the more fashionable end of the market. However, it was not until 1625 that these new methods were introduced into North Somerset by John Ashe - a move which sparked a much-needed revival.

By 1586, the situation inside Bath - set against a background of soaring inflation - had become serious. [During the sixteenth century, national food prices roughly quadrupled, while wages only witnessed a two-fold increase.] In that year, a letter reached the sheriff and justices of Somerset from the privy council stating that 'the poor sort of people inhabiting about the city of Bath' and its neighbourhood, who had previously made their living in the woollen industry, were no longer being set to work. The condition had become so acute, because of harvest failure and food shortages, that public order was now in danger.

The justices were therefore ordered to summon all the local clothiers to a meeting and instruct those who still had stocks of raw material to re-employ their former workers immediately. Those who refused were to be reported to the queen. This pressure seems to have had a salutary effect - at least in the short term. In April 1587, the Earl of Leicester wrote from Bath to Sir Francis Walsingham (the Secretary of State), describing 'the great decay of trade and distress in the country'. Nevertheless, he continued, enormous credit was due to the clothiers, who kept many of the poor people in work in spite of losing a good deal of money themselves in the process.

This gloomy state of affairs within the cloth industry continued until well into the seventeenth century. By 1622, the mayor of Bath was informing the privy council that Bath had become 'a very little, poor city, our clothmen much decayed and many of their workmen amongst us relieved by the city'. (For further details of the cloth industry and its decline, see John Wroughton, *Stuart Bath, 1603-1714*).

A woman spinning outside her cottage - part of a large work force which supplied spun thread for the independent weavers and capitalist clothiers. (By permission of the British Library: ref - Roxburghe Ballads, RAX.Rox. I, pt. 2.353)

Burdens of Taxation: the Subsidies of 1524 and 1541

Quite apart from the need to contribute to purely local taxes (such as collections to support the poor, the church tithe, the trained soldiers' rate or coat-and-conduct money), the citizens of Bath were also subjected to periodic demands from central government. There was, however, a longstanding tradition in England that the king should 'live of his own' in peacetime, covering the costs of government out of his regular income from crown lands, customs and excise duties and surviving feudal dues. It was only during times of war or major crisis that parliament traditionally felt able to grant a specific tax to help with the emergency. For much of the medieval period - from 1290 to 1523 - the most familiar tax employed was known as **'the fifteenth and tenth'**.

This was a charge on all personal property (including household goods, cattle, farm produce, traders' stock, money and valuables), levied at the rate of one fifteenth of its assessed value in country districts and one tenth in towns and cities. In 1334, the king came to an agreement that in future (to avoid unnecessary administration) the tax should become a fixed sum payable by each community whenever the tax was granted. It was then up to the parish officers in town or village to share out the tax locally as appropriate. The figure collected from Somerset, therefore, remained at around £1358 between 1334 and 1625, when the tax was finally abandoned. Out of this sum, Bath's contribution was always £13 6s 8d. Sadly, in view of the fixed and unchanging nature of the tax, detailed lists of taxpayers were not forwarded to central government and have therefore not survived.

Needless to say, with inflation soaring, the total sum raised nationally by the fifteenth and tenth (around £38,000) had plummeted in value by the time Henry VIII had ascended the throne in 1509. Faced by the cost of war and the threat of attack, parliament launched a new tax in 1523 known as **'the subsidy'** to supplement (not replace) the fifteenth and tenth. In the first instance, it was to be paid for just two years (1524 and 1525). Based largely on the value of personal possessions, the subsidy had three main tax bands - plus a further category for less wealthy people, who earned reasonable wages. The local assessments help us to build up a useful picture of comparative levels of affluence within the city.

The 1524 collection raised £43 6s 4d in Bath, which was over three times the amount raised previously by a typical fifteenth and tenth. The detailed returns, which have survived for all five city parishes, indicate that far more people had been drawn into the tax net. Indeed, in a community with a population of around 1500 people living in around 300 households, no fewer than 211 individuals (mostly the heads of households) paid tax, including 44 who were taxed just four pence as major wage earners. Of the remainder, 44 were in the lowest tax band, paying just four pence on possessions worth less than £1; while a mere 11, with possessions worth over £20, fell into the highest category. The other 107 were to be found somewhere in between, including 47 who paid twelve pence. Bearing in mind that the daily wage of a skilled carpenter or mason in 1524 was around six pence, this did not represent an excessive tax burden.

Within the city, the parishes containing the highest number of taxpayers were St Michael's Without (which included Broad Street and Walcot Street) with 69; and St James's (which was centred on Southgate Street and Binbury) with 54. These were followed by St Mary de Stall's (including Cheap Street and Stall Street) with 45; St Mary's by the North Gate (based largely on Northgate Street) with 26; and St Michael

Within (which lay in the area around Westgate Street) with 17. The poorest areas by far were the parish of St James, where the vast majority of taxpayers (83%) - chiefly craftsmen with small workshops and modest homes - paid the lowest rates of either four pence or one shilling; and the parish of St Michael Within, which contained many small workshops in the passages off Westgate Street, where 82% did so. On the other hand, whereas the parish of St Michael Without also contained a high proportion of low taxpayers (66%) - many of whom worked in the cloth industry - it also housed a fair number of businessmen in the middle tax band, who enjoyed a comfortable standard of living. Of the eleven wealthiest inhabitants, paying the highest rate of tax, no fewer than seven lived in the parish of St Mary by the North Gate.

By far **the most affluent individuals**, were the three clothiers who were credited by John Leland (writing after a visit to the city around 1542) as having been largely responsible for the city's prosperity. Alderman John Kent, who lived in the parish of St Michael *without*, was taxed on goods worth £133; Thomas Chapman, who from the parish of St Mary de Stall, on £134 in goods; and Alderman Thomas Style, resident of the parish of St Mary by the North Gate, on £100. To give an idea of the total dominance of these three men in terms of affluence, the next two wealthiest inhabitants were Henry Cavell with £46 in goods and William Chapman with £26.

Eight more subsidies were imposed between 1524 and 1559, when Elizabeth I was crowned queen. The rates of tax and the exemption limit varied considerably. In 1541, for instance, the subsidy - which was paid by a mere 31 inhabitants in Bath (compared with 211 in 1524) - only raised £15 15s 0d (compared with £43 16s 4d). Emanuel Green believed that these statistics provided proof of the sudden decay of the city and the collapse of its cloth-based economy, following the death of Kent, Chapman and Style. He failed to take account, however, of the higher exemption limit which had been set - raised from a mere £1 on the value of goods in 1524 to £20 in 1541. This consequently lifted most people well outside the tax threshold.

Queen Elizabeth I collected a subsidy on twenty occasions during the forty-three years of her reign to assist in underwriting the enormous cost of war and numerous overseas expeditions (see Chapter 3). From 1562, tax rates became standardised with an exemption threshold of £3 on the value of goods. This meant that the high number of taxpayers produced by the 1524 subsidy was never repeated during the Tudor period. For the subsidy of 1581, for example, just fifty Bath citizens were deemed liable to tax, contributing a total of £10 17s 8d. The highest contribution was in fact made by Edmund Colthurst (the benefactor who had donated the Abbey Church to the city) with a sum of £1 6s 8d - a far cry from the £6 13s 4d paid by John Kent in 1524.

It has to be stressed, however, that the assessments bore little relationship to the actual wealth of those involved. Not only were the assessors themselves local people who wished to remain on cordial terms with their neighbours, but the government also found it both convenient and efficient to work on fixed quotas for each parish. The assessors, therefore, simply ensured that they reached their target figure without worrying too much about the detail. Nevertheless, there was one great compensation for all tax payers. To be known in Tudor times as 'a subsidy man' conferred on the individual a trustworthy status in society. So much so, in fact, that juries in trials were often favourably swayed by the knowledge that the accused was, after all, 'a subsidy man'.

The Granting of Corodies

Corodies, which usually gave the recipients long-term benefits in sustenance, proved to be very costly to Bath Priory and a major factor in its financial ruin (see pages 29-30)

Even the reformer, Prior William Bird (see above), bestowed a substantial favour of this nature on his brother, John, when he appointed him principal doorkeeper at the Priory. This office, which was granted for life, was no more than a sinecure, bearing in mind that an 'under janitor' was also appointed at the same time 'to open and shut the gate by day and night'.

John's reward was an annual salary of four marks (c. £10); a special gown bearing 'the livery of our gentlemen' [i.e. those laymen who lived at the Priory, paying for their own board and lodging]; two cartloads of hay for his horse annually; and as much food and drink as he required for his daily dinner and supper, taken 'at the table of our gentlemen'.

Furthermore, he was also appointed 'park keeper' in Lyncombe - for which he was to receive annually twenty shillings and three cartloads of fuel; plus seven convent loaves and seven gallons of convent ale each week - not to mention a house and garden near the North Gate. In return for all these grants, John was expected to be always ready to ride with the prior on his journeys as often as required; and to pay a sum of four marks a year in rent for the house (the cost of which had already been cancelled out by his 'salary'!).

In 1543, four years after the dissolution of the Priory, the Court of Augmentations granted John and his wife a pension of £6 13s 4d for life in compensation for the loss of his benefits.

On the other hand, William Holloway, who was the last incumbent at the Priory, made use of corodies not simply to favour relatives, but to create a powerful group of local allies just prior to the dissolution (see above).

For instance, John Wilman (a Somerset landowner) was granted a corody for life, which included the weekly gift of seven convent loaves and seven gallons of convent ale; daily access to 'as much flesh and fish' as any of the monks received; an annuity of 26s 8d; a house and garden in Southgate Street at a rent of a mere twelve pence; and a yearly supply of four loads of wood.

Source: Richard Warner: *The History of Bath* (1801: appendix)

SOURCES USED IN CHAPTER 2

Printed material

Bettey, J.H: 'Life and Litigation in Bath and its Environs in the Sixteenth Century' (in *Bath History*, vol. 6, 1996)

Bartelot, Grosvenor: 'New Light on Bath Abbey and the Priory Estates' (in *Proceedings of the Somerset Archeological and Natural History Society, Bath Branch*, 1941)

Chapman, Mike & Holland, Elizabeth: 'The Development of the Saw Close from the Middle Ages' (in *Bath History*, vol. 8, 2000)

Coleman, D.C: *Industry in Tudor and Stuart England* (1975)

Cunliffe, Barry: *The City of Bath* (1986)

Davenport, Peter: *Medieval Bath Uncovered* (2002)

Fowler, John C: *The Benedictines in Bath over a Thousand Years* (1895)

Green, Emanuel: 'Bath Lay Subsidies, Henry IV to Henry VIII'; and 'The Earliest Map of Bath' (in *Proceedings of the Bath Natural History and Antiquarian Field Club*, vol. 6, 1889)

Hylson-Smith, Kenneth: *Bath Abbey: a History* (2003)

Keevil, A.J: 'The Barton of Bath' (in *Bath History*, vol. 6, 1996)

Page, William (ed.): *The Victoria County History of Somerset*, vol. 2 (1911)

Lucy T Smith (ed.): *The Itinerary of John Leland, 1535-1543* (1907 edtn.)

Symons, Katharine: *The Grammar School of King Edward VI, Bath and its Ancient Foundation* (1934)

Stoate, T L (ed.): *The Somerset Protestation Returns and Lay Subsidy Rolls* (1975)

Warner, Richard: *The History of Bath* (1801)

Webb, A J: 'Two Stuart Subsidies for the County of Somerset: 1558 & 1581-82' (in *Somerset Record Society*, vol 88, 2002)

Wroughton, John: *Stuart Bath: Life in the Forgotten City, 1603-1714* (2004)

Documentary material

British Library:	Calendar of State Papers Domestic, April 1587 (re unemployment)
National Archives	Letters and Papers, Foreign & Domestic, Henry VIII, 1535, 1539 (re Layton's findings and the abbot of Glastonbury's fate) Acts of the Privy Council, 1586 (re unemployment)
Somerset Record Office:	St Michael's Bath Churchwardens' Accounts, 1349-1575

The author is also indebted to Marta Inskip for her unpublished research on the Prior's Rental, 19 Henry VII, 1504 (Somerset Record Office, DD/x/HY (H/82) and the Augmentation Office Accounts, Edward VI, 1550/51; and to Jean Manco for her unpublished chronology of the development of Bath Abbey in the sixteenth and seventeenth centuries.

CHAPTER 3

1552: Life in the Parish and the School

Daily Life in St Michael's Parish Without

(i) Housing Within the Parish 1552

A good insight into the lives of ordinary people is fortunately provided by the churchwardens' accounts of **the parish of St Michael's Without**, which extended across the suburbs outside the North Gate. Even by the middle of the fourteenth century, the church owned an impressive portfolio of properties - including houses, gardens, closes, coppices and stables - in Walcot Street, Broad Street, Frog lane [where New Bond Street is today], Barton Street and Alford's Lane [later called Slippery lane], as well as a few outside the parish in Walcot and Stall Street. By 1552, its properties - which in part had been bequeathed by devout parishioners - numbered thirty-six in all, producing rents of £11 18s 8d per annum.

The area in question was, of course, one of the less affluent districts of the city, housing a mixture of labourers, weavers, fullers, thatchers, masons, plumbers and carpenters. The churchwardens, therefore, permitted poorer people to make 'pledges' for their rent, either by paying in instalments or by making donations in kind. In 1551-52, for instance, a total of £2 8s 0d was raised through the handing over of such items as 'a gown' (worth ten shillings), 'brass and pewter' (fifteen shillings) and 'a loom' (sixteen shillings). It is abundantly evident from the accounts that the church took great pride in ensuring that the houses were not only maintained in a good state of repair but were also given the occasional face lift in the cause of modernisation. The work undertaken by teams of local craftsmen provides us with a vivid picture of the type of accommodation available to local people in the middle of the sixteenth century.

Although a few of the houses in the parish had been constructed entirely in **stone** - such as the 'tiled house called Stonehouse in Broad Street', which is mentioned in the accounts of 1395 - the majority of people in 1552 still lived in timber-framed buildings. Nevertheless, as Peter Davenport has shown, some of these properties would have consisted of a ground floor constructed in stone with

Although there are few visible remains of Tudor domestic architecture in Bath, this front section of a small stone cottage is to be found actually inside number 7 Broad Street, including the outer wall, window, front door and front room. It is thought that it was built in 1593, but altered later in the mid-seventeenth century.
(Author's photograph)

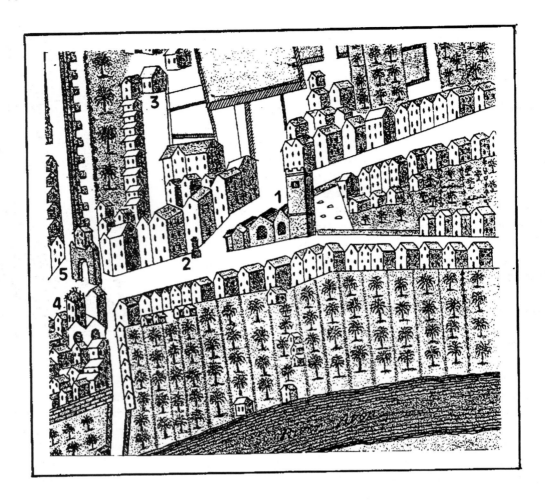

The hub of the parish of St Michael Without. This section of Joseph Gilmore's map show the church itself with its own little churchyard (1); St Michael's Conduit or water fountain (2); the North Gate (4); and two of the early sites of the newly-established grammar school - a house at the end of Frog Lane (3), where the school was based in 1552; and the nave of the disused church of St Mary by the North Gate (4), to which it was transferred in 1583. Also notice that many of the houses in the parish had their own gardens and orchards. (Author's collection)

timber framing above. In 1479, for instance, work undertaken on Philip Strong's tenement included 'raising the walls' as well as 'setting up timbers' for the kitchen. This tradition would therefore help to account for the large amounts of stone brought from quarries in Claverton, Farleigh, Bathampton Down and Englishcombe when repairs or extensions were being carried out. In 1480, for example, the churchwardens paid 10s 8d for eight loads of stone from the Bathampton quarry for building 'a second room' in a house in Broad Street. Masons and labourers were therefore in great demand, both in the quarries and within the parish.

Timber for the whole of the superstructure was obtained locally. Elm, which was used to great extent in Bath, was available in one of the church's own closes ('Elm Hay'), although additional supplies were also brought in from the neighbourhood. Once felled, the tree would first be trimmed of its branches by the carpenter before being

The only visible section of timber framing in Bath (of the sort that was commonplace in St Michael's parish) has been uncovered on the side wall of number 3 Broad Street (right). Inside the shop in question is a simple Elizabethan staircase on the first floor and decorated ceiling beams. (Author's photograph)

squared into a beam over trestles through the use of an axe or adze. Then - according to the needs of the builder - the beam would be sawn into square posts or thinner planks over a saw pit with two men working, one above and one inside the pit below. For the production of smaller items - such as laths, pegs and staves (where total accuracy was less vital) - logs would be cleft and split using wedges. In 1547, the churchwardens paid a total of 10s 4d to a carpenter for 'felling an elm', 'squaring the said elm', 'making the saw pit', 'sawing the said elm into boards' and 'carrying the boards from the said elm'.

Oak - which was the preferred wood for construction in many parts of the country - was also used in Bath, but to a lesser degree. Thus, in 1478, Galfred Carpenter [the carpenter!] was paid a total of 5s 8d for 'two oaks' and 'for squaring, sawing, framing and setting up the same' in the house of John Smythe, the mason. Much of the timber was sawn up inside the city at Saw Close, an open, unpaved area in the north-west corner (see John Speed's map). By the early seventeenth century, there were several saw-pits in use there, as well as stockpiles of timber. The council ruled that each carpenter would face a charge 'for every tree which he should lay at the Saw Close'.

Once the timber had been cut to size, it was the task of the skilled carpenter to assemble **'the frame' of the building** - usually off site in the first instance. The various sections would be laid out on the ground and pieces joined together by carefully-crafted mortise and tenon, dovetail, lap or scarf joints. Wooden pegs would then be used to secure these joints in place, while each piece of timber would be numbered so that the frame could quickly be reassembled after transportation to the building site. The whole construction rested on the sill

This contemporary woodcut shows the various stages of construction a timber-framed house, including the felling of trees, the trimming of branches by axe, the squaring of the beam over a trestle, the sawing of posts or planks and the splitting of logs into pegs by use of a wedge. Also notice that the frame is being first erected at the carpenter's yard before being dismantled and carried to the building site.
From J.A. Comenius, Orbis Sensualum Pictus, *1672 edtn. by permission of the British Library (1607.2351)*

beam, which was placed on top of the lower stone walls, with the main posts rising from it to support the wall plates, which ran across the top of the timber frame. Other prepared pieces of timber were used to provide rafters for the roof, joists to support the floor, curved braces to support the main posts and upright studs or square panels to fill in those areas between the main posts (see illustration). Frames were also constructed for any partition walls (or 'entercloses'), which were used to create separate rooms within the main structure.

The spaces between the exposed timbers on the main walls and inner partitions were usually filled with panels of **wattle and daub**. Upright wooden staves or rods were fixed into slots cut into the horizontal beams of the panels. Then the 'wattle' (i.e. long twigs or thin laths of elm or hazel) was interwoven with the upright staves to create a basket-like effect (see illustration opposite) before both sides of the panel were covered in the 'daub' (i.e. a mixture which included, as available, some of these ingredients - clay, sand, horse-hair, chopped straw, cow dung, water and lime).

It is interesting to note that the practice of painting the beams black and the panels white to gain a more dramatic effect is comparatively modern (i.e. nineteenth to twentieth centuries). Originally the timbers were left to weather naturally in an unpainted form, while the panels were painted with a limewash lighted tinted with natural earthy colours. Many of the houses in St Michael's parish were treated in the manner described above. In 1479, William Mogg was paid two shillings for his work 'at daubing', while his colleague was paid one shilling 'for making the wattle'; in 1473, a 'dauber' repaired the plaster on five houses, while in the same year the church purchased 'three bushels of rods for making the partition in a new tenement'; and in 1541, loads of sand and lime were ordered to enable a worker 'to fresh daub' Mr Baker's house.

A traveller to England (Horatio Busino, Chaplain to the Venetian Ambassador), just after the close of the Tudor period, described his impressions of this fondness for the use of timber in building construction:

> I know not what to commend in their buildings as for the most part they employ timber, driving posts in very deep like a rough scantling [a fairly thin timber beam], which they coat with mortar mixed with the hair of animals; instead of which the poor use very finely chopped straw. The staircases are almost all spiral and the distributions of the rooms sorry and irregular...The timber used by them for building is for the most part oak, but they have a great quantity of elms which they plant along the public roads and walks and even by the side of the field ditches and causeways. They thus derive great profits, converting them into planks and even into beams for various purposes.

During the sixteenth century, houses in Bath were either thatched or tiled - although, as the century progressed, tiles were increasingly preferred - partly because they were rapidly becoming more fashionable and partly because they were less of a fire risk. The thatcher would lay the straw (which was acquired locally from Charlcombe, Bathwick or Walcot) in closely-packed bundles or 'yealms' to ensure that rain was unable to penetrate, holding them in position by means of rods laid across the **thatch** and spikes driven into the rafters. Thus, in 1463, Robert Smythe (thatcher) ordered a wagon load of straw for thirty pence and 1200 spikes for eighteen pence, before spending ten days repairing the thatch on houses in the parish. Thatch continued to be repaired throughout the Tudor period, a thatcher and his man working for five and a half days in 1564 (having previously acquired bundles of elm rods from Bathampton

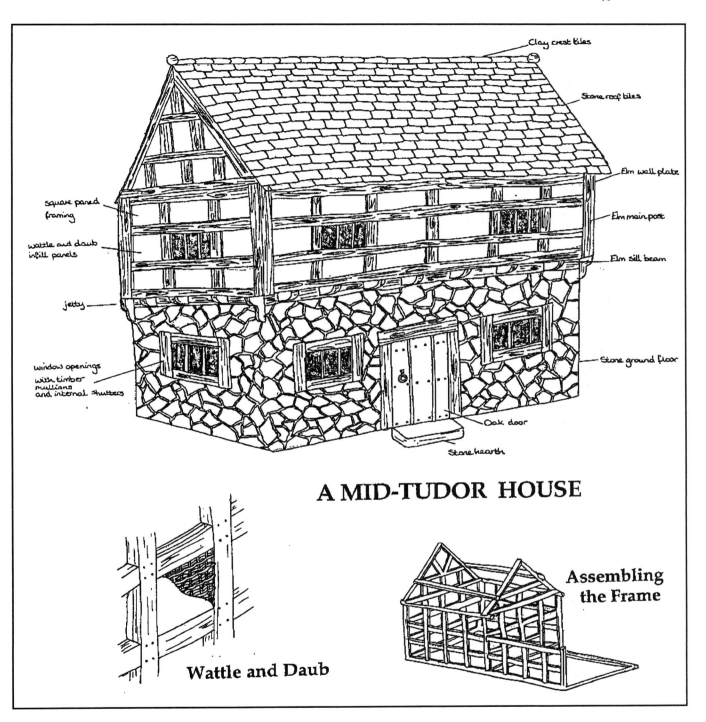

Clay crest tiles

Stone roof tiles

Elm wall plate

Elm main post

Elm sill beam

Stone ground floor

Oak door

Stone hearth

square paned framing

wattle and daub infill panels

jetty

window openings with timber mullions and internal shutters

A MID-TUDOR HOUSE

Wattle and Daub

Assembling the Frame

A mid-Tudor house of the type that would have been found in St Michael's parish.
Notice the stone ground floor with timber framing above.
An original line drawing by Elizabeth Fitzpatrick.

These houses in Lacock provide a good example of the more modest type of homes used by the craftsmen, who lived in Walcot Street and Broad Street in Tudor times (Author's photograph)

hold down the straw and 1600 spikes to fix it).

In spite of the fact that clay **tiles** were more commonplace in many areas of England, 'stone' tiles were frequently used in Bath from medieval times. It is thought quarries on the downs - century, they were also being plundered wholesale from the derelict buildings of the former Priory. The stone used for roof tiles was mined in shallow workings. Above the better quality building stone, the quarriers would find thin layers of hardstone, which could be worked with a tile pick to produce an even thickness. Tiles were traditionally hung on laths, which ran across the rafters, by means of wooden pegs or metal nails driven through carefully positioned holes formed by pointed metal hammers.

In 1479, therefore, the churchwardens paid a tiler 8s 6d for seventeen days work on Philip Strong's house, having previously purchased 350 laths, 1000 lath pins and two 'crests' [the angled tiles which ran across the ridge of the roof]; in 1463, they paid Robert Tyler [the tiler!] 6s 2d for roof repairs on five houses, buying in 600 stone tiles and 200 laths; while in 1468, they invested in 700 'tile pins'. Packets of moss were often bought at the same time to provide greater roof insulation on top of the tiles. There is a good demonstration of the effectiveness of this in the Folk Museum at Voss in Norway. Even as late as 1573, moss was again used on Mr Davis's house when it was undergoing extensive repairs (during the course of which the rungs on the ladder broke).

There is little doubt that some of the houses in St Michael's parish were single-storey cottages, although many boasted at least two floors with the upper floor jettied out over the street below. As time progressed, it was not unusual for a further floor to be added or for extensions to be made at the rear of the house. The smaller properties simply consisted of a shop or workshop in front and living quarters behind. Most single storey houses in medieval times would have relied on an **open hearth** in the middle of the floor for both heating and cooking. In 1463, for instance, the churchwardens paid twenty pence to a mason for 'making a hearth in the cottage of R. Baron'. Smoke from the fire was often left to seep through gaps in the thatch or tiles - as witnessed by the heavily sooted beams and rafters visible in several houses in the Weald and Downland Open Air Museum.

Sometimes, however, special **'smoke holes'** were made in the roof to speed its escape (with possibly a louvre fitted above to keep out the rain). Thus in 1430, the churchwardens authorised the 'making of two smoke holes in the house of William Osborne'. In some parts of the country (including Sussex and Surrey), an improvement to this system and the problem caused by smoke was achieved though the building of a 'smoke bay' at one end of the ground floor. Although there was still an open hearth to provide heat on the ground floor, the smoke from it was channelled up through a specially constructed bay (perhaps four feet wide) to a hole in the roof. Any rooms on

In the absence of glass, many of the windows in small Tudor houses would have looked like this. Notice the vertical wooden bars (or mullions) and wooden shutters, which could be swung into place on hinges. Sometimes the shutters were constructed to slide up and down in groves on either side of the window. Rooms were often draughty in consequence. From the Weald and Downland Open Air Museum at Singleton. (Author's photograph)

upper floors were therefore partitioned off from the smoke. By the sixteenth century, however, homes were often fitted with **chimneys** and proper fireplaces. It could be a costly business, as demonstrated in 1566 when a new chimney was built by a mason and his labourer in Thomas Sander's house, costing a total of £1 5s 10d. [or the equivalent of five weeks wages for a skilled craftsman].

Once the main structure of the house had been built, there was still a need to fix shutters to the windows (glass did not begin to appear in larger domestic buildings until the end of the Tudor period); hang the doors complete with locks, bolts and latches; and secure the lead guttering to the roof. In 1478, therefore, Galfred Carpenter was paid 'for paring, hewing and planing 4 boards and 5 logs of a new door with hinges; and for nailing, hanging and dressing the said door'; while in 1465, the churchwardens not only bought in a supply of latches and bolts for use on doors and windows, but also paid a plumber for 'a leaden gutter weighing 200 pounds' together with the cost of 'solder' and the labour in 'putting it up'.

The front part of the house, of course, was often used as a shop or workshop - hence a payment to a carpenter in 1502 for making 'a stall'. This would almost certainly have been a large shutter, hinged at the bottom, which could be lowered down to create a trestle-style table for the display of goods. Many of the houses in Broad Street or Walcot Street would therefore provide a base for local craftsmen - including shoemakers, tailors, smiths (who provided locks, keys, latches and bolts), turners (who could make a variety of vessels for use in the kitchen) and coopers (who specialised in wooden containers). A typical two-storey

Coopers, such as those featured in this contemporary woodcut, were among the many craftsmen who occupied workshops in the Broad Street and Walcot Street area. From J.A. Comenius, Orbis Sensualum Pictus, *1672 edtn. by permission of the British Library (1607.2351).*

house of modest size in St Michael's parish would also have space for a kitchen behind the shop on the ground floor, a cellar below and living accommodation above.

Many of the houses in that area would also have **a garden plot** behind where herbs and vegetables could be grown or pigs and chickens reared. The gardens were protected by walls or hedges made out of staked thorn bushes. In 1460, therefore, the churchwardens bought 'eight bushels of thorn for a hedge' and 'stakes for the same'; while in 1465, Galfred Carpenter was paid for preparing four elm trees and then sawing out four hundred feet of stakes from them. Small courtyards were also constructed - as illustrated by the purchase in 1502 of 'three sacks of paving stones at John Millward's house'.

(ii) Worship Within the Church: the 1552 Prayer Book

St Michael's Church, which stood outside the North Gate, had been built around the middle of the fourteenth century. It was situated in a bustling part of the town, which contained the official arrival point for visitors, the location of the cloth market and the site of numerous workshops. Seats inside the church had been provided for at least some of the congregation from 1426, when the floor was specially prepared to take them. Members, however, were expected to pay for the privilege with the 'going rate' of two pence in 1494 rising to four pence by 1520. **The bell tower**, which was detached from the building, boasted six bells, which were rung not only for church services, but also to celebrate the arrival of important celebrities (such as the Duke of Norfolk in 1562); or to announce the death of a parishioner (although the charge for ringing a knell was four pence). The first reference to bells, however, was in 1408, when Richard Glover left two marks towards their upkeep.

The tower also housed **a clock** - at least from 1541-42, when the churchwardens paid twenty shillings for the mechanism together with additional sums for making the 'clock house' and 'setting it up'. Then, in 1564, amid great excitement, 'a chime maker' (Mr Whalley) was employed to make and install chimes at a total cost of £5 3s 6d. Needless to say, the bells, the clock and the chimes were in constant need of repair - so much so in fact that the man, who had been employed to 'keep the clock' for four shillings a year in 1542, had his fee increased to eight shillings once the chimes had been added. Apart from this clock at St Michael's, there were three other timing devices in Bath available to passers-by - the 'town clock' in the tower of the church of St Mary de Stall; the clock on the outside wall of St John's Hospital; and, from 1599-1600, a 'horologe' overlooking the King's Bath.

Until the late 1540s, worship inside St Michael's Church continued to be conducted along the lines stipulated by the Roman Catholic faith with a great deal of emphasis on ritual, processions, altars, shrines, expensive ornaments and lavish vestments (see Chapter 1). However, with **the coming of the English Reformation** - prompted by the dissolution of the monasteries in 1536 and 1539 - all this was to change.

Although, in 1538, Henry VIII had ordered the introduction of an English bible in every parish church and the removal of all superstitious images to prevent 'that most detestable offence of idolatry', he had also emphasised his own commitment to the continuation of Catholic teaching in the Six Articles which were issued in the same year. Parishioners at St Michael's would therefore have noticed very little difference in the services until 1547. Indeed, the churchwardens continued to order oil and candles for the

This contemporary drawing shows a Roman Catholic mass being celebrated as the host (the consecrated bread) is raised aloft by the priest. From The Acts and Monuments of John Foxe *(ed. George Townsend, 1843-49 edtn.)*

lamps standing permanently lit on the five side-altars, which were dedicated to various saints - just as they paid men for 'making the paschal' and 'watching the sepulchre' during Lent in 1541-42.

However, in 1547, **the accession of the young Edward VI** (who was guided by two successive Protestant advisers, the Duke of Somerset and the Duke of Northumberland) was to witness a dramatic change in religious policy. Orders were immediately issued for the destruction of images (including stained glass windows); the abolition of many ceremonials; the ending of superstitious practices (including the lighting of candles); and the curtailment of processions to shrines. Furthermore, the two Books of Common Prayer (issued in 1549 and 1552) between them abolished all Latin Services; substantially reduced the number of feast days and holy days; ended the practice of praying for the dead; and substituted the wearing of a simple surplice for that of richly-embroidered vestments.

Of even greater significance, amid all these reforms, was the replacement of the Catholic mass with the service of holy communion - symbolised by the demolition of all stone altars at the east end of the church and the introduction of wooden communion tables in the nave. For, whereas the Catholics believed in the doctrine of transubstantiation (in which the wine and the bread were miraculously transformed into the actual blood and body of Christ before being sacrificed on the altar during the mass), the Protestants believed that, by sharing the bread and wine round the communion table (as He had commanded his followers to do at The Last Supper), they were simply commemorating the sacrifice of Christ made on the cross once and for all.

All this was to have a great impact on the congregation at St Michael's from 1547. A service book in English was purchased; the high altar pulled down; the church interior whitewashed (presumably to eradicate all wall paintings); and a carpet purchased to cover the newly-constructed communion table. The destruction or removal of other items is clearly implied by their sudden restoration during the reign of Queen Mary (see below) - just as the lack of major payments for oil and candles during Edward's reign is indicative of the abolition of the side altars. Further confirmation of this was given in 1548, when the altarpiece with 'an image of Saint Christopher painted on the same' was sold off by the churchwardens for twenty pence. Nevertheless, ordinary parishioners would probably have been most upset by the ending in 1548 of traditional ceremonies during Candlemas, Lent and Rogationtide - ceremonies which had undoubtedly brought an element of colour and pageant to their lives.

Another reform of fundamental importance came with the passing of the **Chantries Act** in 1547. Chantries were the endowments - of which there were many - which had been made for religious, charitable or educational purposes. However, they were chiefly associated with the chantry chapels often found within parish churches. There a priest, who was paid for his services out of income drawn from the endowment, said masses for the souls of the benefactor and his family. By 1547, it is calculated that

This contemporary drawing, which is taken from The Acts and Monuments of John Foxe *(ed. George Townsend, 1843-49 edtn.), shows the destruction or removal of statues, images, vestments and all the trappings of Roman Catholicism from the Anglican Church. This policy formed an important part of the Reformation during Edward VI's reign. (Author's collection)*

these 'obits' (as the masses were called) were celebrated in fifty-one per cent of parishes in Somerset. Sometimes, too, money was left to pay for the continuous burning of lamps or candles on the altar of the chapel on behalf of the deceased (known in contemporary documents as 'lamps and lights').

The Chantries Act roundly condemned the 'superstition and errors' which had been brought into the minds of people 'by devising and fantasising vain opinions of purgatory and masses...for them which be departed' - thus blinding them to 'their very true and perfect salvation through the death of Christ'. Prayers for the dead were therefore to cease and the endowments which maintained such chantries were to be confiscated by the king. It has to be said, however, that - quite apart from any religious considerations - the cash-strapped government also had considerable financial motivation in their abolition. By 1539, for instance, the gross revenue of the 108 chantries in Somerset amounted to some £976.

People living in St Michael's parish would certainly have been affected by this decision - indeed, the very appearance of the church interior would have been radically changed by the disappearance of chantry chapels and the ending of obits, lamps and lights in memory of the dead. Furthermore, St Michael's - along with all the other churches in Bath - held numerous properties which had been bequeathed with the express purpose of endowing masses (see Chapter 1). After a nationwide government survey in 1548, the inspectors visiting Bath found that its five churches possessed numerous 'obits, lights and lamps', which together produced an annual income of £6 12s 0d. Confiscations and sales quickly followed. However, although some eighty per cent of such holdings had been disposed of in Somerset by 1603, an enquiry revealed that there were still a few 'concealed' chantry properties in Bath, which had escaped confiscation - properties which were still producing an income of £4 14s 7d.

The beautiful chantry chapel built by Prior William Birde in the former Priory Cathedral provides a good example of the several chantries which existed inside the Bath churches during medieval times. Whereas most of these were destroyed during the Reformation, Birde's Chapel survived because the Priory fell into disuse and disrepair before the Edwardian Reformation took place. When the church was finally restored (see Chapter 4), the chapel itself was no longer used as a chantry. (photograph by Alan Morley)

Meanwhile, the reform of religious worship had been brought to an abrupt halt by the death of Edward VI in 1553 and **the accession of Queen Mary**. As a practising Roman Catholic, Mary vowed to restore the country to the true religion and to undo the work of the protestant reformers. Many Edwardian Acts of Parliament were therefore repealed. In St Michael's Church, payments made by the churchwardens in 1556-57 indicate quite clearly that many of the old traditions were revived - including prayers for the dead ('a gallon of oil', 'lamps of glass' and 'tapers' to service the lights on altars); processions and holy days ('banners for the church', 'ringing in Rogation week' and 'bearing the banners on divers days'); ceremonial ('mending the sanctus bell', 'holy oil' and 'new vestments'); and revised forms of service, including the mass ('a manual for the church').

This counter-revolution, however, was short-lived. With **the accession of Elizabeth I** in 1558, the parish church again reverted to its Protestant ways (albeit in a slightly less extreme form). The Book of Common Prayer was restored and, through a series of royal injunctions, 'all shrines, candlesticks, pictures, paintings and other monuments of feigned miracles, pilgrimages, idolatry and superstition' were ordered to be destroyed. At St Michael's, the church was again whitewashed; the new English Bible purchased and two panels erected, carrying the text of the Ten Commandments to emphasise the authority of scripture. Church attendance remained compulsory, but with a fine of twelve pence for wilful refusal.

Many of the ceremonies associated with the old ritual year (see Chapter 1) were swept away in this atmosphere of reform. By 1560, therefore, the blessing of the candles at Candlemas, the ashes on Ash Wednesday and the small wooden crosses on Palm Sunday had been banned in order to discourage any superstitious worship of these objects; the Easter ceremonies involving the sepulchre, the new fire and the paschal candle had been omitted from the new liturgy set out in the 1559 Prayer Book; while both the processions on Corpus Christi Day in honour of the real presence of Christ and the ceremonies on behalf of the dead on All Saints' Day had been prohibited.

In place of all this, the Protestant reformers substituted sermons to explain the true meaning of Good Friday and Easter Day; turned Candlemas into a celebration of Christ, 'the Light of the World' (rather than a feast in honour of the Blessed Virgin Mary); and transformed All Saints' Day into a day to commemorate the saints as

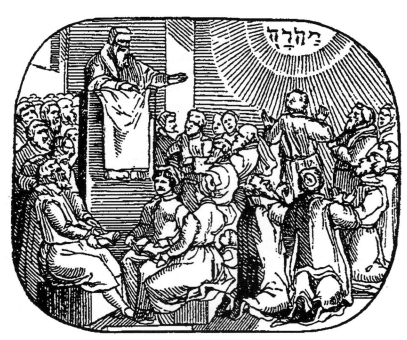

This contemporary line drawing from The Acts and Monuments of John Foxe *(ed. George Townsend, 1843-49 edtn.), which shows a Protestant service in progress, illustrates the central importance of preaching the gospel, reading the bible (note the group beneath the pulpit) and receiving the Holy Spirit (symbolised by the prayerful group on the right). Women are depicted here with open bibles to signify that the gospel is open to all people.*

outstanding human beings (not as intermediaries for the dead). Although the Lenten fast had been retained, meat was the only item that was now proscribed. In Bath - as in towns throughout the country - the mayor was required to conduct a periodic 'inquisition as to flesh eaters on forbidden days'. In April 1572, therefore, Mayor George Pearman duly submitted his return to the Lord Keeper of the Great Seal, certifying that, careful investigations made by himself and a panel of fifteen jurors during Lent and other holy days, they had 'not found any person within the city eating flesh contrary to the form of the statutes'.

There is little doubt that the Reformation had dealt **an immense culture shock** to the congregation at St Michael's Church. As a result of the forced changes, the people had lost much of their traditional form of worship, many of their holidays and most of those colourful ceremonies and processions, which had done so much to unite the community in sociability and neighbourliness. In particular, the stripping out of the altars, the removal of the images of saints and the abolition of obits had had a profound impact on their deepest emotions - for these were the outward symbols of the 'cult of the dead', which had so dominated religious belief in late medieval England. There would be no more masses for dead ancestors, no more intercessions by saints on behalf of deceased relatives. The link of the living with the past had been broken.

Whatever criticism had been levelled within the city at the monks of Bath Priory, the old medieval religion itself had continued to stir the imagination of local people and to command their loyalty. It is perhaps surprising, therefore, that no resistance to these changes has been recorded. There was in fact no mass protest, no street demonstrations, no refusal to implement the new liturgy and no martyrs to the cause. Although the Western Rising of 1649 had witnessed a grass roots rebellion in Devon and Cornwall against the new prayer book and a demand for the return of the 'ancient old ceremonies', it completely failed to spread into Somerset. In Bath, as in most parts of the country, there was - as Eamon Duffy has shown - 'an astonishing degree of conformity' and a grudging acceptance of the will of a highly powerful monarch.

The citizens of Bath were after all led by a strong corporation, whose members also exercised a considerable influence within the parish churches - and the corporation had its eyes firmly fixed on the power and property previously in the hands of the Priory. It is true that, as the years went by, the reforms often caused a fair degree of resentment and division within individual parishes - but in Bath, for the time being at least, Protestantism was beginning to establish itself as an effective force within the city - hence the desire of the corporation in 1573 to build a sufficiently spacious church, where sermons could be preached to the large crowds visiting the spa (see Chapter 4).

A New Grammar School, 1552

(i) The Bath Priory School

The dissolution of Bath Priory in 1539 was to have one unforeseen consequence - namely, the closure of the 'grammar school' which had been run by the monks. Indeed, every monastery in the land had traditionally set up a school to teach Latin to both its own novices and those entering the secular priesthood. Latin, as the universal language of the church, was essential for reading the scriptures, chanting services and writing manuscripts. As Katharine Symonds has shown, Bath Priory had had a school for *oblates* (dedicated boys) from at least the twelfth century.

This is witnessed by the fact that, after the dissolution of the Priory, the sub-prior (John Pytt) claimed a pension of four pounds a year for the loss of his office as master of the school. Although it is known that some such schools also appointed a secular chaplain to teach at the gates of the monastery those other local youngsters who needed Latin for entry into the professions, there is no evidence that this actually happened in Bath. Nevertheless, not all the novices who learnt Latin inside the Priory went on to take vows - some came out to use their knowledge elsewhere. The loss of the Priory school was therefore a loss to the local community.

The boys who entered the Benedictine Priory in Bath were of course subject to the rules of discipline set out in Lanfranc's *Constitutions*. At daybreak - as soon as there was sufficient light to see in the cloisters - the boys were expected to say their prayers and then to read in silence. They were to sit apart from each other and well out of touching distance. Nor were they permitted to speak or signal to each other 'except in the sight and hearing of a master'. Wherever they went, there was always to be a master 'between every two of them'. They were forbidden to put anything into or take anything out of the hand of anyone except the abbot, the prior, their own master or the precentor (who would, of course, hand out the books from which they sang). No-one (except the persons listed above) was permitted to make signs at them or to smile at them.

The punishment of flogging would be administered in the boys' own 'chapter' (or meeting). Although the prior had 'the privilege' of flogging boys who behaved 'with levity', it was normally the abbot alone who issued the order. However, a senior master ('a monk of particular gravity') had power to adjudicate, on those occasions when boys had been caught shouting, whether they should be flogged or treated with indulgence. In order to compensate for the compulsory midnight services, the boys were permitted to rest on their beds at midday.

The novices, of course, were tonsured (i.e. the crown of the head was shaved) - but just as this task was undertaken by their masters, so they in turn were expected to shave the heads of their masters. On 'shaving day' in winter, in view of the fact that this ordeal could apparently cause a feeling of weakness, the boys reported to the refectory after shaving to receive a special medicine. They were each allocated a separate bed - always separated from the next boy's bed, of course, by that of a monk.

(ii) The Foundation of King Edward's School

It has been estimated that between three and four hundred of these grammar schools were in existence by 1539, the majority of which ceased to function after the dissolution of the monasteries and chantries. This considerable loss to the country's education did not go entirely unnoticed. Henry VIII himself, in the Chantries Act of 1545, decreed that charitable funds associated with religious houses should be made available for the re-establishment and development of these old monastic grammar schools. It was not, however, until the reign of Edward VI that anything was actually done. Thanks largely to impassioned pleas made in sermons at court by Bishop Latimer and Thomas Lever, the young king's conscience was eventually wakened to halt 'the putting down of grammar schools' and 'the devilish drowning of youth in ignorance'. As a result, thirty-three schools were established or revived with endowments drawn from old monastic lands after petitions received from local citizens.

It was against this background that, on 28th June 1552, the Mayor (Edward Ludwell) and the Corporation of Bath made **a humble petition** to the king for a grant of the old monastic lands within the bailiwick of Bath for the dual purpose of setting up

This wonderful print (below) shows Bishop Hugh Latimer preaching before Edward VI and his courtiers from a wooden pulpit erected in the privy garden at Westminster, the Chapel Royal being too small to house such a vast crowd. Latimer exercised a strong influence over the young king - not only regarding the direction of the Reformation, but also concerning the need to revive the grammar schools. King Edward's School, Bath, was one of thirty-three such schools established during Edward's reign. By courtesy of the Pepys Library, Magdalene College, Cambridge.

(Right) an engraving by R. Dalton of one of several original drawings by Hans Holbein. This depicts the young Prince Edward at the age of ten, just after his accession in 1547. By courtesy of King Edward's School, Bath.

a grammar school and supporting ten poor people. It has to be said, however, that their motives in doing so were not entirely based on educational or charitable intent. The reality was that the citizens of Bath were at that moment in a state of panic - for a strong rumour was circulating that King Edward was on the point of selling off all the former monastery land still in his possession to settle the crown's enormous debts. This would have created serious problems for the corporation in Bath.

Although the crown had, by 1552, already sold to individual buyers the rich monastic estates outside the city, confiscated property *inside* the city boundaries had remained unsold. Much of the property in question had in fact been let to the corporation by the Priory at a favourably modest rent over a long period of time. Even after the dissolution in 1539, the crown had agreed that a similar arrangement could continue (with rents, of course, now payable to the crown itself). This situation enabled the corporation to manage and develop it in the way it had always done - and to enjoy the considerable profits obtainable from sub-letting. As rumours increased of the likelihood of a sale, the corporation - banned, like all corporations, by the Statute of Mortmain (1279) from actually purchasing any land itself - feared the inevitable and disastrous consequences of purchase by unknown outsiders.

It was therefore to offset this possibility that - with a large measure of cunning - the corporation presented its petition to the king, requesting a total of 102 properties. This schedule of lands, with their values, was drawn up by the mayor himself (Edward Ludwell) who, as deputy crown bailiff, was extremely familiar with crown property within the city. It consisted of all the former Priory lands, which the corporation had previously rented, together with a few additions gained by the crown at the dissolution (with the exception of Ham Meadow, Ambury Meadow and the buildings of the Priory, all of which had been sold in 1542). Although some land within the city walls and immediate suburbs was owned by churches, hospitals, guilds or private individuals, a very substantial portion of Bath was contained within the submitted schedule. The petition, which was presented to the king by the mayor (who was also one of Bath's two members of parliament), was granted by Letters Patent under the Great Seal on 12th July 1552.

This document (which is commonly called **the School Charter**) granted 'that for the future there should be and will be one grammar school in the said city of Bath, which will be called the free grammar school of King Edward VI, which is for the teaching, education and instruction of boys and young men in grammar, to continue for ever'. For the upkeep of the school, the corporation was granted the former Priory's lands as an endowment in return for a fixed charge of just £10 a year in rent payable to the crown. Although much of the property was by then in a dilapidated state and had indeed grown 'very ruinous', its potential for future income was enormous.

An artist's drawing of the initial portrait of King Edward VI and other detail taken from the School's original 'Charter' (or Letters Patent) presented on 12th July 1552. By courtesy of King Edward's School, Bath.

Out of this considerable wealth, the corporation was required to find 'one suitable, able and educated person, who is well instructed and learned at least in Latin and who is to serve in the aforesaid free grammar school and will receive ten pounds a year for his salary'. The corporation was also charged with drawing up rules for the running of the school and the discipline of the students. Furthermore, it was to make funds available to 'help, relieve and comfort for all time for ever ten poor persons dwelling and staying within the aforesaid city of Bath' - a requirement which was to find expression in the form of the Black Alms or St Catherine's Charity (see Chapter 5). The charter concluded by emphasising that the mayor and corporation - as trustees - were to spend 'the profits, incomes, rents and revenues' of all the listed property 'henceforth, forever, totally and entirely for the continuance and maintenance of the free grammar school...and for the relief and support of ten poor persons'.

Sadly the corporation, in the period that followed the Tudor Age, shamefully misappropriated this endowment and totally failed to meet its obligations. For almost two hundred years, therefore, the school was housed in sub-standard accommodation with little money spent on improvements; while a succession of masters received a mere pittance in salary. It was only when the matter was referred to the Court of Chancery in 1734 that the full extent of scandal came to light. The corporation, which was found guilty of 'notoriously misapplying the revenues' of the endowment and 'many other notorious offences in breach of the said trust', was fined £500 and ordered to erect a new school building. Twenty years later, the school was re-housed in Broad Street (see *450 Years: King Edward's School, Bath, 1552-2002*).

(iv) The Schoolroom in Tudor Times

Recent research by Elizabeth Holland and Marta Inskip has shown that King Edward's School was originally situated in a house at the end of **Frog Lane**, just outside the northern wall of the city (near to where New Bond Street is located today). Access to the lane was gained through a narrow passage beneath a house which fronted onto Broad Street. The school house itself was fairly spacious with a garden attached and a fine view to the rear over Rack Close. By the early seventeenth century, this property was being referred to in leases as 'a tenement heretofore known by the name of the School House' - a description which continued into the eighteenth century. As King Edward's School was the only school in Bath during Tudor and Stuart times, it is safe to assume that the house in Frog Lane was indeed its earliest site.

One of the school's earliest benefactors was **Sir Nicholas Jobbyn**. Previously known as Dom Nicholas Bathe, he had been a monk in the Priory before being pensioned off in 1539 to become vicar of St Mary de Stall (which, at that time, was the parish church of the city). A scholarly man, he became chaplain to the corporation, accountant to the city and a close friend of the mayor, Edward Ludwell. It is more than likely, therefore, that Jobbyn worked closely with Ludwell in organising the petition for the foundation of the school. Just before his death in 1553, Jobbyn made a will in which he bequeathed 'for the use of the free grammar school, certain books of grammar and learning, for the use of the schoolmaster and scholars there'. He was particularly generous towards John Short, who had been appointed as the school's first master, leaving him 'my second best gown and, if he continue at the free grammar school, he shall have some of my grammar books'. Furthermore, with the school's property endowment in mind, he added: 'to the maintaining of the tenements belonging to the free school of Bath, all my timber'. In view of the dilapidated state of some of the cottages involved and the high cost of repairs, this was undoubtedly appreciated by the corporation.

In 1583, the corporation moved the school to more spacious premises - the nave of **the disused Church of St Mary** by the North Gate, which had been closed for worship in that year as a result of the consolidation of the city's parishes (see Chapter 4). It was therefore located in that sector of the city which fairly bubbled with life and activity. Not far away were the Guildhall and market, the stocks and the pillory, two water fountains (where travellers refreshed their horses and women did their washing), the North Gate itself (where visiting celebrities were welcomed by the mayor and corporation) and the ferry across the river. Closer still, in the tower of the church, was the city prison. Most of the boys, of course, lived within a stone's throw of the school.

Over the next six years, the old church was gradually converted into a more comfortable home for the school. The first task was to install a new floor - the corporation's treasurer paying fifteen shillings for the sawing of 'one thousand plank of the church timbers and boards' to make 'planking' for the school. Although money had already been spent in 1580 on tiling the roof of schoolmaster's house and insulating it with a covering of moss, further substantial work was undertaken in 1585. Situated behind the old church in the north-eastern angle of the city wall, it was referred to in the city accounts as 'the parsonage house' (implying, of course, that previous rectors of St Mary's had been accommodated

An artist's reconstruction of the North Gate of the city, based on a drawing of a 1630 Plan of Bath. It shows the disused church of St Mary's on the right, in which the School was based. Published in James Tunstall's Rambles about Bath *(1876).*

there). The house was now completely re-roofed with new timbers and tiles; new doors were hung throughout; and the site made more secure through the 'making up of the town wall in the schoolmaster's garden'.

Furthermore, two entries in the accounts suggest that privies had been installed in both the school itself and the master's own house. Certainly the treasurer paid for 'the setting up of the roof and the partition of *the little house* in the school' and 'the making up of *the little house* in the school master's house and tiling'. The improvements made to the master's house suggest that accommodation was probably being provided for a few boarders. This was normal practice in grammar schools of this period and offered a welcome method of supplementing the meagre salary of the master (which had been set at just £10 a year in 1552). Although this figure had risen to £12 by 1568, it was not further increased until 1631 - in spite of soaring inflation during the late sixteenth century.

As the school began to grow in size, further structural work became inevitable. In 1589, therefore, **the school expanded** from the nave into the chancel. This part of the old church was clearly in a broken-down condition and required major refurbishment, including a completely new roof. William Baker, the carpenter, was therefore employed to construct and install a timber frame; while Richard Beacon, the tiler, supplied 'three loads of tile', 550 laths and a large quantity of nails. Fortune, the mason, set to work on 'mending the windows and glazing them', whereas a colleague was hired to insert a completely new window in the gable end of the church. At the same time, the school walls were re-pointed and then replastered; while Gray, the smith, repaired the hinges and catches of the doors. Finally, the corporation paid for the removal of all the old timber and a thorough cleaning of the schoolroom.

All the evidence suggests that the schoolroom, the school yard and the master's house, garden and stable were enclosed, partly by the city wall and partly by a new wall built parallel to the street. Access to the school premises was gained through a door set in this wall. When Anthony à Wood later visited the city, he noted in his diary that there was an engraved tablet set above this door with a Latin inscription. The translation of this reads: *Free Grammar School provided for the education of Bath boys in the Latin language, by the foundation of Edward VI, formerly King of England, in the sixth year of his reign, A.D. 1552.*

In spite of the new window, the school room would undoubtedly have been dark and cold, especially in winter. Most schools at this time were heated by means of a fireplace and chimney built along one side of the room. Thus, in common with normal practice, the boys of King Edward's were probably expected to provide their own share of firewood and coal, and to bring candles for their personal use in school. But conditions would certainly have been spartan. Elizabethan schoolrooms on average measured fifty feet long and twenty-five feet wide, catering for about fifty or sixty boys. The situation was not helped either by the frequency in which windows were mysteriously broken! The corporation therefore sent its glazier along to the school with monotonous regularity.

Inside the schoolroom, the master presided over the whole school from a large chair and desk set on a dais at the end of the room. The boys normally sat on benches or forms, working with the books on their knees. The forms were arranged in rows down the sides of the room with a writing table in a large space in the centre. The master's desk was constructed in 1583, when the corporation paid carpenters twenty-one pence for 'a board' and 'posts for the school desk'. Valuable books, such as the two Latin

The seventeenth-century schoolroom. Details in this drawing by Stephen Beck have been based on the cost of items listed in the Bath Chamberlain's accounts - including the master's desk and chair, the writing board and writing table.

dictionaries purchased in 1594 with strict orders that they were 'to remain in the school', were often chained to the desk for security. In the same year, a blackboard - of the type recommended by educationalists of the period for teaching boys to write - made its first appearance, when a joiner was paid to construct 'a writing board for the school'.

Even greater attention, however, was given to training a boy in **the art of speaking Latin** both fluently and stylishly. This was partly achieved through the performance of plays in Latin - as was certainly the case at King Edward's. In 1583, for instance, John Short (the master) was paid by the corporation for two plays he wrote for performances to local people. Then, in 1602 (when Henry Slyman was master), the corporation granted 6s 8d 'to the young men of our city that played at Christmas' and 5s 0d to 'the children that played at Candlemas' - almost certainly the scholars of King Edward's School. Fluency was also achieved by composing and delivering orations in Latin. As early as 1600, the city gave a reward of five shillings to 'Doctor Sherwood's son for pronouncing an oration'. A scholar of King Edward's, he was the first in a long succession of boys chosen to make a Latin oration to the mayor on mayor-making day. This tradition continued until 1834.

(iv) Life in the Tudor School

Although King Edward's was always referred to as **'The Free School'** until well into the nineteenth century, the boys who attended were actually all fee-paying pupils until 1822, when ten free scholars were elected for the first time. The term 'free' (based on the Latin word *libera*) in fact meant free from all restrictions imposed from outside.

Fees which were therefore paid quarterly to the master ('quarterages'), normally amounted to six pence a quarter for 'grammarians' and threepence for 'petties' or juniors (who were often taught by senior boys, while they continued to improve their reading and writing skills in English). Boarders, of course, would pay an additional fee for board and lodging.

The boys were drawn from a wide spectrum of society - the sons of yeoman farmers, shopkeepers, clergy, skilled craftsmen, local gentry, lawyers and doctors. Many parents - then as now - struggled to pay the fees - as James Howell noticed in 1647:

> Every man strains his fortunes to keep his children at school. The cobbler will clout it till midnight; the porter will carry burdens till his bones crack again; the ploughman will pinch both back and belly to give his son learning; and I find this ambition reigns nowhere so much as in this island.

By the time a boy entered the grammar school at the age of seven or eight (leaving at fifteen for university or work in the neighbourhood), he would normally have learnt to read and write in English at one of the **'petty schools'** run by elderly dames. Instruction was based on the 'horn book', a board covered with transparent horn

which displayed a printed form of the Lord's Prayer and the alphabet. On arrival at the grammar school, the boys would spend most of their time working on Latin which, as the official international language, was an essential subject for all intending lawyers, diplomats, doctors, clergy and clerks. Although the older boys also took in a little Greek and a smattering of Hebrew, there was no tuition in mathematics, science or history. However, from 1553, it became obligatory for all schools to teach the new Greater Catechism, which had been compiled to set out the doctrines of the Reformation (of which Edward VI was an enthusiastic supporter). Religious instruction, therefore, remained an essential part of the curriculum.

A horn book of the type used in the petty schools, where children learned to read and write. From the Elizabethan House Museum, Great Yarmouth.

Although the early records of King Edward's School have long since vanished (with the exception of the charter itself), it is possible to build up a vivid picture of life in a typical Tudor grammar school from the writings of John Brinsley (see also the panel opposite). It is highly probable that the grammar school in Bath followed this general pattern set by Brinsley.

The school would have been structured into **five 'forms'** or classes - all of which would have been housed in the same large classroom. As the boys progressed through the school, they would have been taught the basic rules of Latin grammar and sentence construction. By the fourth form, they would have made a start on writing 'a Latin of their own making', translating sentences given to them by the master. At fifth form level they would have been expected to develop their own style of writing in both prose and verse - and to speak fluently in Latin. Brinsley ruled that 'none of the chiefest forms shall speak English to one another' - on pain of punishment.

The method of teaching was based on a great deal of repetition, learning by heart, testing and note-taking - as Brinsley himself explained:

> The schoolmaster shall give them lessons in the morning, the which lessons shall be examined

in the afternoon the same day. And on the next morning after shall be perfectly repeated without the book...Upon Friday in the afternoon, the scholars shall repeat and say without books and construe their lessons learned the same week...And every scholar shall write their notes in paper books prepared for that purpose, which notes the master shall deliver to them in his reading.

Brinsley appointed reliable senior boys as **monitors** to help him in this process of education. 'In every form, one monitor shall be appointed weekly to note such scholars as in every form shall be either absent or come late after the hours before appointed'. These monitors also had the task of receiving from the master the weekly work assignment for their form and then collecting in from the boys their weekly exercises.

Brinsley stressed the need for the highest **standards of behaviour** from his pupils both inside and outside the school. They were not to 'swear or fight with another or abuse or disturb one another or steal from any'. They were also to show great courtesy to visitors to the school and local people in the town. 'When a stranger cometh into the school, you scholars shall arise, stand and salute them; and likewise civilly give the upper hand to those whom they do meet in the streets and courteously salute as becometh scholars'. Like so many of his contemporaries, Brinsley believed firmly in the use of corporal punishment (see also the panel on page 66). He wrote:

Finally, as God hath sanctified the rod and correction, to cure the evils of their [the boys'] conditions, to drive out that folly which is bound up in their hearts, to save their souls from hell, to give them wisdom: so it is to be used as God's instrument to these purposes. To spare them in these cases is to hate them. To love them is to correct them betime. Do it under God, and for Him to these ends and with these cautions, and you shall never hurt them: you have the Lord for your warrant.

This contemporary woodcut shows a boys being brought to school by his father and handed over to the master. By permission of the British Library (Roxburghe Ballads, RAX.Rox.I, 335)

The Tudor Grammar School: Discipline

John Brinsley, an eminent educationalist of the period, recommended:

Disciplined Recreation: Brinsley believed in the importance of recreation. Therefore part of an afternoon (normally Thursday) was set aside each week for this purpose 'as a reward of their diligence, obedience and profiting'. Dangerous or 'clownish sports' were banned - as was gambling or any 'unlawful games'. They should 'not play in the streets, go into alehouses, break into orchards or rob gardens'. Furthermore,time spent on play was to be strictly controlled - because too much sport 'draweth their minds utterly away from their books that they cannot take pains for longing after their play and talking of it'.

Firm Punishments: Discipline within the school was vital to learning. Reliable senior boys were appointed as 'Prepositors' to keep an eye on the behaviour of pupils and report offenders to the master. On 'the Day of Correction', Brinsley used a graded system of punishments. Minor offences could be dealt with by means of 'reproofs', demotion in place order or loss of playtime. For greater misdemeanours, he recommended 'three or four jerks with a birch'

or, 'for terror' in some notorious fault, half a dozen stripes or more, soundly laid on'.

Nevertheless, he urged caution when administering corporal punishment. First of all, careful preparation was needed: 'To this end appoint three or four of your scholars, whom you know to be honest, and strong enough, or more if need be, to lay hands upon him together, to hold him fast, over some form, so that he cannot stir hand or foot'. Secondly, the reputation of the school was to be safeguarded from 'evil reports' and complaints avoided from 'quarrelling parents'. Thirdly, the master was to ensure that he did not lose his dignity in the process either by struggling with the boy who is to be beaten, or by losing his temper - 'for these things will diminish authority'.

Sources: John Brinsley: *Ludud Literarius, or the Grammar Schoole* (1612); and *Statutes and Orders for the Government of the Grammar School of Ashby-de-la-Zouch* (1575). The contemporary woodcut shows a group of boys with books in their hands under the firm control of the master and his birch. (Author's collection)

Attitudes and Beliefs: the Will of Nicholas Jobbyn, 1552

Quite apart from the generosity of Sir Nicholas Jobbyn towards the new grammar school, his will in 1552 also reveals in vivid detail something of the social conscience and religious beliefs at work in Tudor England. It is true that Jobbyn had almost certainly lived as a monk in Bath Priory, before being installed - after its dissolution in 1539 - as vicar of the church of St Mary de Stall.

Nevertheless, his own pious outlook is more than matched in the wills of twelve other residents of Bath during the first half of the sixteenth century - John Wood (1502), Richard Lacy (1503), Robert Chapman (1504), John Jeffereys, alias Cockes (1510), William Woodhead (1513), Thomas Chapman (1524), Richard Gunn (1531), John Kent (1532), Isabel Chauncellor (1534), Thomas Style (1536), Robert Style (1540) and Henry Cavell (1549). Of these, four were aldermen (John Jeffereys, John Kent, Thomas Style and Robert Style); two were clergy (Richard Gunn and John Wood); and four were wealthy clothiers (Thomas Chapman, John Kent, Thomas Style and Robert Style). The wills also give us glimpse into the dress of the period and the contents of a typical middle-class household.

It is clear that the practice of making arrangements before death for **a specific place of burial** was highly important to this group of people, partly because a prime spot in the church conferred a certain degree of status - status in death, which would confirm in perpetuity the person's status and reputation in life. Therefore, whereas Jobbyn selected a grave 'in the body of Stalls Church *'before the pulpit'*, Wood requested burial in St Mary's by the North Gate *'in the chancel'* and Cavell in the same church *'above the pulpit'*. Side chapels also had their attractions. Lacy, for instance, settled for a spot in the Cathedral Church *'next the entrance of the chapel of the Blessed Virgin Mary'*, while Mrs Chauncellor chose to be buried in the same church *'in St Leonard's Chapel in the north aisle under a stone there already by me prepared'*.

As deeply religious, church-going people, it is hardly surprising that almost all of them left money not only to 'the mother church of Wells', but also to other local churches with which they were connected. Jobbyn, for example left money to pay for 'the making and setting up of the name *Jesus* in goodly colours upon the high front or wainscot' in St Mary de Stall's Church. Although Mrs Chauncellor bequeathed 3s 4d to each of the five parish churches in the city, Jeffereys went one better by donating ten shillings 'to every parish church in the deanery of Bath - and, furthermore, left his house in Cheap Street to St Mary de Stall's Church to fund the cost of candles at Easter each year. Thomas Chapman earmarked money for 'the glazing of a window' in the Cathedral Church, whereas Lacy provided small cash sums to the Chapel of St Catherine and a whole range of local parish churches. Sometimes their consciences gained the upper hand as death approached - particularly in relation to those occasions when they had short-changed the vicar over his rightful dues. Both Woodward and Thomas Chapman fell into this category, the latter bequeathing to the vicar of St Mary de Stall's Church 'my best scarlet gown for my forgotten tithes'.

Given this generosity towards the church, it is hardly surprising that several of the will-makers also made **provision for the poor** of the city. Jobbyn instructed his executors to give, on his death, twopence a week to five people each Friday, plus an additional penny a week during Lent. Mrs Chauncellor was a little less precise, ordering that 'a dole be made to poor people on the day of my burial' and on two subsequent anniversaries. On the other hand - bearing in mind the endless problem of poverty

Middle Class Attitudes

(The life and behaviour of the professionals, businessmen, merchants, clothiers and landowners, who lived in some of the fine houses in Bath)

They all, from time in memorial, wear very fine clothes and are extremely polite in their language...In addition to their civil speeches, they have the incredible courtesy of remaining with their heads uncovered whilst they talk to each other...

The want [i.e. lack] of affection in the English is strongly manifested towards their children: for after having kept them at home till they arrive at the age of seven or nine years at the utmost, they put them out - both males and females - to hard service in the houses of other people, binding them generally for another seven or nine years. And these are called apprentices; and, during that time, they perform all the most menial offices; and few who are born are exempted from this fate, for everyone - however rich he may be - sends away his children into the houses of others, whilst he - in return - receives those of strangers into his own.

And on enquiring the reason for this severity, they answer all that they did it in order that the children might learn better manners. But I, for my part, believe that they do it because they like to enjoy all the comforts themselves, and they are better served by strangers than they would be by their own children. Besides which, the English being great epicures and very avaricious by nature, indulge in the most delicate fare themselves and give their household the coarsest bread, beer and cold meat, baked on Sunday for the whole week; of which, however, they allow them in great abundance.

Source: Andrea Trevisano, *Relation of the Island of England* (1497)

Wives in England are entirely in the power of their husbands, their lives only excepted. Therefore when they marry, they give up the surname of their father and of the family from which they are descended, and take the surname of their husbands...But they are not kept so strictly as they are in Spain or elsewhere. Nor are they shut up, but they have the free management of the house or housekeeping. They go to market to buy what they like best to eat. They are well dressed, fond of taking it easy, and commonly leave the care of household matters and drudgery to their servants. They sit before their doors, decked out in fine clothes, in order to see and be seen by the passers-by. All the rest of their time they employ in walking and riding, in playing cards, in visiting their friends and keeping company, conversing with their equals (whom they term 'gossips') and their neighbours; and all this with the permission and knowledge of their husbands, as such is the custom....This is why England is called the paradise of married women. They wear a hat in the street and in the house; those unmarried go without a hat.

Source: Van Meteren, *Nederlandtsche Historie* (1575)

among the lower classes - Lacy arranged for the distribution of bread to one hundred poor people on the day of his burial, whereas Jeffereys willed that six doles of bread should be distributed annually amongst the poor for seven years following his death.

Similar generosity was shown to particular individuals outside the church. Both Jeffereys and Mrs Chauncellor made numerous cash gifts to servants, apprentices, godchildren and relatives. Gunn, who was unmarried, showed special concern for the education of his nephew by leaving 'Richard Gunn, my brother Robert's son, twenty marks that resteth in Master Bush's hands to help the same Richard to school'. Sometimes the testators tried their best to control the moral behaviour and destiny of their heirs from beyond the grave.

Thus John Kent promised 'Thomas Kent, my son, *if he be a priest*, my best great nut with a cover' [i.e. a silver and gilt drinking cup], stipulating that, after Thomas's death, 'the said nut to be delivered to the [most chaste] and best disposed person of my surname'. In the same way, Isabel Chauncellor promised her son 'the tenement lying within the North Gate' on condition that he continued 'in good disposition and sadness' [i.e. at her death!] following good advice from her executors. Furthermore, 'if God send him issue of his body *lawfully begotten*' [i.e. born in wedlock], then the property was eventually to pass to his heirs.

Five of the thirteen people under review displayed great concern for the future **destiny of their souls** and their speedy passage through purgatory. Lacy therefore promised four pence 'to each priest celebrating a mass for my soul', while Woodhead made a similar amount available for each monk in Bath Priory to say - on behalf of his soul - 'a placebo' [i.e. vespers for the dead] or 'a dirge' [a lament for the dead said at the funeral]. Both Thomas Chapman and Isabel Chauncellor, on the other hand, wanted to ensure more longlasting support of this type - the former by leaving £12 'to a priest to sing for me for two years'; and the latter by paying for a priest to sing continually, for twenty-five days after her death, 'a placebo and dirge with mass' in St Mary's by the North Gate. Furthermore, she required 'a sufficiently able priest to sing and say mass' for four years after burial on behalf of her own soul and those of her father, husband and mother.

A meal in progress. This contemporary woodcut illustrates the use of simple wooden bowls and trenchers for food; the employment of knives (and fingers) for eating - forks were not available until late in the seventeenth century; the linen cloth which covers the table; and the lack of chairs (though stools and benches were sometimes used). (Author's collection)

However, it was Jeffereys who went to the most extraordinary lengths to ensure the safety of his soul. He specified that eight pence should be given to the curate of every church in both the Bath deanery and the Potterne deanery for singing 'a dirge and a mass'; and that those who rang 'a solemn peal' at his funeral should each receive one penny, plus 'a penny for ale to make them drink'. In addition, he bequeathed his home in Cheap Street to the Church of St Mary de Stall, the rent from which was to provide a fund for giving 'a penny dole' to everyone attending his funeral and eight pence to each priest who was present - plus £6 a year for seven years for 'an honest priest' to say regular masses on his behalf.

Quite apart from providing an insight into religious beliefs and practice during the Tudor period, the wills also offer a glimpse of **what the people wore**. Those who enjoyed a comfortable standard of living in Bath as traders, merchants, professionals or craftsmen took great pride in possessing fashionable items of clothing. These invariably featured in their lists of bequests to relations and friends. Jobbyn, for example, specifically allocated his 'best jacket of worsted', his 'gown furred with white', his 'best hose', and his 'red petticoat with grey about the collar'. Lacy left his 'best gown and a doublet' [a short, close-fitting jacket] of blue woollen cloth'; while Cavell picked out his 'doublet of black velvet' - and Gunn his 'black hat'.

Black was a particularly expensive colour because the dye was in short supply. For most men, however, it was the quality of the gown that provided them with an element of distinction and fashion. Their combined list of bequests includes 'one gown of velvet grained', 'a short gown lined with buckram', 'my best blue puckered gown furred with black', 'a black gown furred with fox' and 'my gown of furred black lamb'. Items of jewellery also feature, including 'one crucifix of silver and gilt', 'my wife's wedding ring' and 'my ring of gold with a stone that I used to wear on my forefinger'.

Items from the household provide a few pointers to **daily life** in a middle class home. Nicholas Jobbyn bequeathed 'the best pair of sheets, save one sheet wherein my body shall be wrapped', whereas Isabel Chauncellor left 'a pillow, two cushions and a towel of diaper' [patterned cloth]. Thomas Style specified that 'the third part of the hangings' in his house should go to his son with the rest staying with his wife. Hangings were in fact the curtains which were hung around four-poster beds or across doors to keep out the draft. Windows, on the other hand, were not curtained until later in the seventeenth century. Normally the kitchen and dining room also contained a number of valuable possessions. Nicholas Jobbyn named 'a great crock' [earthenware pot], 'a gridiron and fire pan' and 'a basin of pewter' for special allocation; while Henry Cavell left 'ten crocks and ten pans' to one individual. Other items which featured in the wills included 'one silver goblet with cover'; 'one horn ornamented at the mouth with silver gilt'; 'six silver spoons'; 'one salt cellar of silver'; 'a charger, 12 platters and 12 saucers'; and 'a spice plate of silver and gilt'.

The Rising Standard of Living

Chimneys, Bedding and Tableware

There are old men yet dwelling in the village, where I remain, which have noted three things to be marvellously altered in England within their sound remembrance.

One is the multitude of chimneys lately erected, whereas in their young days, there were not above two or three in most uplandish towns of the realm... but each made his fire against a reredos [a screen] in the hall, where he dined and dressed his meat.

The second is the great improvement in lodging; for, they said, our fathers - and we ourselves also - have lain full oft upon straw pallets, on rough mats covered only with a sheet, under covelets made of dagswain [ie. shaggy cloth] or hopharlots [i.e. coarse coverlets made of shredded cloth], and a good round log under our heads instead of a bolster or pillow. If it were so that our father had, within seven years after his marriage, purchased a mattress or flock bed - and thereto a sack of chaff to rest his head upon - he thought himself to be as well lodged as the lord of the town...so well were they contented and with such base kind of furniture... Pillows, said they, were thought meet only for women in childbed. As for servants, if they had any sheet above them, it was well; for seldom had they any under their bodies to keep them from the pricking straws that ran oft through the canvas of the pallet and razed [i.e. wounded] their hardened hides.

The third thing they tell of is the exchange of vessels, as of wooden platters into pewter, and wooden spoons into silver or tin. For so common were all sorts of wooded stuff in old time that a man should hardly find four pieces of of pewter...in a good farmer's house; and yet for all this frugality, they were scarce able to live and pay their rents in their days without selling of a

cow or a horse or more, although they paid but four pounds [in rent] at the uttermost by the year...

Whereas in my time, the farmer will think his gains very small if he is not able to purchase a fair garnish of pewter in his cupboard, three or four feather beds, so many coverlets and carpets of tapestry, a silver salt [cellar], a bowl for wine, and a dozen spoons to furnish up the suite.

Source: William Harrison: *Description of England*, 1577 (ed. F.J. Furnivall, 1877 edtn.).

(Above) a typical four-poster bed of the Tudor period with curtains or 'hangings' to keep out the draught. The small truckle bed, which is stored beneath, would be pulled out at night for a child or servant.
(Below) the base of a four-poster bed reveals the cords, which support the mattress, and the two mattresses on top - a thin mattress made from plaited straw, above which (folded back) is a softer one filled with flock . Herbs were often scattered between the two to create a sweeter smell. From the Weald and Downland Open Air Museum at Singleton. (Author's photographs)

Woodcuts illustrating typical dress worn by the more affluent during Elizabeth's reign. Note that the unmarried woman is shown bare-breasted. From Richard Warner's History of Bath *(1801).*

A well-dressed family group with the father displaying an air of authority and the children seeking comfort around their mother. Tobacco, though expensive, was being imported from America from the middle of the sixteenth century. A contemporary woodcut by permission of the British Library (Roxburghe Ballads, RAX.Rox.I, 313).

SOURCES USED IN CHAPTER 3

1. Printed Material

Brinsley, John: *Ludud Literarius, or the Grammar Schoole* (1612)

Chapman, Mike & Holland, Elizabeth: 'The Development of the Saw Close from the Middle Ages' (in *Bath History*, vol. 6, 2000)

Davenport, Peter: *Medieval Bath Uncovered* (2002)

Duffy, Eamon: *The Stripping of the Altars:Traditional Religion in England, 1400-1580* (2005 edtn.)

Elton, G.R: *The Tudor Constitution* (1960)

Fox, Levi: *A Country Grammar School: a History of Ashby-de-la-Zouch Grammar School* (1967)

Harris, Richard: *Discovering Timber-framed Buildings* (1993, 3rd edtn.)

Harris, Richard: *Weald & Downland Museum: Guidebook*

Hutton, Ronald: *The Stations of the Sun: A History of the Ritual Year in Britain* (1996)

Loach, Jennifer: *Edward VI* (1999)

Pearson, Prebendary: 'Churchwardens' Accounts, St Michael's, Bath: Introduction' (in *Proceedings of the Somerset Archaeological and Natural History Society*, vol. 23, 1877). For edited transcripts of the accounts see also vol. 26, 1880.

Picard, Lisa: *Elizabethan London* (2003)

Razzell, P. (ed.): *The Journals of Two Travellers in Elizabethan and Early Stuart England* (1995) - for Busino's description

Sims, Alison: *Pleasures & Pastimes in Tudor England* (1999)

Somerset Wills, 1501-1530 (Somerset Record Society, vol. 19, 1903)

Somerset Wills, 1531-1558 (Somerset Record Society, vol. 21, 1905)

Symons, Katharine: *The Grammar School of King Edward VI, Bath and its Ancient Foundation* (1934)

Warner, Richard: *The History of Bath* (1801)

Wilson, Francesca M. (ed.): *Strange Island: Britain through Foreign Eyes, 1395-1942* (1955)

Woodward, G.H. (ed.): *Calendar of Somerset Chantry Grants* (Somerset Record Society, vol. 77, 1982)

Wroughton, John: *King Edward's School at Bath, 1552-1982* (1982)

Wroughton, John: *450 Years: King Edward's School, Bath, 1552-2002* (2002) - including an article by F R Thorn & C M J Thorn: 'The Founding of King Edward's School at Bath'.

2. Documentary Material:

Bath Record Office: No. 43: Commission, 5 November 1584: Inquiry into
             concealed lands

            No. 32: Inquisition as to flesh eaters, 1572

            Bath Chamberlain's Accounts, 1579-1603

            Bath Council Minute Book, 1614

            Edward VI's Letters Patent regarding King Edward's
               School, 7th July 1552 (ie. the School Charter)

Somerset Record Office: St Michael's Bath Churchwardens' Accounts, 1349-1575

This drawing from The Acts and Monuments of John Foxe *(ed. George Townsend, 1843-49 edtn.) illustrates the changes which took place in the liturgy during the reign of Edward VI. Henceforth the preaching of scripture from the pulpit is given prime importance during services (note the woman - bottom left - with an open bible on her lap); a wooden communion table replaces the old stone altar; while the ceremonies and prayers for the expulsion of the Devil are removed from what becomes a simple baptism service - top right. (Author's collection)*

CHAPTER 4

1572 - 74: A New Church, New Houses and a Royal Visit

A Feast for the Bishop, 1572

The year 1572 was a year of great significance for both the city itself and the church in Bath. In response to a petition from the mayor and corporation, Elizabeth I not only granted them permission to complete the building of the former Priory Church, but also to unite the five city centre churches into one rectory with 'the Rector of Bath' responsible for the whole operation (see below). This latter clause, however, was subject to a licence being granted by the Bishop of Bath and Wells (Bishop Gilbert Berkeley). It was therefore not altogether surprising that the corporation decided to invite the bishop to Bath for a discussion on all these matters. During his stay in the city, the councillors seized the chance to impress him with a lavish banquet in the Guildhall to which his wife and a large retinue were also invited.

Judging by the long list of items in the chamberlain's accounts under the heading *Charges upon my Lord Bishop of Bath and others with him*, no effort had been spared in tracking down the very best ingredients from far and wide. Indeed, Perkin was later rewarded with a gift of two pence for scouring the neighbourhood in a search 'for capons and chickens'. His efforts bore fruit with the purchase of twenty-one capons (at 1s 4d each) and twenty-nine chickens (at three pence each) from a number of individuals - including six chickens from 'the parson of Langridge'. Similarly thirty pigeons (at two pence each), one lamb (at two shillings and four pence), a 'bed of beef' (at two shillings and five pence) and two and a half bucks (freely donated) were successfully located - along with fruit, saffron, nutmeg and other spices from Bristol, sugar, salt, butter and cheese.

This contemporary woodcut shows a feast about to start. In the back right-hand corner, a host is greeting one guest, while a servant is helping another guest to wash his hands in a bowl (15). The table is covered with a carpet and tablecloth and is set with trenchers, spoons, knives, napkins and a salt cellar. The master of the feast is already sitting on the right of the table, while the waiters bring in various dishes (10). The butler (21) pours wine out of a flagon into glasses, which have been brought out from the bar at the back. From J.A. Comenius, Orbis Sensualum Pictus, *1672 edtn. by permission of the British Library (1607.2351).*

A large quantity of wine and beer (three kilderkins of double strength beer and one kilderkin of single strength) was acquired 'for the eating of the venison in the hall'. Unfortunately, the two new 'pottle pots' and two 'quart pots', which had been bought specially for the occasion, 'were then lost' somewhat mysteriously. [A kilderkin was a 16-18 gallon cask; a pottle jar contained half a gallon, while a quart pot held a quarter gallon.]

There were other related expenses to the feast, including rewards to those who had fetched the supplies from the countryside; wages for the cooks and the baker who had prepared the food and the maids who had served it; horsemeat to feed the horses in the bishop's retinue; and, instead of a bouquet of flowers, a gift of two capons and a dozen chickens for the bishop's wife. In view of the fact that the search for poultry had taken place over several weeks, there had been a need to obtain 'a cagement' not only to keep the birds safe, but also to keep them alive - hence the purchase of '2 bushels and 3 pecks of barley' and a supply of milk 'to feed the capons and chickens withal'. It was, after all, vital that they remained fresh for the banquet!

The feast itself, which cost a total of £8 11s 3d (almost six per cent of the council's annual budget), would undoubtedly be typical of such celebrations in Tudor times. Although venison was clearly the star item on the menu, the other meats (lamb, beef, chicken and capon) would be offered as *additional* courses, not alternatives. These would often be accompanied by soups and salads, although it will be noticed from the above details that no vegetables had been purchased for the sumptuous feast. In Tudor times, those who could afford it would consume great quantities of meat (often forming up to 75 per cent of each meal) - hence the prevalence of both gout and constipation among the more affluent members of society.

However, in spite of the fact that many local citizens grew vegetables in private back gardens, these were not particularly enjoyed or appreciated as a separate dish - but rather as the basis for soups. After gorging themselves on meat, the guests would then enjoy fruit, cheese and a whole range of sweet desserts in a separate course known as 'the banquet'. This therefore accounts for the large amount of sugar which had been acquired and the employment of John Pearman, the baker, who would have produced a selection of jellies, custards, gingerbreads, pies and puddings.

The Restoration of the Former Priory Church

(i) Royal Permission to Restore, 1572

When **Edmund Colthurst** indicated to the corporation in 1569 that he was willing to donate the site of the former Priory to the city (see Chapter 2), the members of the corporation seized his offer with great eagerness, realising the enormous potential that this presented for future development. It is quite possible, of course, that they had discussed all this with Colthurst long before the offer was made. He was, after all, a well-known local figure, whose father had been member of parliament for the city.

But whatever the background to this dramatic move, the corporation - having carefully worked out its strategy - despatched in 1572 a formal petition to Lord Burleigh, Lord High Treasurer and close adviser to Queen Elizabeth I. It had also wisely taken the precaution of securing a letter from the Bishop of Bath and Wells in support of the petition (the corporation paying two shillings to two of its members 'when they went to Wells for my Lord Bishop's letter to London).

(right) Elizabeth I (1533-1603). A portrait by an unknown artist, c.1588. (By courtesy of the National Portrait Gallery, London)

The dispatch contained **three specific requests** - first, that the corporation should be permitted to complete the building of 'the fair church commenced by the late prior there...Edmund Colthurst, the proprietor, being contented to grant the same to the corporation'; secondly, that authority be given for the amalgamation of 'the three little decayed churches' in the city centre (i.e. St Mary's by the North Gate, St Michael's Within and St Mary de Stall's with its annexed chapel at Widcombe) with the new 'great church' to form one parish (subject to the bishop's permission); and thirdly, that the petitioners be granted the advowsons thereof by the queen. [An advowson was the right to appoint clergy to a particular church. The advowsons of all the Bath churches, which had previously been held by the Priory, were seized by the crown after the dissolution in 1539. Ownership of the advowsons was important, because it brought with it the control of the pulpits - crucial in a largely Protestant city such as Bath.]

By November 1572, the mayor had received the queen's reply - **letters patent** granting the corporation even more than it had requested. For whereas it had originally requested the amalgamation of 'the three little decayed churches', the grant actually conveyed the right to unite all five of the city's churches (including the churches of St James by the South Gate and St Michael's Without) - 'or any of them'. The corporation immediately expressed its gratitude to Edmund Colthurst by making him a freeman of the city and sending him a gift of 'a lamb and a couple of capons' (not to mention a supply of horsemeat for his horse!). Colthurst eventually moved out of Bath and based himself in London, where he greatly impressed the queen with his ideas for a 'New River' to pipe fresh water into the capital (ideas doubtlessly sparked off by his admiration for Bath's own water supply - see Chapter 1). Meanwhile, stung by the queen's description of the former Priory cathedral ('the whole of the church is falling down - even the chancel is ruinous'), the corporation had sprung into action to tackle the immense challenge ahead - a task that proved no less daunting than the creation of a 'new river' for London!

(ii) The Rebuilding of the Church, 1572-1617

By 1572, the 'very ruinous' church was undoubtedly an eyesore in the very centre of the city. Badly plundered at the time of the dissolution and now exposed to the elements, it was frequently used as a stone quarry for building developments or road repairs. However the corporation - anxious to create a city worthy of its growing status as a health resort - was determined to establish a fine new centre, where visitors to the spa could 'hear sermons and other divine services' in comfort. As things stood in 1572, sermons were of necessity preached 'in the open market place', thanks to the lack of space in all the existing churches. With the coming of the Reformation and the decline of Catholic ritual (see Chapter 2), preaching had been given far greater prominence in many churches throughout the land. Bath Corporation - increasingly Protestant in its outlook - was anxious to promote this new trend.

Once permission had been received from the queen, many prominent local citizens set to work on the task of restoring the old building - including Peter Chapman, who repaired the east end of the north aisle at his own expense in order to preserve it from further ravages of the weather (his father, Thomas, having been buried there in 1524). Nevertheless, it was quickly realised that the project was far too extensive and costly to be undertaken in piecemeal fashion by local people.

The corporation therefore petitioned the queen for permission to launch a nationwide appeal for funds. As a result of this request, a licence was issued in April 1573 granting it the right to collect donations over a period of seven years towards the rebuilding of the church and the improvement of St John's Hospital. At the same time, the queen issued a proclamation, which was printed for circulation to all towns and villages throughout England and Wales. This instructed both clergy and local officials to assist the appeal by reading out the proclamation in a convenient public place and then organising a local collection.

As soon as money from the collection had started to trickle in, the corporation immediately undertook the task of re-roofing the chancel with blue slate and rebuilding the north transept - a task which was given increased momentum by the visit of Queen

The opening part of Queen Elizabeth's proclamation of 1573, which launched the appeal for donations towards the restoration of the former Priory Church in Bath. (Author's collection).

Elizabeth in 1574, when the inaugural service was held (see page 91). By 1576 however, in spite of the fact that burials had already taken place in the vault beneath the church, donations towards the work had started to dry up. Sir John Harington, a subsequent benefactor to the church, later suspected that some of the money ear-marked for Bath had been diverted - through an accidental mix-up - to a simultaneous collection being organised for the steeple at St Paul's Cathedral in London.

Whatever the cause of the shortfall, the situation was grave enough to prompt a request from the mayor to the privy council in 1576 for permission to launch a second appeal. After the bishop, on behalf of the privy council, had inspected the corporation's accounts and the progress of the building programme, the request was granted. Nevertheless, although further work was undertaken in fits and starts (including some on the cross aisle and east window in 1577), Thomas Lichfield was to write of the church just two years later that 'at present, it remaineth very ruinous'.

There was now a prolonged pause in activity as the project completely lost its momentum. Sir John Harington commented on this in a letter to Lord Burleigh in 1595: 'Our work at the Bath doth go on hand *passibus aequis* - we sometimes gallop with good presents and then as soon stand still, for lack of a good spurring: but it seems more like a church than it has aforetime, when a man could not pray without danger of having good St Stephen's death, by stones tumbling about his ears'. It was in fact Harington (as godson of the queen with good connections at court) who gave the project 'a good spurring' - with enormous help from Thomas Bellott, steward to Lord Burleigh, and Lord Burleigh himself through a most generous legacy.

Work on the building therefore staged an energetic revival between 1598 and 1600 with the completion and fitting out of the choir; the glazing of the east window; the construction of galleries; the erection of a screen between choir and the nave; and the installation of seating. The chancel and choir areas were now finally ready to take on the role of the city's new parish church. The remainder of the work was completed between 1604 and 1617 (just after the ending of the Tudor period), including the south transept, the tower (complete with both clock and bells), the vestry and the nave (now boasting a fine timber roof).

(iii) The Unification of the Churches, 1583

The Appointment of John Long

The story of the unification of the churches is the story of clever conspiracy, ruthless determination and illegal practice with the corporation itself holding centre stage.

By 1572, it had already achieved two of its main objectives - namely, the power not only to transform the ruined Priory Church into the city's main parish church, but also to appoint clergy to all the churches in Bath. Its third objective, however, proved much more elusive to secure - for although the queen had granted authority to the mayor and corporation to 'unite and consolidate' the five city churches into a single rectory, it was to take a further eleven years before a start could actually be made on the process.

In the first place, the timing of the reform was partly dependent (according to the terms of the grant) on the livings of all the churches being vacant. However, although the church of St James by the South Gate had already become vacant following the death of Thomas Wathall in 1569, a vacancy did not occur at the church of St Mary de

Stall until 1577, when the vicar (Henry Adams) died. Secondly, it was essential from a practical point of view to ensure - before any of the smaller churches were closed down - that sufficient repairs had been undertaken on the former Priory Church for services to be held there. Thirdly, in giving assent, the queen had emphasised that her permission was subject to the approval of the Bishop of Bath and Wells, Bishop Gilbert Berkeley.

Faced with these problems - and in particular the need to avoid making any permanent appointments of clergy to the city's churches while the three conditions were being fulfilled - the corporation secured the services of the Reverend John Long in 1574 as master of its new grammar school. Educated at Eton and Cambridge, he was a young energetic scholar, who was also an able preacher - a rising star destined for high office (ten years later, for instance, he had been appointed Bishop of Armagh). There is little doubt that the corporation saw in this ambitious young man someone who could fill the increasing vacuum in local church life, while at the same time acting as their expert advisor on the amalgamation process.

We certainly know from payments made by the city's chamberlain that Long was used regularly to take services at those churches in Bath, which lacked a permanent priest (in 1576, for instance, he paid twenty shillings to 'Mr Long, the preacher'); and that, by 1579, he had been accommodated by the corporation in 'the parsonage house' of St Mary's by the North Gate. Indeed, the churchwardens there paid 'Mr Long our parisher' the sum of £6 10s 0d for his duties over a four-year period between 1579 and 1583. We also know that he devoted much of his energy to helping the corporation to achieve the unification of the parishes - even to the extent of resigning his mastership of the grammar school in 1582 in order to concentrate more fully on that objective as the matter finally came to a head (see pages 83-4).

The Five Redundant Churches

Long soon realised that the corporation's idea of amalgamation made a lot of sense. Although the churches of St James and St Michael Without enjoyed modest resources, the three city centre churches (St Mary's, St Michael's Within and St Mary de Stall's) were not sufficiently well endowed to support clergy of their own, were far too small to accommodate the increasing number of visitors and were largely in a run-down condition. Indeed, as early as 1554, the churchwardens of St Mary's by the North Gate had actually advocated the idea of an amalgamation during the bishop's visitation. The entry in the visitation book reads:

> *Bath St Mary.* The churchwardens there presenteth that they have had no parson nor curate by the space of one year and half last past and that the revenues of the parsonage are so bare that it is not able to maintain a curate; wherefore they desire the same church to be united to some other.

The lack of affluence within this tiny parish was underlined partly by the fact that its annual income from rents amounted to just £3 17s 4d; and partly by an exchequer document of 1576 which referred to 'the very poor and needy parishioners living and dwelling there'. The extent of its poverty was further confirmed by its exemption from the subsidy tax in the years 1556, 1561 and 1565 on the grounds that it was far too poor to contribute. After the church had finally been made redundant in 1583, it took on a new role by providing accommodation for the grammar school (hardly surprising in

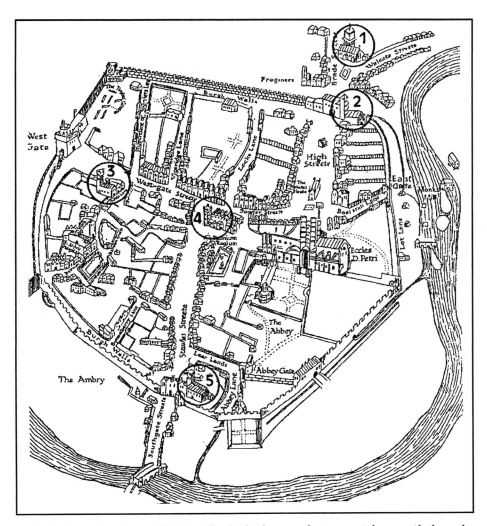

The sites of the five churches of Bath, all of which served tiny parishes until the scheme for amalgamation in 1583. 1 = St Michael's Without; 2 = St Mary's by the North Gate; 3 = St Michael's Within; 4 = St Mary de Stall's; 5 = St James's. Map based on a version of John Speed's map of Bath. (Author's collection)

view of the fact that the master was already living in the parsonage house!). The building itself survived until 1777, when it was demolished during construction work associated with the new Pulteney Bridge.

The second of these churches, St Michael's Within (also known also as Little St Michael's or St Michael's by the Bath), had already been annexed by St John's Hospital by 1548 under the authority of Edward VI - so that the parson of the church was also the master of the hospital. The parish, which covered a very small area in the north-west corner of the city, was one of the poorest in Bath and was populated chiefly by labourers and craftsmen. Little money was therefore available for the maintenance of church fabric, despite its modest size. As Jean Manco has shown, the corporation had largely taken the hospital under its wing (together with the annexed church) by the middle of the century. From 1568 (when the city's account book commences) the now-redundant church was being rented out to a private individuals (in 1588, for instance,

An artist's reconstruction of the Churches of St Michael Within (top) and St Mary de Stall (bottom), based on a drawing of a 1630 Plan of Bath. Published in James Tunstall's Rambles about Bath *(1876)*

Henry Chapman was paying two shillings a year for the privilege). Meanwhile, the corporation had itself taken over responsibility for the payment of any charges connected with the church, including the 'procurations' (or fees) connected with visitations by the bishop or archdeacon.

The third church was that of St Mary de Stall, which stood at the corner of Stall Street and Cheap Street. Always regarded as the official city church, it was used by both the mayor and corporation (who sat together in 'the Mayor's Aisle') and the Guild of Merchant Tailors (which not only maintained its own chapel there, dedicated to St Catherine, but also used the church for the initiation of new members). However, although this was an active and vigorous church, it was only natural that the mayor and corporation should wish to transfer their civic services to the much larger new church - hence the fact that it was being forced into redundancy. All the evidence suggests that Mary de Stall's continued to be used as the official city church until sometime between 1593 and 1600 - by which date the new church had finally been fitted out for divine service. The redundant building was then left to fall into a gradual state of disrepair. In 1656, for instance, the council minute book indicated that that the tower was 'much fallen into decay and cannot be repaired'. It was partly demolished in consequence - only for the minutes to report just three years later that the whole church had 'fallen down'.

The Opposition of the Bishop

In view of all these circumstances, no opposition was voiced to the idea of amalgamation by the parishioners of these three churches. This, however, was not the case with Bishop Berkeley, whose support was crucial to the project's success. For some unknown reason, he withheld his agreement to the proposals - presumably because he actually disapproved of the amalgamation on principle, even though he had warmly supported the restoration of the former Priory Church. It was not therefore until after his death in 1581 that the corporation could renew its attempts to gain authorisation.

(right) Dr William Aubrey (1529-1595). The Archbishop of Canterbury's Vicar-General, he was formerly professor of civil law at Oxford University and master in chancery. He was elected MP for Taunton in 1592. Print by Wenceslaus Hollar; sculptor unknown. (By courtesy of the National Portrait Gallery, London)

Circumstances quickly worked in its favour - for during the vacancy, the diocese was administered by Dr William Aubrey, the archbishop's vicar-general and a man well known to the citizens of Bath.

The corporation eagerly grasped the opportunity to achieve its objective before the appointment of the next bishop - partly by lobbying Aubrey with ceaseless determination and then by bribing him into compliance. In 1583, for instance, the chamberlain released £10 from the city's funds at the mayor's request 'to get Dr Aubrey to secure the uniting of our churches', plus further sums to cover the cost of frequent communications with him in London. Furthermore, between 1584 and 1594, the corporation paid Aubrey an 'annuity' or 'fee' of forty shillings a year - probably as an on-going reward for his services; while in 1593, it sent him a special gift of 'two dozen pigeons, three dozen larks and three live partridges'. Sensing the likelihood of strong objections to what it had in mind, the corporation realised the value of securing the continuing support of such an influential ally. Meanwhile, its tactics had been successful for, on 12th April 1583, Dr Aubrey signed the order of amalgamation.

This stated that the four main churches in Bath - St James's, St Michael's Without, St Mary's and St Mary de Stall's with its annexed chapel at Widcombe - were at last all vacant. [The already redundant church of St Michael Within was clearly excluded from the list for the circumstances outlined above.] For various reasons, argued Dr Aubrey, it now made sense for these churches to be amalgamated into one parish. In the first place, the churches were so close to the church of the former Priory 'that the parishioners of the same may easily and without hindrance' congregate there to hear divine service and receive holy communion. Secondly, the financial resources of the four churches were far too 'meagre' to enable each church to support its own rector. Thirdly, the imposing Priory church was a much more suitable and dignified location 'for the word of God to be preached, prayers to be offered and the sacraments to be administered' than the crumbling old churches had been.

The amalgamation order then went on to promote the newly-restored Priory church as the city's sole parish church. Old parish boundaries were to be removed. Once repairs had finally been completed, every inhabitant of the former parishes would 'be bound to go there and nowhere else to hear divine service and to receive the sacraments' The corporation, which held the right to appoint clergy in Bath (see above), wasted no time in appointing John Long as the first Rector of Bath and dedicating the restored church to Saint Peter and Saint Paul. Dr Aubrey had ruled that the assets of the four redundant churches (including income from property, 'offerings' and the tithes paid annually by parishioners) were to be amalgamated to create a new 'rectory' in support of the new parish church and its rector. The corporation did not, however, react quite as speedily in implementing some of the other stipulations. Indeed, far from bringing about the closure of the four old churches, it actually permitted two of them to survive (St Michael's Without and St James's by the South Gate), although the curates who ministered there worked under the control of the rector (see below).

The Opposition of Widcombe

St Thomas à Becket Church, Widcombe, built by Prior Cantlow between 1490 and 1498. The arms of Bath Priory are carved on the east-facing wall of the tower.
(Author's collection)

The most vociferous resistance to the corporation's plans came from the inhabitants of Widcombe. The old Norman chapel of Widcombe had since 1263 been attached to the vicarage of St Mary de Stall, although - from 1322 - it had enjoyed the privilege of having its own resident chaplain to officiate at services. A more imposing church, dedicated to St Thomas à Becket, had been built by Prior Cantlow between 1490 and 1498 (see Chapter 2), displaying the arms of Bath Priory (a shuttle and mitre) on the east wall of the tower. This church is clearly shown on William Smith's map of 1588, standing beyond Bath Bridge.

Understandably, the residents of the village greatly resented the order for amalgamation, which instructed them to abandon their own chapel and worship instead at the new parish church (trudging across the bridge in order to do so!). Within just two months of the order for amalgamation being made, therefore, they lodged a formal objection with Dr Aubrey in London and succeeded in obtaining a 'sequestration' of the living. This enabled them to divert income from the vicarage of St Mary de Stall to support their own separate priest as before. Then - with impressive speed - they set about the task of appointing such a man (a Mr Gay) to the office, having gained a licence to do so from the diocese. [The bishopric itself remained vacant between the death of Bishop Berkeley in November 1581 and the appointment of Bishop Godwin in September 1584.]

The corporation was furious at this resistance and weighed in heavily with all its might and influence to get the ruling overturned (spending a massive £39 in the process). Its new rector, John Long, was despatched to London with forty shillings in his hands 'to avoid' (as the words of the council minute puts it) 'the sequestration procured forth by the inhabitants of Widcombe'; while Matthew Lloyd (Long's successor as master of the grammar school) was sent post-haste to Wells to persuade the diocese to cancel the licence granted to Mr Gay. These frantic efforts were finally rewarded - the chamberlain simply noting in his accounts that the mayor, John Pearman, had paid 13s 4d for bringing down from London 'a revocation' of the original order. The poor parishioners of Widcombe were therefore forced to succumb to the powerful bullying tactics of the corporation.

However, although the village lost its resident chaplain and did not gain its own independent vicar until 1855, the evidence suggests that services continued to be held in the church (presumably with ministers supplied by the Rector of Bath). Certainly christenings took place there in every year without exception following the 1583 crisis - as did burials from 1592, when that particular register commenced.

The Corporation's Devious Plan

Yet another threat to the corporation's plans surfaced in the November of 1584. The queen appointed a commission to inquire into former monastic lands in Somerset, which might have been 'concealed' in an attempt to escape confiscation by the crown at the time of the dissolution in 1539. Five men of substance from the county were nominated to spearhead the investigations with the help of panels of 'jurors' drawn from each locality. Proceedings were duly held in Bath in January 1585 under the leadership of three of those commissioners - William Walley, William Cavell and Thomas Harington.

They eventually reported their findings - namely, that fifty-six properties (mainly small cottages, meadows and barns) had been identified in Bath as having been 'concealed and unjustly kept back' from the crown. Thirty-six of the tenements in question represented the total property holding of the church of St Michael's Without, with the remainder almost certainly belonging to the church of St Mary de Stall (which, of course, was already destined for closure). Confiscation, it seemed, was now inevitable. At first sight, this represented a serious blow to the finances of the new rectory.

The story now takes on the nature of a political mystery involving all kinds of intrigue, subterfuge and collusion. Two groups of people had vital interests which were now at stake - the corporation, whose secret agenda was based on its desire to control all the property in Bath; and the parishioners of St Michael's Without, who wanted to salvage their active church from closure and their ownership of the thirty-six tenements. It so happened that several leading members of the congregations at St Michael's and St Mary de Stall's were also highly influential members of the corporation. Indeed, at least seven of them had already held high office on the council, including William Sherston, a former churchwarden at St Michael's (who was mayor at the time of the findings in 1585), and John Sachfield, a former churchwarden at St Mary's (who was city chamberlain).

This contemporary print, entitled Street Cries, *illustrates some of the ordinary basket traders and workers who would have been a familiar sight around the markets and streets of Bath in Tudor times (see also next page). By courtesy of the Pepys Library, Magdalene College, Cambridge.*

Furthermore, six of these leading councillors actually rented parts of this 'concealed' property at St Michael's, including John Walley, who became mayor at the end of 1585 having served as churchwarden of St Michael's in 1563. Even more surprisingly, however, was the fact that another of the tenants was William Cavell, one of the queen's inquiry commissioners! With such an overlap of interests, it is hardly surprising that private agreements were quickly reached by all the affected parties.

There were also suspicious circumstances surrounding the inquiry itself. In the first place, the tenants of the fifty-six properties under investigation made absolutely no attempt to put forward any arguments in favour of the claims of the two churches to retain possession - even though many of them were highly articulate businessmen and councillors, who were also members of the congregations. Furthermore, there would in fact have been a strong case to support the argument that these properties had always been owned by the churches (having been bequeathed in many instances by faithful parishioners from as far back as 1349) and not by the Priory.

Indeed, the chief link with the Priory had simply been that it owned the advowson of all the city churches and therefore the right to appoint all the clergy. Although it is true that one rector of St Michael's in 1242 had negotiated from the Priory one daily pot of ale and one freshly-baked loaf - plus a dish of meat three times a week and a dish of whatever the monks were eating in the refectory on the other four days - there is no evidence to suggest that the Priory had endowed the church with property. The parishioners' case was therefore strong. Furthermore, the inquiry commissioners had actually encouraged the tenants 'to say what they could in support of their title' - but 'none did'. All this rather smacks of a conspiracy of silence, suggesting that there had been a prior agreement amongst them not to resist the confiscation.

Suspicions were also heightened by the fact that the commissioners grossly - and perhaps deliberately - under-assessed the properties, fixing the rentable values at truly laughable rates. These ranged from between one penny and twelve pence a year (with the vast majority being set at between two pence and four pence). Therefore, whereas the churchwardens of St Michael's had actually collected £11 8s 0d in rent for their thirty-six properties in 1572, the commissioners set the rentable value at just 19s 4d for all fifty-six of those under review!

The mystery deepened even further two months later when, following a petition by Sir James Croft, the queen granted William Sherston, clothier, and John Sachfield, baker, all fifty-six properties which had been listed in Bath. In return, they were to pay the measly sum of just £1 14s 4d a year in rent. Croft, who was controller of the royal

household, had been granted a patent (or sole right) to search for concealed lands over a period of four years. In other words, he was in it to make money for both himself and the queen. There is little doubt that he had put in a special plea to the queen over the matter of the Bath properties and was granted his request as a favour 'in consideration of the faithful and acceptable service hitherto rendered'.

Nor is there any doubt that Croft had been actively lobbied by Bath corporation, the chamberlain paying for 'the hire of a mare for Peter Chapman to ride to London to Sir James Croft about the church land' - a mare which, incidentally, had been provided by William Sherston. Although there is no record of the conversations which took place between these two men, there is little doubt that Chapman, a distinguished soldier, persuaded Croft to support the intricate and devious scheme which the corporation had now devised. Nor do we know just how much money changed hands in the process - although we do know that the enterprise was to cost Sherston the enormous sum of £326 in expenses' (see below).

It is highly probable, however, that the solution to this deepening mystery was to be found in the heart of the Guildhall, where a most daring plot had been devised. Faced with the crown's threat to confiscate 'concealed' priory property, Bath Corporation had secretly vowed to prevent that property being sold to outsiders. Indeed, it was crucial for the success of its own ambitious plans both to develop the city and to fund the amalgamation of the parishes into a united rectory that its own property portfolio should be enlarged.

Unfortunately, under the terms of the Statute of Mortmain of 1279, corporations were banned from purchasing property. In order to circumvent these regulations, therefore, it was unofficially agreed that the mayor (William Sherston) and the chamberlain (John Sachfield) should act in a private capacity - but as secret trustees of the corporation - in obtaining the fifty-six properties at stake. This is confirmed by the fact that, very shortly afterwards the transaction had gone through (i.e. by 1586), the corporation reimbursed Sherston with the £326 which he had invested from his own money.

All this helps to explain not only why the corporation had despatched Peter Chapman to London to lobby Sir James Croft, but also why the tenants in St Michael's parish had not resisted the confiscation. Under the terms of the private deal struck with the parish, the churchwardens were guaranteed the continuing right to collect the rents of the properties for the use of the parish (thus ensuring its long term survival) in return for the nominal payment of £1 14s 4d a year to the crown as head rent. For its own part, while the corporation agreed to maintain the fabric of the church, it was to enjoy all other income from the property, including the large 'fines' which were imposed when a lease was renewed or changed hands.

It is also interesting to note in this connection that, in 1585, twenty-one of the tenants of 'church lands' in St Michael's parish suddenly paid the chamberlain substantial 'fines' totalling £114 16s 8d (without any indication that leases had changed hands or expired). Indeed, as Katherine Symons has suggested, this almost unprecedented yearly total reads far more like a subscription list than a renewal-of-lease list - with the wealthier residents clubbing together to help pay the cost of the acquisition.

All this 'devious procedure' (as P.R. James has described it) was strictly illegal. In fact it was not until the new Elizabethan charter had been granted to the city in 1590 that the corporation actually received the legal right to purchase additional property.

Even then the mystery continued for several more years before the dwellings in the two parishes, which had been held in trust by Sherston and Sachfield, were finally transferred to the corporation. Although a conveyance was drawn up in 1598, it was not finally signed until 1618. Through this deal the corporation acquired another substantial slice of city-centre property to add to that which they had already secured through the endowment of the grammar school in 1552 (see Chapter 3) and the take-over of St John's Hospital. However, in spite of these successes, its insatiable appetite continued undiminished as a new target came into view.

(iv) The Lease of the Rectory, 1590

After ten years of dedicated work on behalf of the corporation, John Long resigned as Rector of Bath in 1584 to take up an appointment as Bishop of Armagh and Primate of All Ireland. The corporation expressed its heartfelt thanks by by presenting him with a gift of ten pounds, most of which had been 'gathered' in a collection. It then proceeded to use its freshly-acquired powers to appoint the Reverend Richard Meredith as Long's successor, choosing without doubt a man who would be sufficiently subservient to its wishes. A former pupil of King Edward's School, he - like Long - was also appointed as master of the school for at least one year during his incumbency (the chamberlain paying him £12 in 1586-87 'for keeping the school').

In 1590 - six years after his appointment as rector - the true intentions of the corporation were revealed when it persuaded or bullied Meredith into signing a most extraordinary lease. In it he agreed to surrender to the mayor and citizens of Bath 'his rectory of Saints Peter and Paul with all the glebe lands, meadows and pastures - and all manner of tithes' - together with his rights to all associated churchyards and waste ground. The agreement was also to include all such property associated with the chapel in Widcombe or 'any other church within the said city'.

In return, he was to receive an annual rent of £52 (which, in reality, became his stipend) and the right to retain the parsonage with its adjoining garden and orchard. Although the lease was granted for a term of just sixty years, the corporation continued in possession of this church property until the early nineteenth century. While at first sight, the income allocated to Meredith by the lease seems generous, it is interesting to note that, by 1631, the stipend of the rector had been reduced to just £10 - a situation which forced incumbents to become 'pluralists' by taking responsibility for a number of other churches in order to boost their income.

By taking this action, the corporation had merely underlined its intention to enlarge its own assets through - if necessary - the ruthless exploitation of institutions as opportunity arose. The 1590 lease had finally ensured that all former church property was now firmly under its control. The closure of St Mary de Stall's, of course, enabled the corporation - from 1616 - to develop the churchyard (and, later, the site of the church itself) for new housing - just as it had already done with the land immediately adjacent to the new church, which Edmund Colthurst had donated in 1572. This was to result in the unsightly building of tightly-packed houses right up to the northern wall of the new church - much to the inconvenience of residents and the discomfort of the congregation. They were not finally removed until the 1830s.

*****

By the end of the Tudor period, therefore, three of the old city churches had been closed down and the Rector of Bath installed in his new parish church (later to be styled Bath Abbey). The churches of St Michael's Without and St James by the South Gate had been reprieved. Although these continued to survive with their own congregations, therefore, they were now served by curates appointed by the Rector of Bath (a situation which continued until 1843).

For its own part, the corporation had succeeded in building a prestigious church worthy of the new reformed religion and the city's growing national fame - although, in the process, it had behaved at times like a disreputable property developer, crushing those who dared to stand in its way. Nevertheless, it has to be admitted that - as a landlord - it was conscientious in maintaining the fabric of its churches (the chamberlain paying, for instance, for repairs to the chancel at St James's in 1590, the leads on the roof of St Mary's in 1589 and the tiles on the 'Great Church' in 1593) - just as it was generous in its treatment of St John's Hospital. Indeed, the corporation actually enlarged the hospital in 1580 with the addition of an upper floor, attic and master's lodgings (see Jean Manco, *The Spirit of Care*).

A Royal Visit, 1574

In the summer of 1574, excitement reached fever pitch around the streets of Bath as its citizens eagerly awaited the expected arrival of their queen. Indeed, it was Elizabeth I's custom to make a short 'progress' or tour each year to a different part of the country so that she could become better acquainted with as many towns and cities as possible. Somewhat belatedly, therefore, she suddenly decided in the July of that year to visit the west country in the company of her court. Yeomen ushers were hurriedly despatched to make arrangements for her majesty to stay in the houses of selected nobility and gentry along the route, making sure that these were properly furnished in time for her arrival - each of which properties took several days to prepare.

Such was the haste of her departure, however, that several items crucial to the queen's comfort and appearance were inevitably forgotten. At one stage, therefore, the yeoman of the wardrobe of the beds was sent back to London to fetch not only 'stools, cushions and other stuff', but also 'a chair of cloth of gold' for her majesty to use as a dining chair. Later still, the yeoman of the robes was twice despatched to the capital - once for 'a gown and two hats' and later for an embroidered gown of white satin.

It was customary for the royal court to transport a considerable amount of baggage in order to ensure maximum comfort throughout the trip. Many carts were therefore required to carry furniture, soft furnishings, bed curtains, pewter tableware, clothing and provisions (bearing in mind that the royal entourage was considerable in size). Indeed, following a visit to England in 1597, the Duke of Wurttemberg wrote:

> When the Queen breaks up her court with the intention of visiting another place, there commonly follow more than 300 carts laden with bag and baggage; for you must know that in England, besides coaches, they use no wagons for the goods, but have only two-wheeled carts; which are however so large that they carry quite as much as wagons, and as many as five or six strong horses draw them.

It was the task of the master of the posts to ensure that fresh horses were available for the use of this baggage train at every stage along the route - for it was essential that the goods arrived at each destination well ahead of Her Majesty.

Leaving Greenwich in early July, Elizabeth continued her tour via Richmond, Windsor, Reading, Woodstock, Sherborne, Sudeley, Gloucester, Berkeley Castle and Bristol, where she arrived on 15th August. There, after a welcome by the mayor and corporation, she was treated to speeches and poems delivered by some of the boys of the city. A guard of three hundred soldiers then escorted her to her lodgings (the house of John Young in St Augustine's Back) before firing a musket volley in salute. On her departure after a week's stay, the queen was presented with a fabulous 'jewel', made out of rubies and diamonds, by her host (who was duly knighted for his generosity). She then proceeded to Keynsham, where she dined, before progressing to Bath later that day (Saturday 21st August).

Judging by a series of entries in the Bath Chamberlain's accounts, the corporation had made a frantic effort to tidy up the city in anticipation of the queen's visit. A specialist painter had been brought over from Salisbury to re-paint the statues and emblems at the King's Bath, the Guildhall, the North Gate and the West Gate; the Guildhall itself had been extensively repaired; the road had been mended by the West Gate; the area around the city wall had been thoroughly cleared of litter; new butchers' stalls had been constructed; a new public privy had been built; extensive repairs had been undertaken on the network of water pipes; and windows in the churches of St Mary de Stall and St Michael Without had been re-glazed 'at the Queen's Majesty's being here'.

At least on this occasion, the corporation had received ample notice of the visit - unlike the situation which was to occur in 1602, when rumours swept through the city of an imminent and unheralded visit by the queen. The corporation, realising the deplorable state of its streets and the depleted nature of its own workforce, was plunged into an instant state of undisguised panic. Messengers were therefore urgently despatched to Tetbury, Cirencester, Frome, Bristol, Sodbury, Warminster and Chippenham 'to get paviours against the queen's coming'. Emergency repairs were then quickly undertaken by these reinforcements in both the High Street and Westgate Street. Sadly - after great sums had been expended - the rumours eventually proved to be false!

There is no exact record of where Elizabeth stayed during her visit in August 1574, although it is probable that she was either based in Westgate House or in Abbey House (the former Prior's residence), which Joseph Gilmore labelled 'the royal lodgings' on his map of 1694. What we do know is that a gentleman

An artist's view of Abbey House (the former Prior's lodgings), which was finally demolished in 1755, was possibly the base used by the queen during her stay in 1574. From a sepia drawing by R.W. M. Wright. (Author's collection)

usher of the queen's chamber (Symon Bowyer) - accompanied by one yeoman usher, three yeomen of the queen's chamber, two grooms of the chamber, two grooms of the wardrobe and one groom porter - had been sent on in advance to oversee preparations at Her Majesty's lodgings. Bowyer was eventually reimbursed for his outlay on accomplishing this task the sum of £7 17s 4d. During their stay these officials were entertained to dinner at the city's expense, the chamberlain paying 'the tapster of The Hart for the gentleman usher and his company's dinner' a total of 12s 8d. One other court official - a page, Charles Smith, with two assistants - was also sent ahead 'to make ready the office of the robes', thus ensuring that the queen had suitable attire for her visit to Bath.

It is important to realise that Queen Elizabeth was anxious that these official visits should not normally become an expensive burden either on the town itself or on the owner of the house in which she stayed. Her treasurer's accounts therefore reveal that she largely bore the cost of the two-day visit to Bath herself. In all, she paid out a total of £373 16s 0d on the costs incurred by the whole court, including *stabulum* (the stabling and feeding of horse) £19 18s 9d; *garderoba* (wardrobe - probably the cleaning and repair of garments) £46 19s 9d; and *elemosyna* (alms) 8s 0d. It was Elizabeth's custom to donate four shillings a day towards the local poor during each of her visits.

The remainder of her expenditure covered the cost of food and drink consumed - *cenam* (the ingredients of the main meals) £12 1s 6d; *butteria* (the provision of liquor) £94 7s 1d; *coquina* (kitchen - preparation and cooking) £111 19s 8d; *pulletria* (poultry) £36 13s 7d; *scuttleria* (the laying out and washing of dishes) £9 5s 4d; *salseria* (salt and sauces) £1 18s 4d; *aula* (hire and preparation of the hall where the courtiers ate their meals) £7 19s 0d; and *vadia* (wages) £20 0s 0d. As a result of this policy, the corporation was not required to stage an expensive banquet of the kind arranged for the bishop in 1572 (see above) - indeed, according to eyewitnesses, the queen normally preferred to dine alone with just a handful of attendants.

There is little doubt, however, that the mayor and corporation in all their finery would have met the queen and her courtiers most graciously at the North Gate and that - accompanied by the city's newly-formed trained bands (see Chapter 5) - this spectacular procession would then have made its way through cheering crowds along the High Street. For there, in the spacious area outside the Market House, a special platform had been erected and roped off to keep the crowds at bay (the chamberlain having already paid a carpenter for 'making the oration place'). A formal speech of welcome would then have been made by the mayor (accompanied no doubt - as in Bristol - by other greetings in verse), before the procession moved on to the queen's lodgings.

On the following day (Sunday), we know that Elizabeth attended a service in the Abbey Church, curious no doubt to inspect for herself the condition of the building for which she had already launched a restoration appeal (see above). The newly-constituted 'parish church', which the queen herself had authorised in 1572, was simply housed in the chancel (the rest of the structure being in a state of disrepair). All we know of the service itself is that the corporation had paid for fresh rushes to be strewn over the floor and for choristers to be brought from Wells to sing for the queen on what was, in effect, the church's formal opening. Furthermore, it had chosen a distinguished preacher for this momentous occasion - Mr Huntingdon, who had gained a fine reputation in 1559 after preaching before large crowds at St Paul's Cross in London. The chamberlain subsequently paid Perkin twelve pence 'for going to Bristol' to escort him; and Mr Huntingdon a fee of 6s 8d 'for preaching the first sermon in the new church' - plus a

A Royal Procession

This contemporary account of an event in 1598 gives a good idea of what Queen Elizabeth I's procession in Bath would have been like on her arrival at the North Gate in 1574.

First went Gentlemen, Barons, Earls, Knights of the Garter, all richly dressed and bare-headed; next came the Chancellor, bearing the Seals in a red silk purse - between two, one of which carried the Royal Sceptre, the other the Sword of State in a red scabbard studded with golden fleurs-de-lis, the point upwards. Next came the Queen, in the sixty-fifth year of her age, as we were told, very majestic; her face oblong, fair but wrinkled; her eyes small, yet black and pleasant; her nose a little hooked; her lips narrow, and her teeth black (a defect the English seem subject to, from their too great use of sugar); she had in her ears two pearls, with very rich drops; she wore false hair, and that red.

Upon her head she had a small crown, reported to be made of some of the gold of the celebrated Luneburg table. Her bosom was uncovered, as all the English ladies have it till they marry; and she had on a necklace of exceeding fine jewels; her hands were small, her fingers long, and her stature neither tall nor low; her air was stately, her manner of speaking mild and obliging. That day she was dressed in white silk, bordered with pearls the size of beans, and over it a mantle of black silk, shot with silver threads; her train was very long, and the end of it borne by a Marchioness; instead of a chain she had an oblong collar of gold and jewels.

As she went along in all this state and magnificence, she spoke very graciously, first to one, then to another, whether foreign ministers, or those who attended for different reasons, in English, French and Italian; for besides being well skilled in Greek, Latin and the languages I have mentioned, she is mistress of Spanish, Scotch and Dutch. Whoever speaks to her, it is kneeling; now and then she raises some with her hand. While we were there, a Bohemian baron had letters to present to her; and she, after pulling off her glove, gave him her right hand to kiss, sparkling with rings and jewels, a mark of particular favour. Wherever she turned her face, as she was going along, everybody fell down on their knees.

The Ladies of the Court followed next to her, very handsome and well-shaped, and for the most part dressed in white; she was guarded on each side by the Gentlemen Pensioners, fifty in number, with gilt battle-axes. In the antechapel next the hall where we were, petitions were presented to her, and she received them most graciously, which occasioned the acclamation of *Long live Queen Elizabeth!* She answered it with, *I thank you, my good people.*

From Paul Hentzner: *A Journey into England in the year 1598* (ed. Horace Walpole in *Aungervyle Society Reprints*, 1881)

further sixpence for horsemeat!

At some time during her stay in Bath, Elizabeth found an opportunity to hold a meeting of her privy council - an indication that she was accompanied by most of the key members of her court. She left the city on Monday 23rd August and returned to London via Lacock, Longleat, Wilton, Salisbury, Amesbury, Winchester, Farnham and Bagshot. She arrived back at Hampton Court on 25th September. Meanwhile, the citizens of Bath were no doubt rejoicing that the queen had witnessed at first hand the plight of their Abbey Church, that her courtiers had been both intrigued and impressed by the hot water baths and that the visit had not been too costly to stage.

There is some indication that a special tax had in fact been raised to pay for the improvements and repairs associated with her visit. Although, sadly, the chamberlain's accounts for the mayoral year 1573-74 have not survived (the year in which the tax would probably have been charged), there is one solitary reference in the following year (1574-75) to what might well have been a back payment: *William Acton, for tax money against the queen's coming, 3s 0d*. Nevertheless, in terms of national publicity, this had been a major success for the city's public relations. Its future economy had been given an enormous boost just at the moment when the corporation was commencing the development of the health resort. It is no coincidence, therefore, that courtiers now begin to flock to the spa to seek health benefits from its waters. Bath had suddenly become fashionable (see Chapter 6).

The city's recently-formed trained bands would undoubtedly have provided a ceremonial guard for the queen during her visit in 1574. Here a company of musketeers is on the march - but also see the company of pikemen on page 109. A contemporary woodcut by permission of the British Library (Roxburghe Ballads, RAX.Rox.III, 63).

An impression by Shane Feeney of the arrival of Queen Elizabeth outside the North Gate of the city in 1574. In the background are St Michael's Church Without and some of the houses in Broad Street. She is accompanied by members of her privy council and other courtiers. The detail shown here of the procession itself is based on an original oil painting (c.1580) of the queen's visit to Berwick upon Tweed.

A New Row of Houses, 1570

Faced with a steady rise in the city's resident population by the 1560s and a predicted increase in the number of visitors to the developing health resort, Bath Corporation decided to expand the amount of accommodation available. Between August 1569 and the early summer of 1570, therefore, teams of craftsmen worked furiously to complete a group of 'new houses' within the walled area. Although the chamberlain did not reveal in his accounts either the number of houses being built or **their location** (in spite of the large amount of other detail provided), there has been some speculation that the houses might well have been those which were built about this time against the north wall of the Abbey.

There are one or two clues in the accounts which might lend support to this theory. For instance, the old Guildhall (standing in the lane leading down to the East Gate) was used as a storage base for a large number of sacks of lime; while the former Bishop's Palace was used extensively as a quarry for building stone. Both sites were extremely convenient, of course, for any building work taking place outside the Abbey. This, however, is an unlikely theory - especially in view of the fact that the queen's licence in 1572 for the land in question to be transferred from Edmund Colthurst to the corporation was not granted until after the houses had been built (see below). There is, however, another vital clue to their actual location in the chamberlain's accounts of 1569. Robert Stevens paid a 'fine' or fee of ten pounds on signing his lease for 'one of the new houses' - and, as Elizabeth Holland has discovered, his property holding was concentrated on the west side of the High Street and the south side of Cheap Street. The latter area is considered by far the most likely situation for the new buildings - and it was extremely close to both the 'storage base' and the 'quarry' (as mentioned above).

The methods used in this building operation were in many respects very similar to those financed earlier by the churchwardens of St Michael's parish (see Chapter 3). There were, however, some important differences - including, as the houses rose from their foundations, the **use of scaffolding** (hence the frequent purchase of hurdles, nails and cord 'for the scaffolds'). The corporation also had its own source of raw materials, preferring to obtain these wherever possible from its own lands in the vicinity. Timber was cut and prepared chiefly in Hinton and Newton, where saw pits were specially dug for that purpose - although preparation work also took place in Bathwick, Walcot and Saw Close (an area set aside for the use of carpenters near the West Gate). A plentiful supply of 'stone' roof tiles reached the site from quarries in Farleigh. On the other hand, straw for thatching was noticeably absent from the shopping list.

Furthermore, there are clear indications that the houses were **mainly built of stone** (rather than timber), judging by the large amounts purchased. In all, the builders received 134 loads of stone from 'the quarry' - plus the spoil taken from nine raids on the former Bishop's Palace, one of which produced no fewer than twenty loads of stone. The chamberlain always kept the quarriers well supplied with 'meat and drink' to sustain them throughout their gruelling work. [By 1575, the corporation was actually paying five shillings a year in 'rent' for a quarry, which the town clerk, Mr Britten, was entrusted to deliver to the queen's receivers. Although its location is unclear, it is possible that this is the same quarry on the common land, which was used in the seventeenth century.]

The accounts also reveal that the chamberlain paid for a total of 1305 man/days of work by free masons (whose task was to work the best freestone into building blocks) and 'rough masons or layers' (whose duty was to work with the refuse of the freestone in constructing common stone walls etc); plus a further 1379 man/days by labourers, who not only undertook ground clearance and carrying work, but also mixed the mortar (no fewer than 531 sacks of lime arrived together with fifteen cartloads of sand). By contrast, the wage bill only accounted for 156 man/days of carpenters' time. It seems likely, therefore, that these particular craftsmen concentrated on the frames for the roofs and the inner partitions, rather than on timber for the outer walls. Nor is there any reference to 'wattle and daub', which would have indicated timber framing of the upper storeys.

The 'new houses' were altogether more modern in appearance - built in stone rather than wood, tiled rather than thatched, equipped with chimneys rather than smoke holes, fitted with lead gutters and paved thresholds - and, at least in some instances, supplied with fresh spring water via the city's network of pipes. Certainly a plumber was paid the princely sum of twenty shillings for 'making of the pipes', plus eighteen shillings for 'solder', five shillings for 'a load of hardwood' and fourteen pence for 'nails for the cisterns and pipes'. This was luxury indeed.

*****

Sadly - unlike in many cities - an exploration of modern Bath reveals little of the distinctive medieval and sixteenth-century houses which lined the streets in Tudor times. However, as Peter Davenport has shown, some fragments have survived. An excavation of the basement of Sally Lunn's teashop in 1984 uncovered the partial remains of a medieval stone wall. This would probably have supported the timber framework of one of the Priory's outbuildings. Similarly the stone cellar, which lies beneath Abbey Church House, is the undercroft of a substantial medieval building (possibly with a timber superstructure). This was rebuilt in about 1590 by Dr Robert Baker and is shown as Mrs Savil's lodgings in a drawing on Joseph Gilmore's map of the city in 1694. It will be seen from this that the modern building still contains a great deal of the original Elizabethan structure. Although it was bombed during the Second World War, much of the Great Hall on the first floor has survived, including the fine Elizabethan fireplace and wooden panelling (see opposite page) .

The only visible section of timber framing in Bath has been uncovered on the side wall of number 3 Broad Street. Inside the shop is an Elizabethan staircase on the first floor and decorated ceiling beams. A little further up the street (actually inside number 7) can be seen the outer wall, window, front door and front room of a small stone cottage. It is thought that this was built in 1593, but was altered later in the seventeenth century. (See also the illustrations of buildings in Broad Street in Chapter 3.)

Abbey Church House

Abbey Church House (above), which was rebuilt in c.1590 by Dr Robert Baker. After Queen Elizabeth's visit to Bath in 1574, the hot water baths were given nationwide publicity as members of the court flocked to the city for their cures. Houses situated close to the baths, therefore, were suddenly in great demand by physicians anxious to accommodate their patients as near as possible to the healing waters. (Author's collection).

The house was described on Joseph Gilmore's map of 1694 as 'Mrs Savil's Lodgings near the Hot Bath' (below). It was partly rebuilt after extensive bomb damage during World War 2.

The Great Chamber on the first floor still contains some of the original Elizabethan panelling as well as this impressive original fireplace (left). The overmantle carries the arms of Dr Sherwood's wife, a member of the Clarke family of Wookey. (Author's collection)

Staying at an Inn

The courtiers, who accompanied the Queen on her visit to Bath in 1574, would have stayed at some of the many inns available in the city.

The world affords not such inns as England hath, either for good and cheap entertainment after the guest's own pleasure, or for humble attendance on passengers; yea, even in very poor villages. . . . For as soon as a passenger comes to an inn, the servants run to him, and one takes his horse, and walks him till he be cold, then rubs him and gives him meat - yet I must say that they are not much to be trusted in this last point, without the eye of the master or his servant to oversee them. Another servant gives the passenger his private chamber, and kindles his fire ; the third pulls off his boots, and makes them clean.

Then the host or hostess visits him; and, if he will eat with the host or at a common table with others, his meal will cost him six pence, or in some places but four pence; but if he will eat in his chamber, he commands what meat he will, according to his appetite, and as much as he thinks fit for him and his company. Yea, the kitchen is open to him to command the meat to be dressed as he best likes.

And when he sits at table, the host or hostess will accompany him - or, if they have many guests, will at least visit him. While he eats, if he have company especially, he shall be offered music, which he may freely take or refuse; and if he be solitary, the musicians will give him the good day with music in the morning. It is the custom, and no way disgraceful, to set up part of supper for his breakfast.

Source: Fynes Moryson, *An Itinerary Containing his Ten Years of Travel, 1617*, 4 vols, 1907-8 edtn.)

Those towns have great and sumptuous inns builded in them, for the receiving of such travellers and strangers as pass to and fro... Our inns are also very well furnished with napery *[household linen]*, bedding, and tapestry, especially with napery: for beside the linen used at the tables, which is commonly washed daily, is such and so much as belongeth unto the estate and calling of the guest.

Each comer is sure to lie in clean sheets, wherein no man hath been lodged since they came from the laundress, or out of the water wherein they were last washed... Whether he be horseman or footman, if his chamber be once appointed, he may carry the key with him, as of his own house so long as lodgeth there. If he lose ought whilst he abideth in the inn, the host is bound by a general custom to restore the damage, so that there is no greater security anywhere for travellers than in the greatest inns of England.

Source: Paul Hentzer: *A Journey into England in the Year 1598*, edited by Horace Walpole in the Aungervyle Society Reprints, 1881

SOURCES USED IN CHAPTER 4

1. Printed Material

Bartelot, Grosvenor: 'New Light on Bath Abbey and the Priory Estates' (in *Proceedings of the Somerset Archeological and Natural History Society, Bath Branch*, 1941)

Cunliffe, Barry: *The City of Bath* (1986)

Davenport, Peter: *Medieval Bath Uncovered* (2002)

Green, Emanuel: 'Did Queen Elizabeth visit Bath in the Years 1574 and 1592?' (in *Proceedings of the Natural History & Antiquarian Field Club*, vol.4, 1881) with reference to The Chamber Treasurer's Accounts and the Queen's Wardrobe Accounts for 1574-75.

Harris, Richard: *Discovering Timber-framed Buildings* (1993, 3rd edtn.)

Harris, Richard: *Weald & Downland Museum: Guidebook*

Hentzner, Paul: *A Journey into England in the year 1598* (ed.Horace Walpole in *Aungervyle Society Reprints*, 1881)

Holland, Elizabeth: 'The Earliest Guildhall' (in *Bath History*, vol. 2, 1988)

Hylson-Smith, Kenneth: *Bath Abbey: a History* (2003)

*James, P.R. (ed.): *The Charters of the City of Bath*, vol. 2 (1942)

*King, A.J: 'The Destruction of the two Churches of St Mary in Bath' (in *Proceedings of the Bath Natural History and Antiquarian Field Club*, vol. 6 (1889)

*King, A.J. & Watts, B.H: *Municipal Records of Bath, 1189-1604* (1885)

Manco, Jean: *Guidelines,* no. 44 (1992)

Manco, Jean: 'Bath's Lost Era' (in *Bath City Life,* Summer 1992*)

Manco, Jean: *The Spirit of Care: The 800-Year Story of St John's Hospital, Bath* (1998)

McNeil, Cameron: *The Story of a Bath Parish: St Michael's Church outside the North Gate* (1936)

Page, William (ed.): *The Victoria County History of Somerset*, vol. 2 (1911)

Picard, Lisa: *Elizabethan London* (2003)

Pritchard, R.E: *Shakespeare's England: Life in Elizabethan & Jacobean Times* (1999)

Rye, W.B: *England as Seen by Foreigners* (1865)

Shickle, C.W. (ed.): *The Register of the Parish of Widcombe, 1574-1812* (transcripts, c.1910)

*Symons, Katharine: *The Grammar School of King Edward VI, Bath and its Ancient Foundation* (1934)

Wardle, F.D. (ed.): 'Bath Chamberlain's Accounts' (in Somerset Record Society, vol. 38, 1923)

Warner, Richard: *The History of Bath* (1801)

Wroughton, John: *Stuart Bath: Life in the Forgotten City, 1603-1714* (2004)

2. Documentary Material:

Bath Central Library:	*Rents of Assize of St Mary's within the Gate (Mss file of the Bath Literary Club - various papers)
Bath Record Office:	*Chamberlain's Accounts, 1568-1603
	Council Minute Book, 1656, 1569
	*Lease of Rectory of Bath Abbey, 1590
	*Petition to Dr Aubrey to consolidate the churches, 1583 (Acc.59/2/12/1)
British Library:	Calendar of Patent Rolls, 10, 12, 15 & 18 Elizabeth I
	Calendar of State Papers Domestic, 1547, 1576
Somerset Record Office:	Visitation Books - Act Books
St John's Hospital Archive:	*Shickle, C.W; *Introduction to the History of St John's Hospital,* vol. 1 (typed mss, including various transcripts of documents)

* The items marked with an asterisk are particularly valuable in researching the rebuilding of the former Priory Church and the amalgamation of the Bath churches into a single rectory.

The author is also indebted to Jean Manco for her unpublished chronology of the development of Bath Abbey in the sixteenth and seventeenth centuries; Peter Davenport for providing access to the English Heritage Listings Report on number 7 Broad Street; Rodney Morant for supplying a new translation from the Latin of the Amalgamation Order of 1583; and Frank Thorn for offering meaning to the Latin terms used in the queen's treasurer's accounts.

A VIEW OF BATH, c1540

Or ever I came to the bridge of Bath that is over the Avon, I came down [from Beechen Cliff] by a rocky hill full of fair springs of water: and on this rocky hill is set a long street as a suburb to the city of Bath; and [in] this street is a chapel of St Mary Magdalen.

There is a great gate with a stone arch at the entry of the bridge. The bridge has five fair stone arches. Betwixt the bridge and the south gate of Bath I marked fair meadows on each hand [i.e. Ambury Meadow and Ham Meadow], but especially on the left hand, and they lie by south-west of the town.

The city of Bath is set both in a fruitful and pleasant bottom, the which is environed on every side with great hills; out of which come many springs of pure water that be conveyed by divers ways to serve the city. Insomuch that lead, being made near at hand [i.e. on the Mendips], many houses in the town have pipes of lead to convey water from place to place.

There be four gates in the town by the names of east, west, north and south. The town wall within the town is of no great height to the eyes; but without, it is *à fundamentis* [i.e. from the foundations] of a reasonable height; and it standeth almost all, lacking but a piece about Gascoyn's Tower. In the walls, at this time, be no towers saving over the town gates. One Gascoyn, an inhabitant of the town *in hominum memoria* [i.e. in living memory], made a little piece of the wall that was in decay, as a fine for a fight that he had committed in the city: whereof one part, as at a corner, riseth higher than the residue of the wall - whereby it is commonly called Gascoyne's Tower...

There be two springs of hot water in the south west part of the town. Whereof the bigger is called the Cross Bath, because it hath a cross erected in the middle of it. This bath is much frequented of people diseased with leprosy, pox, scabs and great aches; and is temperate and pleasant, having 11 or 12 arches of stone in the side for men to stand under in time of rain. Many be helped by this bath from scabs and aches.

The other bath... is less in compass within the wall than the other, having but 7 arches in the wall. This is called the Hot Bath; for coming into it men think that it would scold the flesh at the first, but after that the flesh is warmed it is more tolerant and pleasant...

The King's Bath is very fair and large standing almost in the middle of the town and at the west end of the cathedral church. The area that this bath is in is compassed with a high stone wall. The brims of this bath have a little wall encompassing them; and in this wall be 32 arches for men and women to stand separately in. To this bath do gentlemen resort...The colour of the water of the baths is, as it were, a deep blue sea water, and reeketh like a seething pot continually, having a somewhat sulphureous and somewhat unpleasant savour.

Source: Lucy T Smith (ed.): *The Itinerary of John Leland, 1535-1543* (1907 edtn.)

CHAPTER 5

1588: Threat to Security

Security against Spanish Invasion

(i) The Tradition of National Defence

Throughout the Tudor period, governments of the day - with no standing army or regular police force on which to call - relied heavily on the ability of each county to turn out a large body of ordinary people to offset foreign attack. Whereas normal breaches of the peace, including riots and other serious disturbances, could be contained by the sheriff's officers, local constables and justices of the peace, the tradition of national defence - from the days of the Anglo-Saxon fyrd - had always been based on the principle that it was the duty of every man to serve in the hour of need. By the fifteenth century, the monarch had assumed the right to issue a 'commission of array' for the urgent assembly of all able men within a county for military purposes. By the sixteenth century, the task of putting such a commission into effect had been placed in the hands of the county's lord lieutenant.

Under Tudor monarchs, this ancient idea was expanded further through an insistence that men should be properly trained for this duty *before* the country found itself under threat of attack. In Mary's reign, for instance, parliament actually specified the quantity of weapons and equipment which members of the upper classes - according to their wealth - were to maintain in readiness. Then in 1573, Elizabeth I established the notion of '**the trained bands**', when parliament decreed that each county should organise a select group of able-bodied volunteers, between the ages of 16 and 60, into regularly trained units. It was the task of the deputy lieutenants in each county to oversee a programme of training, aimed at transforming groups of farm workers, shopkeepers and craftsmen into soldiers, who were both disciplined and experienced in the use of weapons. Training was therefore organised for such groups on a local basis, usually after church on Sundays, whereas general musters of all the county's bands were called once or twice a year (see below). The cost of both equipment and training fell on the local community through a parish rate.

Quite apart from service in the trained bands (which in peacetime, at least, was a somewhat pleasurable social activity), local people could also find themselves pressed into service for one of the monarch's overseas campaigns. It was the task of the constable of each hundred [i.e. a local administrative unit within the county] to specify to each of its parishes how many men it was forced to provide. A local tax, called 'coat and conduct money', was then collected to cover the cost of supplying each pressed man with a good coat, plus eight pence a day - sufficient to provide him with an escort to the port or place of rendezvous and food for the journey. **Pressed men** were also given twelve pence in 'press money' as an incentive at the time of recruitment. Throughout the Tudor period, there were in fact many expeditions of this nature - some to suppress the rebels in Ireland or the Scilly Isles; and others to offset the threat of

Spanish attacks from the Low Countries or Brittany. On each occasion, a force of a few hundred pressed men was sent from Somerset, including a small quota from the city of Bath.

In 1596-97, for instance, when a man named Jesper was pressed into service in Ireland as a musketeer, the corporation's chamberlain (or treasurer) paid for 'a satchel to carry his powder and shots in' and 'a bandolier of brass' [a wide belt worn across the chest from which hung twelve containers, each carrying a charge of powder]. Furthermore, he not only paid Jesper twelve pence in press money and the cost of carrying his armour to Wells (the point of rendezvous), but also supplied an additional twelve pence to provide him with an escort as far as Keynsham, where he was officially enrolled by a justice of the peace. Escorts were required to ensure that the pressed man did not run away - a circumstance which would have rebounded heavily on the corporation.

Similarly, in 1601-02, two local men - John Morgan and Robert Everett - were also pressed into service on an expedition to Ireland. Quite apart from the press money issued, this venture was extremely costly to Bath Corporation in other respects. To cover the expense of uniform, equipment and weapons, its treasurer paid out £3 6s 4d to the city constable, who had made all the practical arrangements when these soldiers 'went into Ireland for the city'; and an additional £1 15s 0d to the justices at Wells, where the rendezvous again took place. Furthermore, he hired horses 'to bring our soldiers and our money to Wells'. Once enlisted, the pressed soldier would in theory be allowed eight pence a day (or 4s 8d per week), a substantial proportion of which would be taken by the victual master to cover the cost of lodging and food (usually carried in bulk on horseback). On the march, the soldier's diet consisted of biscuit, boiled beef and cheese.

Nevertheless, no matter how inconvenient it was to select, finance and dispatch small numbers of conscripts on expeditions, this paled into insignificance alongside the major disruption caused by preparations to offset **the threat of a Spanish invasion** - a threat which had been a growing reality since 1547. To highlight the danger, Elizabeth I - on her accession in November 1558 - ordered a complete muster of all able-bodied men in each county. No fewer than 4,326 responded in Somerset alone - a figure which had increased to 5,330 one year later and to 12,000 in 1580. By 1586, the county was on a high state of alert. The Somerset coastline was heavily protected with a line of watch towers supported by cannon; heavy artillery guarded its ports; coastal lookouts were organised around the clock with beacons poised to signal an early warning of imminent attack; and posthorses or footposts were put on standby in every town or village to relay messages.

In short, the whole country took on the appearance of a military camp. Indeed, such was the state of nervous anxiety, that a false alarm was sounded in 1586 as a result of an incident near Bath. The privy council in London quickly voiced its concern that following 'a casual fire happening about the city of Bath', the men who had been in charge of the beacons in the area had wrongly assumed that an official beacon had been fired. A few other beacons had therefore been lit in response - with the result that the whole county's forces had been on the point of being called out before the mistake was realised. The council therefore urged those who guarded the beacons to take careful note of the actual location of all beacons along the coast, so that in future they would not be confused by 'any casual fire'.

By 1587, musters of the trained bands were being called with great frequency in

Somerset. Captains were appointed to inspect the efficiency of local preparations against attack under the supervision of the deputy lieutenants. In a report to the privy council, the inspecting officer (Captain Thomas Howard) declared that he had found the county 'beyond my expectation and unto my great comfort so excellently furnished with all sorts of armour and weapons, and that in such perfect readiness, the men so well sorted and chosen... that I assure your lordships it doth exceed any county that ever I came in'. A year later, he reported that he found the trained bands 'brave and well furnished' and that 'it is a most gallant county for men, armour and readiness'.

In the summer of 1587, that state of readiness was almost put to the test, when 3350 men from the Somerset bands were put on a heightened state of alert to move at one hour's notice - especially if Plymouth and Falmouth were attacked. Although this tension inevitably subsided after the defeat of the Spanish Armada in 1588, defensive measures were nevertheless kept in place for the remainder of the Tudor period. There was, after all, the worrying danger that Spain might still attack England through its back door in Ireland.

(ii) Equipping the Local Bands

Until the 1590s, the trained band infantry consisted of archers, billmen, arquebusiers and pikemen. **The bill**, which originated as a farmer's scythe, consisted of a broad, hooked blade with two protruding pikes set into a short staff. It was most effective when used to unhorse cavalry by cutting through the bridle. **The heavy arquebus**, which was an ancient type of matchlock musket with a three-foot long barrel and a short stock, required the use of a forked-shape rest (or 'lintock') to support its weight when firing a two-ounce bullet. With an effective range of no more than fifty yards, it was a notoriously inaccurate weapon (as was its heavier version - the caliver). **The pike**, which made its appearance during the reign of Edward VI, consisted of a twelve-inch flat steel spike set on a heavy wooden shaft (usually made of ash) some sixteen feet long. Although requiring a strong man to wield it on the field of battle, it soon became a formidable device for piercing armour in the cut-and-thrust of hand-to-hand fighting.

The long bow, however, remained by far the most popular weapon. Made preferably of birch, oak or ash, it boasted three hempen strings and had an effective range of 240 yards when using the heavier arrows. An archer, who normally carried sixteen of these together with eight of the lighter arrows, traditionally wore a 'sallett' or steel cap and a 'war brace' to protect his wrist when firing. For body armour, he usually wore a 'jack' made of leather or canvas over stout quilting. With the introduction of firearms, the jack was often strengthened by the addition of squares of iron plate sewn into the quilting. A trained archer could shoot twelve arrows in a minute - or five in the time it took a musketeer to fire one bullet.

The pikeman wore an oval-shaped helmet (known as a morion), which was ridged along the top with a wide brim around its base. He was also equipped with two further pieces of metal armour - a 'corslet' (consisting of linked back and breast plates) and a 'gorget' to protect the neck and shoulders. In the sixteenth century, pikemen were in fact often nicknamed 'corslets' after their armour. Helmets, of course, needed an inner lining to act as a shock absorber, when subjected to heavy blows from a sword or the butt of a musket. In Bath, therefore, the corporation's armourer frequently invested in such items as 'one pound of wool to stuff the morions' or 'new caps to put in headpieces'. The two other weapons, which were evident on the field of battle, were

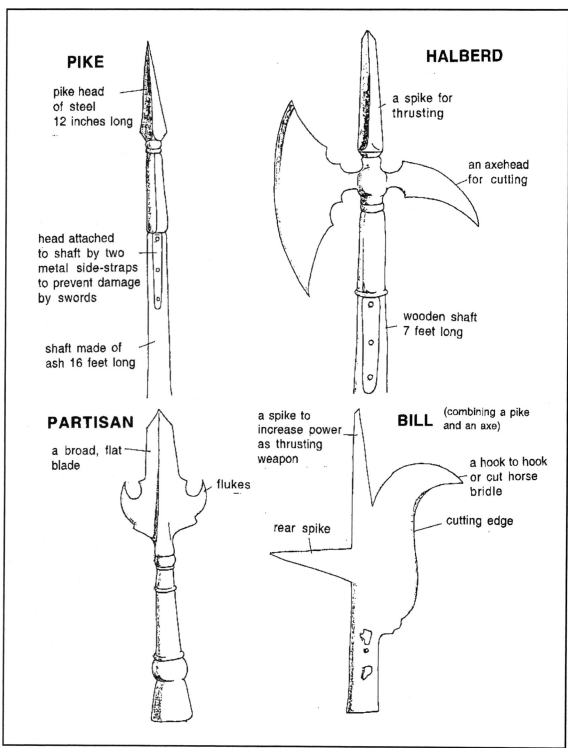

PIKE

pike head
of steel
12 inches long

head attached
to shaft by two
metal side-straps
to prevent damage
by swords

shaft made of
ash 16 feet long

HALBERD

a spike for
thrusting

an axehead
for cutting

wooden shaft
7 feet long

PARTISAN

a broad, flat
blade

flukes

a spike to
increase power
as thrusting
weapon

BILL (combining a pike
and an axe)

a hook to hook
or cut horse
bridle

cutting edge

rear spike

Some of the weapons used by the local trained bands at the time of the Spanish Armada in 1588. Line drawings by Elizabeth Fitzpatrick.

used increasingly as badges of rank. **The halberd** (for sergeants), which was useful in both cutting and thrusting, consisted of a spike on top with an axehead below mounted on a shaft some seven feet long. By contrast, **the partisan** (for officers) had a broad flat blade with upturned flukes on either side (see drawing on page 104). Most soldiers carried, in addition to their chief weapon, a sword and a dagger.

The mid-1590s, however, witnessed a transition in the type of weapons being used. Whereas Bath's own armourer was still repairing bows, purchasing 'shooting gloves', mending 'arrow cases' and replacing bow strings in 1589, such items had been made totally redundant by 1595. The bill, too, had completely disappeared. During the latter years of the Tudor period, therefore, the local trained bands relied increasingly on the pike and the new type of **matchlock musket**, which was much more powerful - although a few old calivers were still in use as late as 1601. The armourer's shopping list now featured such items as '18 pounds of lead to make bullets for the soldiers'; 'three bullet bags'; 'a leather flask' [to hold the powder]; 'three-and-half yards of fringe to arm the pikes'; 'two musket scourers' [to clean out the barrels]; 'a musket rest'; and 'a pair of moulds' [for casting the lead bullets]. The latest technology had arrived!

From the time of King Alfred, there had been a traditional expectation in England that every man should possess his own weapon for use in battle if danger threatened. This notion was made even more specific in the reign of Edward IV, when it was decreed that each man would in future be required not only to keep a bow 'of his own height', but also to use it in practice on every Sunday and holiday. During the early years of Elizabeth I's reign - faced as she was by the ongoing threat of a Spanish invasion - the government issued detailed instructions to all its more affluent citizens requiring them (according to their actual wealth) to keep a specific number of horses, weapons and pieces of armour in readiness.

Even the poorer sort (who were excluded from the above regulation) were encouraged to join together for 'love of their country' to provide either a pike, a bow or an arquebus. Further instructions threatened heavy fines on any father, who permitted his son under the age of seventeen 'to lack a bow and two arrows for the space of a month'; any man between the ages of seventeen and fifty-nine who, being

A contemporary woodcut, which depicts two archers - one with a long bow and a quiver of arrows (right) - and a sergeant carrying a halberd (centre). By permission of the British Library (Roxburghe Ballads, RAX.Rox.III, 11).

able to shoot, should 'lack a bow and four arrows' for a month; and any bow-maker, who tried to profiteer when selling bows to children under fourteen or youths under twenty-one. Acceptable prices were in fact listed. Although there is little evidence to suggest that these regulations were strictly enforced, they did nevertheless re-establish the principle of the personal ownership of weapons in readiness for war.

This principle was clearly at work in Bath. Although, as we shall see below, Bath Corporation kept a stock of its own weapons in **the Guildhall armoury** for general use, many citizens had already purchased their own. These were then named and stored in the armoury, but repaired when necessary at the expense of the corporation. In 1600-01, for instance, William Doulton (the armourer) invested in 'a new scabbard for Rendel Bennett's dagger'; 'a new pommel for William Morford's sword'; 'a new scabbard and chape [the metal cap of the scabbard point] for the sword of Roger Lovell'; and a new fitting 'for George Kingston's caliver'. Furthermore, the corporation was always happy to sell individuals items from its own stock. In 1572-73, for example, it raised £1 7s 11d through the sale of one halberd, one bow and one black bill - together with a number of bowstrings and a quantity of gunpowder. It would also appear that the Bath armoury was also used as magazine for other local companies of trained bands. In 1587-88, for example, the hundred of Bathforum purchased a supply of powder for 8s 9d.

In view of the fact that the chamberlain's accounts do not exist before the year 1569, it is not possible to know how large an armoury Bath Corporation maintained during the first half of the Tudor period. What is abundantly clear, however, is that any possible lethargy on the part of the corporation was quickly swept away during the early years of Elizabeth I's reign. Two measures in particular were sufficient to jolt them out of complacency as the new monarch made clear the very real threat posed by Spain - first, the appointment of commissioners in 1565 to make a survey of what weapons were held in store and the numbers of men under training for possible service; and second, the receipt by the mayor and aldermen in June 1573 of specific instructions to 'array, inspect and arm' both infantry and cavalry. Enclosed were instructions 'very meet and necessary for the mustering and training of soldiers in cities'. Furthermore, other orders were issued, which insisted that a suitable place was to be established in each locality where weapons could be 'safely kept, stored and preserved' with specific individuals appointed to maintain the store and keep the armour clean.

Bath's response was immediate. In the very same year (1573), William Moore was appointed 'to keep the armour clean' (the forerunner of Richard Gray and William Doulton, who became successive armourers later in the century at a salary of twenty shillings); new stock was ordered from suppliers outside the city (4 dozen bills; 6 bows; 6 sheafs of arrows; 6 halberd heads; 4 dozen bill heads; 4 dozen bill staves; and 'two skins of vellum for the drum', which had been purchased in 1569); and the city's defences were thoroughly checked. The West Gate was extensively repaired, using large quantities of stone, timber, sand and 'iron work'; and the gate at the end of the bridge was made to fasten properly. Thereafter the walls and gates were maintained in a good state of repair for the remainder of the century. In 1598-99, for instance, a mason was employed 'for hewing of stone and setting up five top stones which were lacking upon the borough walls; while other workers attended to faults on Gascoin's Tower, the strong point of the defences in the north-western corner of the city.

The armoury itself, which was based in a room on the first floor of the Guildhall, was steadily improved over the years to take in more and more equipment. In 1580-81,

The armoury (right), which was accommodated on the first floor of the Guildhall, had purpose-made racks for storing the pikes and muskets. Helmets and other items of armour were hung from the walls.
Line drawing by Stephen Beck.

for instance three large mats were purchased 'to hang the armour on' - presumably as a form of damp-proofing to prevent corrosion. In fact, the armourer, regularly invested in 'sallett oil' to smear on the corslets and helmets as a protection against rust. Then, in 1601-02, a special new room was constructed to contain the armour (possibly as an extension to the Guildhall) - the chamberlain paying for the timber frame, tiles for the roof and plaster for the walls of 'the house over the armour'.

Although some items were bought in from outside (such as the eight new pikes purchased in 1600-01), the corporation tried wherever possible to use local craftsmen. In 1568-69, for instance, John Dallamy, the carpenter, was employed to make the stock of a musket; John Broad, the leather worker, to produce the leathers for three powder flasks and the cords, which were used to tighten the skin on the town drum; John Stowell, the metal worker, for 'mending a headpiece'; Benedict Gray, the carpenter, for 'mending two touchboxes' [the flasks which contained fine powder for priming the matchlock muskets]; and Fletcher, the bowyer, for mending two bows and supplying six bow strings. Furthermore, Richard Gray, the locksmith (who lived just outside the city in Walcot) was often paid for specific repairs to weapons and armour over and above his salary 'for keeping the armour clean'. In 1583-84, for example, he was rewarded for 'mending the calivers which were broken'.

One other improvement to the equipment of the trained bands came right at the end of the century with the arrival in 1597 of **a distinctive uniform**. This consisted of a blue cloth coat, trimmed with silk and lace, over a doublet and hose. Consequently, in 1600-01, Richard Story (the tailor) was paid for 'making nine coats', 'new lacing nine soldiers' coats', repairing sixteen coats and 'making John Hancock's doublet and hose'. In the same year, '21 yards of blue broadcloth for solders' coats were purchased along with 'two pieces of silk seam for coats'.

(iii) Selecting the Local Bands

As a result of the new legislation at the start of Elizabeth I's reign, commissioners were quickly appointed to make **a survey of the human resources** in each county and, at the same time, to gain a clear idea of the quantity of armour and weapons available for immediate use. With the help of the constables of each hundred, the names of all male householders, apprentices, journeymen, servants and labourers between the ages of

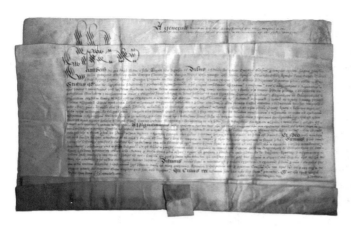

The 'commission of muster' of 1573, which ordered Bath corporation to list, muster, arm and train all able men in the city. (By courtesy of the Bath Record Office, Bath & North-East Somerset Council)

sixteen and sixty were listed. These were then mustered before the commissioners and divided roughly into the 'able' (i.e. those who were in theory capable of serving in war) and the 'unable'. A note was also taken of those who would be suitable to serve as labourers or pioneers to construct fortifications; metal smiths to repair equipment on the field of battle; or carpenters - so that 'their abilities may be used as cause shall require'. These non-combatants would not of course be issued with weapons or armour.

Surveys of this kind were taken periodically in the years leading up to the Spanish Armada. The commission of muster, issued to the mayor and aldermen of Bath in 1573, still survives in Bath Record Office (see illustration above). This not only ordered the corporation to muster and list 'all men-at-arms and men capable of bearing arms', but to assign weapons to them and 'teach, instruct and exercise in the art of war all recruits, unwarlike men and those ignorant of military matters'. Furthermore, future musters were to take place 'from time to time' at their own discretion.

The information assembled in 1573 quickly highlighted a major problem facing the commissioners. The figures for Somerset revealed that no fewer than 6,770 had been deemed to be 'able', thus presenting the local authorities with the almost impossible task of equipping and training such an enormous number of men from scratch. Common sense quickly prevailed. By later that year, it had been agreed that it was much more sensible for the commissioners to concentrate on 'a convenient number' of **the most suitable men for training**.

They therefore began the process of weeding out all marginal cases 'without partiality, malice, injury or distemperence' according to physique, strength, character and age (those between eighteen and forty-six were preferred). Once chosen, each man was firmly enlisted into the trained bands, swearing to serve his captain for at least six months. Although the recruit was still in one sense a part-time volunteer, he was now just as much under military discipline as the conscript. Indeed, failure to attend a muster could result in a fine of forty shillings or ten days in prison.

Those enlisted were by no means drawn exclusively from the lower classes - indeed, many companies were made up of businessmen, skilled craftsmen, yeomen farmers and members of the professions. After all, membership carried with it a certain degree of local prestige - not to mention exemption from the dreaded risk of being conscripted for an overseas expedition. It is interesting to note that the muster list for Bath in 1569 was headed by George Pearman (archer), who not only became mayor of the city in 1581, but also paid one of the largest amounts of tax in the government subsidy of that year - a clear sign that he was a man of substance and distinction.

The result of this double selection process was illustrated in 1580, when - out of nearly 7,000 'able' men in Somerset - only 4,000 were actually selected for training. The remainder were held as an untrained reserve. Locally, in **the company drawn for the city of Bath** and the hundred of Bathforum, only 120 men were provisionally selected out of an initial list of 360. The final figure was actually made up of 24 'corslets' (or pikemen) furnished with armour, pikes, swords and daggers; 37 'arquebusiers' with guns, morion helmets, swords and daggers; 20 archers with bows, sheafs of arrows, swords and daggers; and 5 billmen with bills, swords and daggers.

Throughout the county, the selected men were grouped into local companies of about one hundred - partly to facilitate training and partly to engender a community spirit. They were then trained in bands of twenty-four by a corporal, who was also responsible for knowing where each of his men could be contacted in an emergency. By 1585, the county had been divided into six separate areas, each with its own regiment of (ideally) 800 men divided into eight local companies. The company drawn from the city of Bath and the hundred of Bathforum was part of what later became known as 'the Bath Regiment', recruited from the north-eastern sector of the county. During Elizabeth I's reign, it was commanded at various times by Sir John Horner, Sir Maurice Berkley and Sir Arthur Hopton (all members of the local gentry).

The muster roll of 1569 provided a detailed list of those enlisted from the city Bath. It read as follows:

George Pearman	archer	John Style	billman
Richard Pearman	billman	William Keevil	archer
Richard Chapman	billman	Thomas Ridge	gunner
William Masters	billman	Edward Cornish	archer
John Turner	gunner	Thomas Raynold	archer
Edward Spice	billman	John Garlyoke	gunner
William Botewyke	pikeman	Henry Newman	gunner
Thomas Newport	billman	Henry Grenefeld	archer
John Burd	archer	William Pytte	billman
John Pylton	billman	John Towne	archer
Walter Acary	billman	William Wilman	archer
Henry Garnessye	archer		

A company of pikemen from the Bath Regiment of Trained Bands marching at one of its regular training musters. A woodcut by permission of the British Library (Roxburghe Ballads, RAX.Rox.II, 56).

This gave a total for Bath of twenty-three recruits out of a population of possibly some 1500. The amount of armour available for the city in 1569 was also listed as consisting of just seven corslets (two of which were owned by private individuals) and two 'almain rivets' [i.e. a type of German armour with riveted sections to provide more manoeuvrability]. In addition, there were just three calivers for the 'gunners' to use. From these dismal figures, which uncover an appalling lack of equipment, it is easy to see why the corporation took such urgent steps in 1573 to establish a proper armoury.

It will also be noted that the city did not provide any cavalry (nor, indeed, did the hundred of Bathforum). The government mainly relied on the nobility and wealthier gentry with country estates to undertake this task - even though a pursuivant did visit the city in 1580 to read a proclamation urging citizens to breed heavy horses for the war effort. There was indeed an alarming shortage. The muster list of 1569, for instance, had revealed that - in Somerset - there were just 20 'great horses' furnished with armour and demi-lances; and 125 'light horses' furnished with pistols. This could hardly be said to represent an impressive cavalry force. In Tudor times, horses were used at the trot to gain manoeuvrability on the field of battle and to provide their heavily-armed riders with a raised platform from which to fire their pistols or use their lances and swords. It was not until the Thirty Years War on the continent (1618-48) had completely transformed cavalry tactics that horses were used in a compact body at the charge as a shock tactic to break up enemy formations.

(iv) Training the Local Bands

Just as legislation in the early years of Elizabeth's reign had ruled on the selection and equipping of the trained bands, so it also gave instruction on the methods of training to be adopted. In the first place, local companies were to meet twice a month for **drill and target practice** - either on holidays or work days, but not on Sundays. Suitable butts were to be erected not far from the place where the weapons were stored, so that members of the band could practise their skills with either the long bow or the arquebus. It was considered important that each arquebusier should be allowed at least five shots at each practice session. Contributions towards the predicted monthly cost of bullets and armour (3s 8d per man) could reasonably be expected from local inhabitants.

In order to encourage the development of excellence in shooting, it was further recommended that prizes should be awarded each time to the best shots with each type of weapon - the awards to be funded, if necessary, from the proceeds of the betting that would naturally take place, 'as in other games', on the likely winners. The organisation of rival sports, which might tempt men away from their duty with the bands, was strictly forbidden on practice days - especially such games as dicing, cards, ninepins and tennis. Local town officials were instructed to ensure that order was maintained throughout. However, realising that large crowds would gather to watch the shooting and that spirits could well run high among the local youth, a further safeguard was built into the regulations. For the first year of operation, 'until order should be established', a justice of the peace was to accompany the officials to deal promptly with any troublemakers on the spot.

The butts, which ideally were to be twenty feet broad and sixteen feet high, were to be constructed of earth with the targets set in front - namely, boards between four and five feet wide with black painted roundels and a white bull's-eye in the centre. In Bath, shooting butts had been a well-established feature of city life over many

Target practice became a regular feature of training for the arquebusiers and musketeers of the Bath Regiment. This line drawing by Stephen Beck shows a session in progress at the butts situated in an area known as the Litten, just outside the Abbey.

generations. Indeed one field, which stood outside the south-western wall of the city, was actually named 'Butt Haies' - a reminder that this was the traditional site for archery practice. However, with an increase in the use of fire arms and the continuing threat from Spain, two new sites were established inside the city for use by arquebusiers (and, later, musketeers). The first hint of this appears in the corporation's accounts for 1585-86, when payments were incurred 'for making the butts and bringing the turves'. Cut sections of turf were used to top the mounds of earth - partly to prevent erosion and partly to create an element of landscaping on such prominent sites.

The actual site of one of these two new butts was revealed in the 1592-93 accounts, when the chamberlain not only paid for digging out and carrying the turves, but also for making the butts 'in the Litten'. This area [now Orange Grove], which had been the location of the former Priory's cemetery, was - by the end of the Tudor period - being used as a recreational space. Then in 1596-97, while some labourers were busy reconstructing the butts in the Litten, the corporation employed others 'to make the butts in Timber Green'. This area in the north-western angle of the city wall [now called Saw Close] was where carpenters traditionally prepared their timber for use in house construction. The butts here were made from a slightly different design with a stone wall topped with turves instead of a bank of earth.

Quite apart from the twice-monthly target practices for the local company, the Bath members of the trained bands were also required to attend **general musters of the whole Bath Regiment**. The purpose of these was to enable the soldiers to gain experience in battlefield tactics, formations and drill in larger numbers. By 1584, the musters had increased in frequency from annual to monthly occasions. However, with tension mounting in the country at large, it was decided in the following year that each regiment in Somerset should muster once a fortnight (on different days of the week, so that the 'muster master' for the county could attend each muster in person).

This decision met with some resistance in commercial centres such as Bath - especially in view of the fact that the days allocated (Mondays, Thursdays and Saturdays) were normal working days. This was seen to be harmful to trade. Furthermore, musters like this imposed a considerable financial burden on the community (bearing in mind the cost not only of new equipment and repairs, but also of transportation). For instance, a series of six musters in Wells in 1596-97 cost the corporation £17 12s 8d, which represented almost ten per cent of its total budget for the year. In view of all this, many cities tried to gain exemption - with Bath itself failing to enter a muster return for 1584. The lord lieutenant of the county was furious at this defiance, ordering the corporation to understand that his royal commission demanded total obedience.

Musters for the Bath Regiment, which took place either in Wells, Mells or Bath, were complicated in the extreme to organise. Each company first needed to collect its weapons, armour and powder from the armoury, before making its way to the point of rendezvous. A roll call was then taken, after which the muster master inspected the regiment to highlight any faults in equipment. It was only at this point that exercises and drill could commence. Many contemporary observers commented on the inefficiency of the whole operation. Far too much time was often wasted as they waited first for the various companies to dribble onto the field from outlying villages; and then, (even longer) for the arrival of their weapons and armour.

The responsibility for this (at least in the case of the Bath company) was in the hands of the city constables, who hired horses to transport the equipment and powder in bulk from the armoury. In 1601-02, for instance, the chamberlain paid eight pence 'for cords to bind the pikes and the armour that was carried to Wells for the muster'. Even

In the days before the musketeer took over from the archer as a key element in the infantry regiment, men were expected to practise regularly in using their bows. It had long been traditional for all males to possess a bow at home for use in emergencies. A woodcut by permission of the British Library (Roxburghe Ballads, RAX.Rox.I, 360).

after the arrival of the equipment, the roll call took ages to complete with lists of absentees being carefully drawn up for later punishment. On a brighter note, however, members of the bands were paid eight pence a day for time spent at the musters (a rate which compared favourably with that paid to unskilled workers at the time). This at least meant that they did not suffer financially from the performance of their duty.

It was hardly surprising that Bath Corporation relied heavily, in preparing for the musters, on the advice of one of its few professional soldiers - Peter Chapman. He had fought in the French wars during Henry VIII's reign and, although eighty-two years of age by the time the Armada sailed in 1588, he was vastly experienced in military matters. In 1573, therefore, the corporation paid him 'for riding to Bruton about the musters' - just as it did in 1589 'for sending a letter to Mr Hopton about the muster'. Chapman's task was clearly to liaise with the captain of the Bath Regiment about arrangements for the muster day (by 1589, Sir Arthur Hopton had succeeded to that position).

The chamberlain's accounts give a good idea of what was involved. For instance, in the spring of 1588 he 'laid out for the muster' (which was on that occasion held in Kingsmead in Bath) a total sum of £7 2s 6d. This not only covered the repair of many old items of equipment and the purchase of various new ones, but also the cost of entertaining the troops. An 18-gallon barrel of beer and 'a dozen ale' were 'carried out unto the meadow amongst the soldiers' at a cost of 7s 6d. Normally, it was just the officers who tended to benefit from this type of hospitality.

At the Bath muster in May 1596, for example, the corporation paid £1 2s 7d 'for Mr Hopton's dinner' (which presumably would have involved all the other officers together with local dignitaries). Other expenses in 1588 included the hire of the five horses 'that brought the muster master out of Bath' (the inspecting officer was in fact Captain Thomas Howard, the muster master for both Somerset and Wiltshire); and the payment of eight pence each to those members of the bands who came from the city. The total expense for this item of fourteen shillings (representing 21 soldiers) is confirmation that the size of Bath's representation had not increased since the 1569 muster (see above). To help defray the cost of maintaining the trained bands in this way, a 'trained soldiers' rate was regularly imposed on the local community.

In many ways, it was understandable - given the speed with which arrangements were made - that the Bath Regiment was something of a hotchpotch of men and equipment; and that the musters tended to be at best slightly shambolic. After all, the country had had no experience of professional soldiering. Nevertheless, by the end of the Tudor period, weapons had been modernised, shooting butts improved, uniforms introduced and community spirit enhanced. Of course, as it turned out - with the defeat of the Armada at sea - the regiment was never actually required to face up to the realities of war on the field of battle. Perhaps it was just as well. The men who had been recruited, as we have seen, were often drawn (particularly in towns like Bath) from the more comfortable sector of society - a point noted by Lord Burleigh in 1590. Men of this type, he commented, were 'too daintily fed and warm lodged' to be of real value in the tough conditions of front-line action.

Nevertheless, the regiment had played its part both as an immediate deterrent to would-be attackers and as an investment for the future security of the country. For unlike many county contingents, the Somerset regiments were not disbanded as tension eventually eased, but were kept under training well into the Stuart period. In consequence, the Bath Regiment did eventually see action on the outbreak of the Civil War in 1642, when trained troops on both sides were in short supply. Furthermore, the New Model Army - the country's first professional army, which was established in 1645 - was drawn initially at least from those who had seen service in the bands.

Security against Catholic Rebellion

(i) The National Background

The Elizabethan church settlement of 1559 had attempted to achieve a 'middle way' between the extremes of staunch Catholicism and ardent Puritanism - a compromise designed to accommodate all citizens within one English church with the queen herself styled as its 'Supreme Governor'. Regular attendance at the local parish church, therefore, became compulsory on pain of a twelve pence fine. The majority of English Catholics, in an attempt to avoid harassment and financial loss, paid at least lip service to these arrangements, becoming known as 'church papists' (i.e. those who dutifully attended church, but nevertheless held on to their inner beliefs and avoided taking communion whenever possible). Catholic clergy, who refused to conform to the new Book of Common Prayer, were deprived of their livings (including, in the area around Bath, those at Weston, Bathford, Saltford and Keynsham). Many fled abroad in consequence.

The harmonious operation of these new arrangements, however, was soon undermined by a number of external factors, which combined to pose a considerable **threat to the security of the country** and the survival of the government. In 1570, Pope Pius V not only excommunicated Elizabeth I, but also called on Catholics to bring about her deposition as queen. At the same time, two colleges were established on the continent with the sole aim of launching a Catholic mission to England - one at Douai in Flanders, founded by William Allen to train 'seminary priests' who would seek new converts within their native country; and the other at Rome, set up in 1579 by the Jesuits with the task of working among established Catholic families.

From the mid-1570s, therefore, waves of priests and Jesuits hit the country's shores and quickly found themselves at the heart of conspiracies to bring down the government. These included the Throckmorton Plot in 1583, which aimed to launch a French invasion; and the Babington Plot of 1586 to murder Elizabeth and install the Catholic Mary Queen of Scots in her place. Indeed, Mary - who was in fact Elizabeth's legal heir - had for many years been a focus for Catholic conspiracy, following her abdication of the Scottish throne and her flight to England and imprisonment in 1568. To aggravate the situation for the government even further, a serious Catholic rebellion had broken out in Ireland in 1579, while a rapid decline in relations with Spain during the mid-1580s greatly increased the prospect of a Catholic invasion led by Philip II.

Under all these circumstances, it is hardly surprising that the government was driven to introduce a series of increasingly fierce **measures against Catholics** in England. In 1577, for example, all Catholic 'recusants' (i.e. those refusing to attend church) were to be officially listed in all dioceses. Four years later, an Act of Parliament stipulated that priests saying mass or persons hearing mass were to face a year's imprisonment and a heavy fine; recusants were to be fined twenty pounds a month; while those who converted others to Catholicism were to be deemed guilty of treason.

Additional legislation in 1585 ruled that all Catholic priests were to leave the country within forty days or suffer death as traitors. Furthermore, an Act of 1593 stipulated that all avowed Catholic recusants were to return to their home parishes, where they were to register and make an undertaking not to make journeys of more than five miles in distance from home (except under special licence). These and other similar measures were accompanied by a wave of executions, including those of twelve priests and three laymen in 1586; thirty-one priests in 1586; and Margaret Clitheroe, who was pressed to death in 1586 for hiding priests.

(ii) The Local Scene

Given the increased threat to national security during the 1570s and 1580s, it was inevitable that Catholics in Bath and its surrounding area would suffer, at least in part, from the restrictions and penalties imposed. In point of fact, there were very few resident Catholics within the area of North-East Somerset at any time between the accession of Queen Elizabeth in 1558 and the restoration of the monarchy in 1660. Indeed, whereas a mere ten names were recorded from the city in early lists of recusants, the number had only increased to twelve 'reputed papists' in a return by local churchwardens in 1662.

Nevertheless, when the churchwardens of the three Bath parishes presented offenders at the archdeacon's visitation in 1593, twenty-seven people were accused of being non-communicants over a twelve-month period. It has to be stressed, however, that many of those charged were in all probability not Catholics at all, but rather Puritans who disagreed with the liturgy as set out in the Book of Common Prayer. Although John Stibbs, for instance, had refused to attend St Mary de Stall's Church in 1594, he had nevertheless been going 'to other churches' instead (presumably because he preferred the form of worship on offer there). Similarly, whereas Thomas Clement normally refused to go to church and receive the sacrament, he was quite happy to hear sermons being preached.

It is therefore likely that the hard core of **Catholic recusants in Bath** was largely represented by those six individuals presented for non-attendance offences in 1594, when Bishop John Still conducted his own visitation of the Bath and Wells Diocese. Of these, Paul Poole was excommunicated 'for refusing to come to his parish church'; Richard Marcombe 'for not receiving communion these two years' (although his punishment was later changed to a twelve pence fine); and John Baker 'for not receiving communion at Easter'. Henry Dolomer and his wife, on the other hand, were ordered to do penance 'for not coming to church above once a month' - a punishment later increased to excommunication when they failed to conform.

In actual fact, excommunication (or official exclusion from participation in the sacraments), which represented a most terrible punishment to devout churchmen, was never regarded as a serious penalty by people who were already out of sympathy with the newly-formed English church. Indeed, a fair number of those punished in this way within the diocese were to remain under sentence for several years without any sign of remorse. The penalty of penance, on the other hand, was much more personal. For a lesser offence, the guilty person was ordered to confess his fault in front of the pulpit wearing his normal clothes. More serious offenders, however, were ordered to enter the church in bare feet, wearing

John Still, Bishop of Bath and Wells, 1593-1608, who conducted a visitation of the diocese in 1594. Photograph by Michael Blandford by courtesy of the Bishop's Palace, Wells.

a large white sheet and carrying a white wand; they were then to stand by the pulpit while the rector read out a homily against their particular offence - following which they were to make a public confession of their offence, ask for forgiveness and seek the prayers of the congregation.

If the threat from resident Catholics in Bath was regarded as minimal, the threat from convicted **recusants visiting the city** was perceived to be very real. The government was particularly concerned that the health resort provided an ideal cover for conspirators wishing to discuss their latest schemes. Furthermore, the dependence of the local economy on a steady flow of visitors meant that local businessmen, producers, innkeepers and spa guides would be unlikely to refuse hospitality to such guests. In 1569, after a twenty-day visit to Bath, Thomas Churchyard sent a report to William Cecil (secretary of state and master spy of his day) warning him that he had witnessed 'much assembly and company of gentlemen...under the colour of coming to the bath' - known papists, who were acting suspiciously, including Sir Thomas Stradling, who had recently been released from prison; and Sir John Southworth, leader of the Catholic rebels in the north.

In one sense, the government had become a victim of its own policy of granting special licences, which enabled sick or infirm papists to gain temporary release from prison in order to visit the healing waters of Bath. In 1574, for instance, John and Nicholas Harpesfield, prisoners at the Fleet in London, were granted a two-month visit 'for the recovery of their healths' - on condition that they did not undermine 'the laws of religion' during their stay. Many others followed, including Evan Fludde from Cambridge in 1580, a man imprisoned for ' his obstinacy in popery'; and William Hassey from Yorkshire, 'an irreconcilable papist'.

Some were granted licences with a considerable degree of reluctance - such as John Whitmore in 1591, who had been 'restrained for recusancy' in Chester Castle. Although the privy council realised that he was 'very unworthy of favour', it agreed to his visit to avoid complaints 'by any of his sort' that the government was uncompassionate over serious matters of health. Similar concern was shown in 1582 over Lady Cecily Stonar, a committed papist. Fearing that she would become a subversive influence in Bath, the privy council stipulated that 'no person known to be evil affected in religion shall have access unto her or to confer with her' and that her appointed physician at the baths should be 'of good religion'.

Sometimes, however, government agents and local authorities took decisive action against individual Catholics. In 1581, for instance, after a royal proclamation against Jesuit priests had been read out in Bath, William Pitts was charged with distributing literature published by Edmund Campion, the leading Jesuit missionary in England. The privy council, therefore, was not at all pleased when it was subsequently informed that Pitts 'had escaped from Bath gaol'. On the other hand, Henry Clarke had been successfully apprehended in the city in the same year 'for popery and massing' (i.e secretly attending the Catholic mass). He was duly punished by the confiscation of five pounds in cash and a gelding worth four pounds. Later, however, the former Mayor of Bath - John Sherstone, who had been involved in the trial - was informed by the privy council that Clarke had recanted publicly in Salisbury Cathedral and had therefore been released. Sherstone was immediately instructed to restore the man's possessions.

Not all visiting papists brought dishonour or anxiety to the local community. **Dr John Feckenham** (the former Abbot of Westminster), for example, devoted himself to charitable works rather than conspiracy after he had been deprived of his living.

When, therefore, he visited Bath for health reasons in 1575 and 1576, he not only compiled a book of medicines for the use of poor people visiting the baths, but even built a 'lepers' hostel' with seven beds alongside the Hot Bath for the benefit of those 'most miserable of objects [i.e. with serious skin disease] who fly to Bath for relief from the hot waters'.

It is more than likely that mass was said in secret within the city throughout the period by visiting recusant clergy. It has often been alleged that the home of **Dr John Sherwood** (who lived in Abbey House from 1593) provided a base for these illegal services under the cloak of medicine. He was later described by Anthony Wood, for instance, as 'an eminent practitioner....in the City of Bath....much resorted to by those of the Roman Catholic religion, he himself being of that profession.' There is however little real evidence for this allegation.

The name of Dr Sherwood himself never appeared on any of the official lists of recusants and he certainly did his best to dissuade one of his sons from becoming a Catholic priest. On the other hand, it is true that his own father, mother and wife were devout papists; his brother, Thomas, became an Elizabethan martyr for his faith; and three other brothers became Catholic priests. Furthermore, his daughter, Mary, and four of his seven sons were converted to the Catholic faith - Thomas (who joined the Society of Jesus), Robert and William (both of whom entered the Benedictine Order) and John (who was a practising Catholic in Ireland).

Quite apart from investigating non-attendance at church, **Bishop John Still's visitation** of the diocese in 1594 also looked into other matters of concern within each parish. Clergy were chastised for failing to follow the Book of Common Prayer or the Articles of Religion - the vicar of South Stoke, for instance, for not wearing a surplice, not making the sign of the cross at baptism and leaving out parts of the service to make room for his sermon; and the curate of St Michael's, Bath for not preaching a sermon every quarter and failing to catechise the children. Churchwardens were censured for neglect - at Bathford, for failure to provide 'a bible of the largest volume'; at Freshford, because 'the chest in the church does not have three locks according to the article'; and at South Stoke, because 'the chancel is in decay'. Members of the congregation were dealt with for immoral behaviour - Agnes Harris at Swainswick for being 'begotten with child by Richard Pitt'; and Richard Tapp and his wife at Widcombe for 'living asunder'.

Individuals were punished for unseemly behaviour - at Bathford, John Bradley who had felled trees 'for the most part of the day' on May Day; at St Mary de Stall's Church in Bath, Henry Blackledge who was 'a drunkard and disturber of his neighbours by night and day'; at Freshford, the rector himself who was 'a common visitor of alehouses'; and - worst of all - at Priston, Joan Blackborough who was 'suspected to be a witch'. Although unable to attend the court - she was 'old, lame and sick' - she was thought 'to have bewitched Widow Launsden of Priston, who died thereupon'. Joan, however, died of natural causes shortly after the hearing, thus avoiding the usual trial by ordeal to ascertain whether she was indeed a witch. The likely penalty, if found guilty, would have been death by either hanging or burning.

By dying immediately after the hearing, Joan Blackborough avoided being subjected to a trial by ordeal (i.e. trial by water) to ascertain whether she was indeed a witch. It was believed that a true witch could not sink, even when tied up. The sow on the right was clearly believed to be the witch's 'familiar' sent by the Devil to assist her in inflicting damage on her neighbours and their property (note the cart in the background which has come to grief). From Witches Apprehended, Examined and Executed, 1613. *(Author's collection)*

Security against Beggars and Vagabonds

(i) The National Background

During the sixteenth century, the whole nation was plagued by **widespread vagrancy** as bands of hungry beggars, armed with wooden staves, roamed the countryside in search of both food and shelter. The children's nursery rhyme, *Hark! hark! the dogs do bark. The beggars are coming to town*, was no simple expression of a youngster's delight at the approach of visitors, but rather a fearful warning to neighbours to batten down their shutters in readiness for assault. There were many reasons for the development of this threatening situation, including the return of swarms of unemployed soldiers after the ending of wars, rebellions or foreign expeditions. Chiefly, however, the root cause lay in the ever-changing economic scene over which the authorities at the time had little control.

In the first place, a rapid and unprecedented explosion in the population of England and Wales, which rose from three million in 1550 to just over four million in 1601, created a burgeoning surplus in the labour market. The consequences of this were seriously exacerbated by a prolonged period of rampant inflation in Europe brought about by debasement of the coinage in many countries, large-scale bullion imports from the New World, repeated harvest failure (particularly an extended sequence from 1594 to 1597) and the inflationary pressures of war. Between 1500 and 1640, it is estimated that the price of food rose by 700% and that of industrial goods by over 300%. Wage increases inevitably fell short of the rate of inflation by a huge margin - with the result that the remuneration earned by farm workers approximately halved in real terms during the same period.

To make matters worse, the first part of the sixteenth century witnessed widespread enclosure of the open fields as more and more of the larger farmers - attracted by high profits to be gained from the expanding cloth trade - turned to sheep farming. This resulted in a serious depopulation of the countryside in many areas. Agricultural workers, driven off the arable strips which had been farmed by their families for generations, now took to the roads as landless labourers in search of employment in the more industrial towns. The later years of the Tudor period, however, witnessed a further economic upheaval brought about by the prolonged decline of the cloth industry in the face of strong competition from abroad. This resulted in the mass unemployment of spinners, weavers and fullers in most of the traditional cloth making districts.

Elizabeth I's reign was therefore marked in part by deep-seated problems of unemployment, poverty and hunger. Successive governments tried their best to contain the situation without ever fully understanding the complex causes of poverty. Frustrated by their inevitable lack of success, they turned increasingly at first to harsh and inhumane methods of treatment. **The Beggars Act of 1551**, for instance, noted that 'vagabonds and beggars have of long time increased and daily do increase in great and excessive numbers, by the occasion of idleness, mother and root of all vices'. Although local magistrates were therefore empowered to license any genuine 'aged, poor and impotent persons' to beg locally, they were also instructed to deal firmly with any able-

Groups of armed vagabonds such as these posed a serious threat to villages and towns alike. A woodcut by permission of the British Library (Roxburghe Ballads, RAX.Rox.III, 10).

bodied beggar who was caught wandering through the parish. He was 'to be tied to the end of a cart naked and beaten with whips...till his body be bloody' and then escorted back to his rightful place of residence.

A second Beggars Act five years later encouraged parishes to look after their own genuine poor by taking voluntary collections in church each week in an attempt to prevent the 'poor, impotent, lame, feeble, sick and diseased' from being forced into begging. However, after this voluntary system had met with limited success, parliament eventually called for weekly payments to be recorded and for any reluctant subscribers to appear before the priest or even the Quarter Sessions to be 'charitably and gently persuaded'. Meanwhile, a short-lived Act of Parliament in 1547 had imposed even harsher punishments on 'sturdy vagabonds and valiant beggars'. A first offence was to be punishable by branding on the chest and two years slavery with a local farmer, while the second offence was to warrant branding on the cheek or forehead and slavery for life.

The Poor Law Relief Act of 1576 brought a little more compassion onto the scene. Local magistrates were to keep stocks of material in towns so that beggars could be set to work. Those who refused were to be confined in specially constructed 'houses of correction', where conditions were harsh and hours of labour long. It was not, however, until the **Poor Law Act of 1601** that a well thought-out system was introduced based on the best features of the previous legislation - a system which was to last in fact until 1929. This made a clear distinction between the various types of pauper and the type of action needed in each category. Orphans and children from pauper homes were to be apprenticed; the aged and infirm were to be looked after in almshouses; the fit, but genuinely unemployed were to be set to work by the parish; while wilfully idle rogues and vagabonds were to be whipped and sent back to their home parishes. It was also established that the cost of maintaining the genuine poor was to be borne by the inhabitants of each parish through the raising of a compulsory poor rate - tasks undertaken by overseers of the poor.

(ii) The Local Scene

By 1550, Bath Corporation was facing a major social and economic crisis with a daily influx of threatening beggars - a mixture of rogues, vagabonds, pedlars, runaway apprentices, unemployed soldiers and so-called minstrels. 'You cannot be without peril at Bath', wrote one visitor to Lord Burleigh in 1552, 'whither there is a daily resort from Bristol and specially of beggars and poor folks'. **'The Beggars of Bath'** gained such national notoriety that the very reputation of the health resort was placed in jeopardy. The corporation felt grave anxiety in two ways - first, that an increasing crime rate centred on petty theft, burglary, poaching and aggressive harassment would frighten its citizens and scare away its visitors; secondly, that any attempt by these beggars to remain in the city (where the potential pickings from wealthy 'health tourists' were considerable) would put an unsustainable burden on the relief already provided by churches for their own poor parishioners.

Although documentary evidence is slight on this subject, there is little doubt that the corporation would have used the powers granted by the poor law legislation (see above) to whip the vagabonds out of town and drive them back to their own parishes. There is also a clear hint that branding irons were used on this type of beggar, as permitted by the 1547 Act. Certainly, in 1613, the council paid William Doulton, the metal smith, twelve pence 'for an iron to burn rogues with' - probably as a replacement for a similar tool used previously. The chamberlain's accounts show that the council never hesitated in protecting its citizens from the threat of outside danger. William Ford was therefore employed 'to keep out wanderers' from the city, while an escort was paid 'for sending a mad man back to his country' [i.e. his place of birth].

However, sturdy beggars such as these formed only one part of a regular influx to the city. Whereas the unemployed from other parts of the country were attracted by the comparative affluence of the resort, those who were seriously ill or incapacitated recognised in its healing waters their final chance of a cure. Scores of them in consequence descended on Bath each month. In desperation, the corporation petitioned parliament for urgent help in tackling this menace, which was putting the city's relief funds under considerable pressure.

Pedlars, who wandered the countryside in an attempt to sell their wares, were regarded as vagabonds and treated accordingly. A woodcut by permission of the British Library Roxburghe Ballads, RAX.Rox.II, 404).

The Poor Relief Act of 1572, therefore, gave recognition to Bath's unique problem (namely that 'a great number of poor and diseased people do resort to the City of Bath...for some ease and relief of their diseases', which resulted in the inhabitants being 'greatly overcharged'). In future, therefore, any 'diseased or impotent' person would be banned from visiting the city, unless licensed to do so by two justices in his native county. The licence gave a guarantee that his own parish would eventually take him back and continue to support him financially. Failure to produce this licence at the city gate, however, would result in instant punishment as a vagabond - and, in 1572, this

A poor man begging from a well-dressed citizen in a non-threatening manner. Genuine poor from within the parish were normally treated with compassion, but those from outside ran the risk of being treated as vagabonds. (Author's collection)

meant being branded on the chest with a 'V' and then being handed over to a farmer for
slavery.

Nevertheless, as P.R. James has shown, those sick people who had obtained
genuine licences together with financial support from their own parishes were always
welcomed at the resort. Four lame men, for instance, were each granted twelve pence in
Nottingham to cover their expenses in 1579; a poor lame boy from Oxford received
ten shillings to visit Bath for a cure; and William Porter, 'a broken-down soldier' had
expenses amounting to thirty shillings funded by a rate on the inhabitants of Droitwich.
Private charity also helped to subsidise the needs of sick visitors. Lord Shaftesbury, for
example, gave a lump sum to realise four pounds a week for the sick poor; while Lady
Anne Sherington donated forty pounds, the interest of which was to be used for the
benefit of lame and diseased people staying in the city.

Quite apart from tackling the problem of unemployed vagabonds and diseased
migrants, the corporation was also faced with the routine task of catering for **the city's
own poor** whether aged, sick or unemployed. Residents in Bath, of course, were not
immune from all the economic pressures outlined above - a population explosion, rising
prices, inadequate wages, food shortages and unemployment in the local woollen cloth
industry. It is estimated that, in the country at large, 4-5% of the population would be
receiving poor relief at any one time during this period, but that this would increase to
up to 20% in terms of severe crisis.

The corporation responded to this
escalation of poverty with a great
deal of compassion. For instance, the
chamberlain's accounts from 1568
show that the elderly and infirm
received a regular supply of annual
gifts to ease their distress - 'bread
given to the poor in Lent'; 'forty
sacks of coal to the poor at
Christmas'; and 'wood to the poor at
Christmas and carrying it home to
their houses'. Similar compassion
was shown through a whole sequence
of small acts of kindness offered to
individuals in need. Money was
therefore released 'for a smock for
Westfield's daughter and for making
her a petticoat and waistcoat'; 'for
the apparelling of Fortune Welsh's
son'; 'for Gillian Forrester's coat';
'for a pair of shoes for Owen
Colloway'; 'for a shroud and burial
for Hugh Hill'; 'for a shroud cloth
for one Bush, a poor man that died
at the bath'; and 'for making Julia
Forrest's bastard son's coat'. Support
was also offered to those who

*Bath corporation helped to ease the poverty of numbers
of its own residents by providing gifts of bread and fuel
at Christmas and Lent. A line drawing by Mark Withers.*

fostered orphans or looked after those in particular trouble. Mr Cox, therefore, received ten shillings 'for keeping a mad woman', while Mr Box was paid five shillings for accommodating 'Westfield's child'.

Quite apart from the benevolence of the corporation, the churches in Bath also distributed relief to the poor of the parish in line with the responsibility placed on them by Tudor legislation (see page 120). Although recorded evidence for this is thin on the ground, the churchwardens of St Michael's Church distributed 21s 4d 'to poor people' in both 1551 and 1563 - presumably after collections had been taken in response to the terms of the 1552 Act. Assistance of this kind, however, was essentially of a temporary nature and intended to support an individual facing a particular crisis. The able-bodied poor desperately needed the opportunity to work.

Among the hundreds of visitors who came to the health resort each year were a few individuals (as Jean Manco has shown) who were greatly moved by the sight of poverty and distress - individuals who subsequently decided to become benefactors by making a gift to the corporation for the relief of the poor. These included several contributions which were intended to stimulate the creation of work for the unemployed. For instance, Bath (along with twenty-two other towns on a rota system) benefited from Sir Thomas White's Charity, established in 1566 by a wealthy London clothier. The city qualified for its first payment in 1595, when £100 was allocated. This proved an enormous boon to four selected freemen (or 'poor artificers', as they were styled), who each received a £25 interest-free loan for ten years to help them expand their businesses. Thereafter, the city qualified for further repayments from the charity very twenty-four years.

On the other hand, the elderly and infirm (i.e. those who were no longer able to fend for themselves) required more long-term care. By the end of the Tudor period, Bath was in a strong position to accommodate poor people of this type in the sort of **almshouses** envisaged in the Poor Law Act of 1601 (even though it did not build its first 'house of correction' for putting the able-bodied unemployed to work until 1634). The city did in fact already own two almshouses (or 'hospitals') by 1572 - soon to be increased to three after the opening of Bellott's Hospital in 1609, built through the generosity of Thomas Bellott (steward to William Cecil, Lord Burleigh). **St John's Hospital**, situated near the Cross Bath, had originally been administered by Bath Priory, but had escaped closure at the time of the dissolution of the monasteries because a layman (and not a monk) had been in charge as master. After briefly being annexed to St Michael's Church by the West Gate, it eventually became the responsibility of the corporation following a petition to Queen Elizabeth in 1572.

This resulted not only in the Corporation being granted the right to appoint the Master of the Hospital, but also in the launch of a nationwide appeal for funds both to complete the building of Bath Abbey and to enlarge the hospital. By 1580, therefore, an additional floor had been created, enabling it to accommodate four poor men and four poor women each with a weekly allowance of 4s 2d. Clothed in blue gowns with white cotton linings and clasps, the residents were under the care of three paid officials - the master, the reader (who took the services) and the washer (who cleaned and took care of the laundry).

Not far away in Binbury Lane, near the South Gate, stood **St Catherine's Hospital** or the Black Alms House, which was originally endowed in about 1444. Rebuilt by the corporation in 1553, it was (according to John Wood in 1642) 'a mean structure, two stories high and containing fourteen tenements'. The intention was to support ten poor people of either sex (made possible by the further funding offered by

Edward VI's substantial grant of property in 1552 for the founding of a grammar school and the maintenance of ten poor people - see Chapter 3). The residents received a weekly allowance of three shillings and sixpence each, plus a black coat with red lining once every two years. In return they were expected to attend (in their gowns) two services in the Abbey each Sunday, including one communion a month - and to live a sober and respectable life.

There was in fact a fourth hospital just outside the city - the **Hospital of St Mary Magdalen** (or Magdalen's Hospital, as it was known) on Holloway. This was not owned by the corporation, but was under the jurisdiction of the crown, which appointed the master. Nevertheless, the corporation did send an annual gift of four shillings at Christmas for the benefit of the poor people in residence. [For a more detailed description of the hospitals see Jean Manco, *The Spirit of Care*.]

Sir Thomas White, founder of his own charity in 1566, which helped to create work for the unemployed in Bath. An engraving from Richard Warner's History of Bath, *1801.*

SOURCES USED IN CHAPTER 3

1. Printed Material

Bagley, J.J. & A.J: *The English Poor Law* (1966)

Barnes, Thomas G: *Somerset, 1625-1640: a County's Government during the Personal Rule* (1961)

Chapman, Mike: 'When Bath prepared to fight the Armada' (in Holland, Elizabeth: *Citizens of Bath,* 1988)

Day, Rosemary: *The Tudor Age* (1995)

Green, Emanuel: *The Preparations of Somerset against the Spanish Armada, 1558-1588* (1888)

Green, Emanuel (ed.): 'Certificates of the Musters, 1569, in the County of Somerset' (in *Somerset Record Society,* vol. 20, 1904)

James, P.R: *The Charters of the City of Bath*, vol. 2 (1942 typescript, BRO)

Manco, Jean: *The Spirit of Care* (1998)

Page, William (ed.): *The Victorian History of Somerset*, vol. 2 (1911)

Powell, Ken & Cook, Chris: *English Historical Facts, 1485-1603* (1977)

Pritchard, R.E (ed.): *Shakespeare's England: Life in Elizabethan and Jacobean Times* (1999)

Shickle, C W: 'Accounts of the City Trained Bands' (in *Proceedings of the Bath Natural History and Antiquarian Field Club*, vol. 10, 1905)

Shorrocks, Derek (ed.): 'Bishop Still's Visitation, 1594' (in *Somerset Record Society*, vol. 84, 1998)

Tucker, John & Winstock, Lewis (eds.): *The English Civil War: a Military Handbook* (1972)

Williams, J.A: *Post-Reformation Catholicism in Bath*, vol. 1 (1975)

Wroughton, John: *Stuart Bath: Life in the Forgotten City* (2004)

2. Documentary Material:

Bath Record Office: No. 26: Letters Patent, 6 June, 15 Eliz., 1573

                            Bath Chamberlain's Accounts, 1568-1603

National Archives: Acts of the Privy Council, 1574, 1575, 1579, 1580, 1581, 1582, 1586, 1596

                            Calendars of State Papers Domestic, Elizabeth

CHAPTER 6

1602: Life in the Emerging Spa

Entertainment

(i) Feasting and Merrymaking

Some of the most eagerly-awaited events in the local community were the days of feasting and merrymaking which followed the major religious festivals. Although vivid accounts of what went on are often lacking for individual towns (including Bath), hints are sometimes provided in city or parish accounts when payments are made in relation to a particular celebration. Furthermore, historians have gleaned evidence from around the country to demonstrate what normally took place in parishes great and small throughout the land. This is particularly true in relation to Christmas, Shrovetide, Whitsuntide and Midsummer.

The end of the church service on Christmas morning heralded the start of the **Twelve Days of Christmas** - a period of merriment and partying, which concluded on Twelfth Night. As everyone had endured a restricted diet of soups, fish and stews during the four weeks of Advent leading up to Christmas, the meal on Christmas Day was eagerly anticipated. With their houses decorated with holly, ivy and mistletoe, those who could afford it would certainly enjoy a feast of roast meat, poultry and frumenty (the forerunner of Christmas pudding - a mixture of porridge, nuts, spices and dried fruits).

The days that followed were not only given over to parties at home with board and card games, but also included public entertainments provided by the town or city. We know, for instance, that Bath Corporation paid 6s 8d in 1602 'to the young men of our city that played at Christmas' - and it is more than likely that some of the recorded visits by travelling players, minstrels and bear wardens (see below) took place during this time of celebration at the corporation's expense. In many places, too, it was normal for 'mummers', wearing masks or other disguises, to perform traditional mimes or folk plays on Boxing Day.

Shrovetide in February provided people with their last opportunity to have fun before the start of Lent imposed a period of fasting and self-denial. Families therefore feasted on

Travelling players and minstrels often joined in the fun during the Twelve Days of Christmas. This contemporary woodcut shows Will Kemp, who danced all the way from Norwich to London to the sound of pipe and tabor in nine days - for a bet! (Author's collection)

their remaining stocks of salted meat, cheese and eggs (foods which were forbidden during the fast). 'Pan cakes' or 'pan puffs', as they were sometimes called, therefore became a popular dish at this season. However, for many people, as one preacher pointed out in 1571, Shrovetide had become a time of 'great gluttony, surfeiting and drunkenness'.

Shrove Tuesday (the day before the solemn church service of Ash Wednesday - see Chapter 1), was traditionally the day for public entertainment. Although the corporation would normally sponsor a programme of bearbaiting, music and performances by travelling players, much of the entertainment was organised unofficially by the youth of the city. Fuelled by an excess of alcohol, it often became an excuse for rowdy and riotous behaviour. According to John Wood, writing in 1742, two sports had for many years dominated all entertainment in Bath on Shrove Tuesday - cock-threshing and football, which was played on Ham meadow. Cock-threshing was a particularly cruel and barbaric activity, which involved the brutal killing of the birds - as was described by the Dutchman, William Schellinks, who visited England in 1662.

COCK-THRESHING

Shrove Tuesday in England and their Lent or fasts start - and one eats pancakes. Their entertainment then is to throw at the cock. In London one sees in every street, wherever one goes, many apprentice boys running with - under their arms - a cock with a string on its foot, on which is a spike, which they push firmly into the ground between the stones.

They always look for an open space and, for a penny, let people throw their cudgel from a good distance at the cock; and he who kills the cock gets it. In the country, or with countryfolk, they bury the cock with only its head above the ground, and blindfold a person and turn him two or three times around himself, and then he tries to hit the cock with a flail; and the one who hits it or comes closest to it gets the prize.

Source: Maurice Exwood & H.L. Lehmann (eds.): *The Journal of William Schellinks' Travels in England, 1661-63* (Camden Society, 5th Series, vol. 1, 1993)

Football, on the other hand, was also violent in nature - but only dangerous to those involved. Bearing no possible resemblance to the modern game, it featured large numbers of youths, who fought vigorously for the possession of the ball. There were no effective rules, no recognisable teams and little particular purpose other than to allow local hooligans the chance to let off steam, settle old scores and voice their protest against authority (see the description by Philip Stubbes in the panel opposite). Inevitably - then as now - violent disorder continued in the streets long after the football had ended. In 1598, for instance, a complaint was made to the Mayor of Bath that 'certain lewd and disordered persons of base sort and condition, upon Shrove Tuesday last, did in tumultuous sort assemble themselves together' and then proceeded to vandalise the private hot water supply leading into the house of Dr Sherwood, near the Hot Bath, digging up the pipe in the process.

FOOTBALL

As concerning football playing, I protest unto you it may rather be called a friendly kind of fight than a play or recreation; a bloody and murdering practice than a fellowly sport or pastime.

For doth not everyone lie in wait for his adversary, seeking to overthrow him and to pitch him on his nose, though it be upon hard stones in ditch or dale, in valley or hill? What place soever it be, he careth not, so he [may] have him down. And he that can serve the most of this fashion, he is counted the only fellow.

So that by this means, sometimes their necks are broken, sometimes their backs, sometimes their legs, sometimes their arms; sometimes one part thrust out of joint, sometimes another; sometimes their noses gush out with blood, sometimes their eyes start out [of their heads]; and sometimes [they are] hurt in one place, sometimes in another. But whosoever escapeth away the best, goeth not scotfree, but is either sore wounded, crushed and bruised, so as he dieth of it, or else escapeth very hardly.

And no marvel, for they have the sleights [cunning] to meet one betwixt two, to dash him against the heart with their elbows, to hit him under the short ribs with their gripped fists; and with their knees to catch him upon the hip, and to pitch him on his neck, with an hundred such murdering devices.

And hereof groweth every, malice, rancour, choler [anger], hatred, displeasure, enmity, and what not else: and sometimes fighting, brawling, contention, quarrel-picking, murder, homicide, and great effusion of blood, as experience daily teacheth.

Source: Philip Stubbes: *Anatomy of Abuses in England*, 1583 (1877-79 edtn., pt. 1, edited by Frederick J Furnivall). Picture by permission of the Mary Evans Picture Library.

Whitsuntide provided another opportunity for merrymaking in the two days following Whit Sunday. Many parishes up and down the country held traditional 'church ales', a fund-raising event in support of the church with ale, food, music and dancing on offer. Although existing records do not indicate whether or not the churches in Bath followed this tradition (there is no mention of in in the accounts of St Michael's Church), we do know that one particular ceremony was regularly undertaken during this festival - namely, the election and crowning of a 'mock king'. This Bath tradition is briefly described by John Leland, who visited the city twice between 1533 and 1542:

> And at Whitsunday-tide, at the which time men say that Edgar was there crowned, there is a king elected at Bath every year by the townsmen in joyful remembrance of King Edgar and the privileges given to the town by him. This king is feasted and his adherents by the richest men of the town.

We certainly know from the city chamberlain's accounts that the corporation entertained the freemen of the city to a treat of ale, bread, cheese and cakes in the Guildhall each Whitsuntide - and it is more than likely that the elected 'king' and his followers were invited to this feast. In the country at large, these mock kings were expected to preside over the summer games, which took place during the warmer weather in May (although there is no specific evidence for this in Bath). In some places, the election merely became the excuse for the youth of the parish to indulge in another round of drunken and riotous behaviour. Philip Stubbes, who describes one such episode (see panel opposite), also links the ceremony to the tradition of morris dancing.

Midsummer Day on 24th June - the feast of St John and the longest day of the year - prompted several further displays of merrymaking in the warmth of the sun. Doors of houses were decked with foliage and garlands of flowers; parties and family feasts were held; and drink flowed freely throughout the city. It was traditional for city corporations to sponsor the great bonfires, which were lit on St John's Eve, together with performances by minstrels and morris dancers. In Bristol, Gloucester and Salisbury, 'marching watches' of armed men, torchbearers and musicians paraded through the streets. For its own part, Bath Corporation certainly took the lead in organising public entertainment, judging by a generous payment of 40s 4d in 1569 to cover 'the charges of Midsummer night'. Furthermore, we know that music and dancing were also part of the tradition in Bath during these celebrations, because in 1606 Robert Corbett, a minstrel, was censured by the bishop (along with three of his companions) for playing 'upon their instruments' and dancing 'to the evil example of others' on Midsummer Day. Their only crime, however, was that they had performed 'during the time of divine service in the afternoon'. There is further evidence that bull-baiting was also a local tradition during this festival.

(ii) Popular Sports

Quite apart from the opportunity provided by these annual events, **animal-baiting** was a popular sport in Bath throughout the year - in spite of the fact that it was increasingly frowned upon by Puritan factions within the church. According to entries made in the chamberlain's accounts, Bath Corporation regularly sponsored bear-baiting performances by groups of bear wardens (or 'bearwards'), who brought the unfortunate animals with them in something resembling a travelling circus. A visit to the city in

ELECTION OF THE MOCK KING

First, all the wild-heads of the parish, conventing together, choose them a Grand Captain of all mischief whom they ennoble with the title of 'my Lord of Misrule', and him they crown with great solemnity, and adopt for their king. This king anointed, chooseth forth twenty, forty, threescore or a hundred lusty guts like to himself to wait upon his lordly majesty, and to guard his noble person.

Then every one of these his men he investeth with his liveries, of green, yellow or some other light wanton colour. And as though that were not gaudy enough, they bedeck themselves with scarves, ribbons and laces hanged all over with gold rings, precious stones and other jewels; this done, they tie about either leg twenty or forty bells, with rich handkerchiefs in their hands, borrowed for the most part from their pretty Mopsies and loving Besses, for bussing [kissing] them in the dark.

Thus, all things set in order, then have they their hobby-horses, dragons and other antiques, together with their bawdy pipers and thundering drummers to strike up the devil's dance withal. Then march these heathen company towards the church and churchyard, their pipers piping, their drummers thundering, their stumps dancing, their bells jingling, their handkerchiefs swinging about their heads like madmen, their hobby-horses and other monsters skirmishing amongst the route [throng]... And so forth into the churchyard, where they have commonly their summer halls, their bowers, arbours and banqueting houses set up, wherein they feast, banquet and dance all that day, and, peradventure, all the night too. And thus these terrestrial furies spend the sabbath day.

Source: Philip Stubbes: *Anatomy of Abuses in England*, 1583 (1877-79 edtn., pt. 1, edited by Frederick J Furnivall). Picture from J.R. Green: *A Short History of the English People* (1907 edtn.) by permission of the Guildhall Library, Corporation of London.

1576 by Lord Warwick's bearward was followed in 1592 by that of the Queen (who returned in 1601) and Lord Dudley's in 1594.

Furthermore, it is clear that some bears were kept locally by residents - the corporation paying a subsidy of twelve pence in 1577 for 'the baiting of John Chapman's bear'. Chapman was a prominent member of the council. The baitings, which would normally be held in the courtyard of local inns, were highly popular throughout the sixteenth century and were patronised by both Henry VIII and Elizabeth I. The bears, who performed on the touring circuit, had often had their claws removed; many were already severely scarred from previous injuries; and some were blind. After the animal had been tied to a post - amid noisy scenes of frenzied betting - fierce mastiffs were set loose within the arena as a prelude to an almighty scrap (see below).

ANIMAL BAITING

In the middle of this place a large bear on a rope was bound to a stake; then a number of great English mastiffs were brought in and shown first to the bear, which they afterwards baited one after another...

When the first bear was weary, another was supplied and fresh dogs to bait him, first one at a time, then more and more till they had overpowered the bear. Then only did they come to its aid. This second bear was very big and old, and kept the dogs at bay so artfully with his paws that they could not score a point off him until there were more of them. When this bear was tired, a large white powerful bull was brought in, and likewise bound in the centre of the theatre. One dog only was set on him at a time, which he speared with his horns and tossed in such masterly fashion that they could not get the better of him. As the dogs fell to the floor again, several men held the sticks under them to break their fall, so that they would not be killed...Lastly they brought in an old blind bear which the boys hit with canes and sticks; but he knew how to untie his leash and he ran back to his stall.

On leaving we descended the steps, went behind the theatre and saw the English mastiffs, of which there were one hundred and twenty together in one enclosure, each chained up to his own separate kennel however. And the place was evil-smelling because of the lights and meat on which the butchers feed the said dogs. In a stall adjoining were some twelve large bears, and several bulls in another, all of them kept there merely for the sport described above.

Taken from the experiences of Thomas Platter during his travels in England, 1599, in P. Razzell (ed.): *The Journals of Two Travellers in England in Elizabethan and Early Stuart Times* 1998)

The same courtyards were also used for other forms of animal sports. Even the Rector of Bathwick (William Powell), who kept his own pack of mastiffs for the purpose, organised a bull-baiting event in Bath in 1606. He was apparently a regular attender of baiting sessions of both bulls and bears - much to his bishop's fury! Cockfighting, too, had also made its appearance, although the specially-built 'cockpit' in Saw Close (shown on Joseph Gilmore's map of 1694) was not constructed until later in the next century. Nevertheless, as early as 1562, Dr William Turner (an eminent local physician) had complained that, even though there was serious under-funding of the hot water baths, 'there is money enough spent upon cock fightings, tennisplays, parks, banquetings, pageants and plays' - a concise summary indeed of the entertainment opportunities available in Tudor Bath!

There were in fact two courts available in Bath for 'tennisplay'. This was royal or **'real' tennis**, a sport popularised by Henry VIII, who had built no fewer than four such courts at Whitehall. One of the Bath courts was situated on the eastern side of the King's Bath (shown clearly on John Speed's map of 1610); the other, 'one wood barton called Tennisplay' by the South gate, which was leased to Alderman Thomas Gibbs in 1585. The game, which was played indoors, involved serving a ball (made of sheepskin and stuffed with sawdust) with a racquet (constructed out of yew with cat-gut strings) onto a sloping roof, which ran along one side of the court - and thence across the net (or even a piece of string).

(iii) Travelling Players

Visits by groups of **travelling players**, which have already been mentioned above, reached a peak of popularity during Elizabeth's reign. P.R. James has actually identified from various sources no fewer than ninety-five such visits between 1569 and 1603 from a total of thirty-four different companies (i.e. averaging almost three a year). These were each sponsored and licensed by a high-ranking patron such as the queen herself or the lord chamberlain. Indeed, by 1598, these licensed groups were the only touring companies permitted by an Act of Parliament, which had otherwise forbidden 'all fencers, bearwards, common players of interludes and minstrels from wandering abroad'. This was in response to widespread public anxiety over the numerous groups of sturdy beggars - often posing as entertainers - who roamed the country. Without a licence, each player would henceforth be treated as a vagabond and therefore 'stripped naked from the middle upwards and openly whipped till his body be bloody'.

On the other hand, official touring companies who visited Bath were well organised, each boasting a cast of around twelve male actors (female parts were played by boys) who perfumed a small repertoire of two or three plays. The productions normally took place either in the Guildhall or in the courtyards of inns - or, in summer, in the open market place. In Bath, most companies were paid a flat-rate fee by the corporation for their performance. However, a different system operated for visits by the most prestigious company of all - the Queen's Players, of which Shakespeare was a member.

On these occasions, the performers themselves first made a collection from the audience ('the gathering') and then the corporation, from city funds, made up the amount to the pre-arranged fee. Thus, in 1581, the chamberlain paid 19s 4d to make up what 'was gathered at the bench' to a total of 26s 4d. Furthermore, when the Queen's Players stayed in Bath after their performance in 1601, the corporation even paid 11s

2d for their 'kitching' (i.e. the bread, beer, wine and sugar they consumed - not to mention horsemeat for their mounts). Among groups of players performing in Bath, the Queen's Players were by far the most regular, attending almost annually between 1583 and 1607. Other groups included the Lord Admiral's, the Lord of Derby's, the Lord of Worcester's, the Lord Chamberlain's, the Lord of Pembroke's, the Earl of Hertford's, the Lord of Leicester's, the Lord of Oxford's and many more - including a troupe belonging to the Master of the Revels.

Thomas Platter, who visited England in 1599, described the scene he witnessed in one such performance:

> They play on a raised platform, so that everyone has a good view...Whoever cares to stand below only pays one English penny; but if he wishes to sit, he pays another penny...And during the performance, food and drink are carried round the audience. The actors are most expensively and elaborately costumed.

It was very much 'theatre in the round'. A large crowd of 'groundlings' jostled for position around the stage with others packed along narrow benches in tiers behind, noisily eating the snacks which they had purchased from hawkers. As many of them could hardly see the stage, they had to be content with just listening to the words being spoken. After all, the origin of the word 'audience' implies listening rather than seeing! Nevertheless, the atmosphere in these crowded conditions for viewers and listeners alike was distinctly sordid and oppressive - there was no interval; ale was generously consumed throughout the performance; and yet no provision was ever made for the installation of a temporary privy. The consequences were most unpleasant. The plays were performed in broad daylight with props and furniture, but without scenery. However, in spite of all those disadvantages, the performances in Bath were hugely popular with the local community.

(iv) Musicians

Another type of travelling entertainer was **the minstrel** or musician, although such people were always regarded with suspicion by the Elizabethan government. Indeed, parliament had specifically included minstrels in an Act of 1572 against vagabonds, authorising local magistrates to punish them with a spell in the pillory, branding them with a 'V', whipping them until they were bloody or cutting off their ears. Nevertheless, some genuine musicians did manage to visit Bath during this period. Thomas Whythorne describes in his autobiography, written about 1576, what sort of service these men offered:

> There be persons who used to go with their instruments about the country to cities, towns and villages, where also they do go to private houses to such as will hear them either publicly or privately; or else to fairs, markets, marriages, assemblies, taverns, alehouses and such like places; and there, to those that will hear them, will sell the sound of their voices and instruments.

When a bagpipe player visited Bath in 1569, the corporation was so impressed that it presented him with a special cotton garment worth 8s 6d. Musicians were certainly on hand to provide additional entertainment in 1603, when a fencer, who 'did play with his sword' in celebration of the accession of James I, was also rewarded by the corporation - as were the Lord of Warwick's 'tumblers' (or acrobats), who performed in 1587, and 'the Queen's men that were tumblers' in 1589.

Musicians of a wholly more respectable kind, however, were officially employed by corporations up and down the country to add colour and dignity to important occasions. **The 'waits'**, who wore city livery, performed at official functions and were also available for outside hire by private individuals. For much of the Tudor and Stuart periods, the Mayor of Bath normally brought in the 'Waits of Bristol' for special ceremonies in the Guildhall - as in 1569, when he paid them 5s 0d for the visit of the Earl of Pembroke.

However, in a brief experiment between 1569 and 1581, the corporation actually recruited its own in-house team of waits - paying 32s 0d in 1569 'for liveries for the waits' and 18s 9d in 1572

Bagpipe players such as this travelled the country offering their services. Bath corporation was generous in its reward of one in 1569. A woodcut by permission of the British Library (Roxburghe Ballads, RAX.Rox.I, pt. 2, 349).

for making 'the musicians' coats'. One local man, who took out a new lease on his property in 1569, was actually styled on the document 'William the Wait'. The fate of the local waits, however, was sealed in 1581 when William Amie was paid 'for taking down the place where the waits did use to stand in the Guildhall'. They had clearly proved themselves to be too much of an expensive luxury. The corporation therefore quickly reverted to its old policy, paying 6s 8d in 1587 'to the Waits of Bristol for playing at my Lord of Warwick's coming'.

Nevertheless, music continued to play an important role in Bath throughout the century, particularly in the life of the church. By the sixteenth century around fifty monasteries supported their own choirs of men and boys. In 1524, for instance, the former Bath Priory had appointed William Cooper in 1524 as organist and choirmaster to assist the precentor in building on its tradition of choral music. His task was to play at all the services and teach boys (both novices and those who came in from outside) how to read music and sing in a choir. He was rewarded for his loyal service in 1537 when he was granted a corody, which provided him with free meals, clothing, fuel, candles and an annuity. This grant was converted into a life-long pension when the Priory was dissolved two years later.

With the establishment of Bath Abbey as the city's parish church in 1572, the musical tradition was revived - although it was thought wise just two years later to import choristers from Wells Cathedral to sing in honour of Queen Elizabeth's visit to the city (see Chapter 4). Nevertheless, young **choristers** were certainly in evidence in 1601, when the corporation paid men to escort 'certain pursuivants [officers of the College of Arms] that did take up boys for the Queen's Chapel - and for a horse to carry

Two musicians entertain a group of people outside a tavern. A woodcut by permission of the British Library (Roxburghe Ballads, RAX.Rox.I, 389).

one of the boys'. At first sight, this recruitment of local choristers to perform in the choir of the Queen's Chapel in London appears to have been a great privilege for the boys themselves and a great honour for the city. Nothing, however, could have been further from the truth!

By 1600, as Antonia Southern has shown, there were two choir schools in London - namely, St Paul's (under Edward Pierce, the master) and the Chapel Royal (with Henry Evans as the manager of the 'Chapel Children'). These men were authorised by royal warrant 'to take up such apt and meet children to be instructed and formed in the art and science of music and singing as may be had and found within any place in this our realm...Such children from churches, cathedrals and every other place or places *may be brought away without let or interruption*'. In other words, this system for recruitment amounted to a legalised form of press-gang - the parents, the children and the local rector having no say whatsoever in the matter.

It was, however, much worse than this. Both Pierce and Evans had established their own theatres in London, each with its own company of child actors. From 1600, both men set about 'taking up' boys ostensibly as choristers, but in reality as actors. Their agents therefore travelled the country in a grand recruitment campaign, often kidnapping the youngsters in a violent manner. Although these rough-house methods were clearly not employed in Bath, we do not know what actually happened to the boys concerned. What we do know, however, is that - after a sustained public outcry - the St Paul's company was closed down in 1606, followed by that of the Chapel Children two years later.

(v) Alehouses and Celebrities

For most people in Bath, life tended to be a somewhat monotonous existence, in spite of the occasional bursts of entertainment which have been described. Many people therefore whiled away their free time by resorting to one or other of the numerous **alehouses**, which lined the streets of the city. A description of the sordid conditions, which resulted from human excess, is given in the panel opposite. Binge-drinking, it would appear, is by no means a modern phenomenon - nor are health warnings over the consumption of tobacco! Smoking was in fact first recorded in England in 1573, although its initial scarcity ensured that it could only be afforded by the more affluent members of society.

One other source of colour in the lives of the local community came in the form

LIFE IN THE ALEHOUSE

Every country, city, town and village hath abundance of alehouses, taverns and inns, which are so haunted with maltworms night and day that you would wonder to see them. You shall have them there sitting at the wine and good ale all the day long; yea, and all the night too - peradventure a whole week together - so long as any money is left; swilling, gulling and carousing from one to another till never one can speak a ready word.

Then, with the spirit of the buttery they are thus possessed, a wonder it is to consider their gestures and demeanours; how they stut and stammer, stagger and reel to and fro like madmen: some vomiting, spewing and disgorging their filthy stomachs; other some pissing under the board as they sit, which is most horrible; some fall to swearing and cursing, interlacing their speeches with curious terms of blasphemy to the great dishonour of God and offence of the godly ears present.

Source: Philip Stubbes: *Anatomy of Abuses in England*, 1583 (1877-79 edtn., pt. 1, edited by Frederick J Furnivall)

In the alehouse, tobacco or a species of woundwort is also available for one's money. The powder is lit in a small pipe, the smoke sucked into the mouth, and the saliva is allowed to run freely; after which a good draught of Spanish wine follows. This they regard as a curious medicine for defluctions and as a pleasure. The habit is so common with them that they always carry the instrument on them and light up on all occasions - at the play, in taverns or elsewhere, drinking as well as smoking together, as we sit over the wine.

It makes them riotous and merry, and rather drowsy, just as if they were drunk, though the effect soon passes - and they use it so abundantly, because of the pleasure it gives, that their preachers cry out on them for their self-destruction. I am told that the inside of one man's veins after death was found to be covered in soot just like a chimney.

Taken from the experiences of Thomas Platter during his travels in England, 1599, in P. Razzell (ed.): *The Journals of Two Travellers in England in Elizabethan and Early Stuart Times* 1998).
Woodcut by permission of the British Library (Roxburghe Ballads, RAX.Rox.II, pt. 2, 376)

of **visiting celebrities**, some of whom came to the spa seeking a cure for their ailments. The corporation always took the opportunity to create something of a spectacle out of their arrival, greeting them in ceremonial robes at the North Gate and presenting them with gifts in keeping with their status. The gifts themselves make interesting reading as a revelation of what was considered luxurious at the time.

A great variety of different types of wine regularly featured on the lists, including claret, canary, madeira, gascon, malaga and rhenish. When the new Bishop of Bath and Wells (Bishop Thomas Godwin) arrived in 1584, however, he was presented with an ox; whereas his successor in 1593 - the distinguished preacher and scholar, Dr John Still - received three pounds of quinces 'bought from Bristol', a dozen pigeons, two capons, a sugar loaf, canary wine costing 22s 0d - plus a barrel to put it in! On the other hand, Sir Walter Raleigh, who visited Bath in 1587, 1589 and 1599, was on one occasion presented with a calf and a quantity of mutton; while the Earl of Warwick received two sheep, a calf and a lamb. At a lower end of the scale, the Earl of Pembroke was forced to be content with 'a box of marmalade'!

Public Health

(i) The Spread of Disease

Terror stalked the streets of Bath in 1597, when an alarming number of citizens were suddenly struck down by a fatal disease (almost certainly the plague). No fewer than 101 burials services were held at the three city churches, compared with an average of just 41 in the years between 1569 and 1603. Several families suffered agonising distress as the disease rampaged its way through the house - three members of the Brown family, for instance, in St Michael's parish died, three of the Pope household in St James's parish and three of the Norway family at the Abbey. St Michael's Church (with forty-five deaths) and St James's Church (with thirty-three) each recorded the highest number of burials for any one year during the thirty-five year period between 1569 and 1603 -

against an average of nine a year for the former and just over fourteen for the latter.

This was without doubt the worst human suffering experienced by the city during Queen Elizabeth's reign, although the year 1570 had already witnessed what proved to be the second highest total of burials

Disease was a constant fear for people living in Tudor towns, where pestilence could spread with alarming rapidity. This contemporary woodcut, with 'death' ringing the knell as he prepares to strike down a sick patient, was a solemn reminder of man's frailty. By permission of the British Library (Roxburghe Ballads, R.A.X.Rox.I, 93).

(sixty-one) with disease particularly prevalent in the parishes of St James and the Abbey. The two poorer parishes of St Michael *without* and St James, which lay in the overspill areas outside the city walls, inevitably suffered periodic epidemics of their own as disease spread rapidly through the more crowded housing conditions. In 1575, for instance, there were seventeen burials at St Michael's (its second highest total), when five members of the Clement household died and two individuals (John Riball and a servant of John Holmes) were hastily buried 'both in one pit'. Similarly, St James's Church buried twenty-four people in 1582 and twenty-seven in 1600 (almost twice the annual average) at a time when the other parishes were experiencing nothing abnormal.

The absence of documentary evidence - particularly eyewitness descriptions by visitors to the city or references to sickness in council minute books etc - makes it impossible to ascertain the exact cause of these sudden increases in the death rate. There were, however, several new diseases which caused havoc in towns and villages up and down the country throughout the Tudor period. **'Sweating sickness'**, for instance, which had suddenly appeared in 1485 and was to recur periodically, was particularly deadly in 1517, 1528 and 1555 (when 800 people died in London in one week). The disease, which caused its victims to sweat profusely, struck seemingly healthy citizens without warning, but at lightening speed. Doctors were powerless to act in the face of such new challenges for there had been little advance in medicine since the time of the Greeks. For the individual, therefore, there was no defence other than seclusion or flight. Many, including Thomas Whythorne in 1576, were fatalistic in their attitude, sensing that plagues were 'sent unto us from God for our sins'.

There was, of course, no shortage of theories. Erasmus, writing to Cardinal Wolsey's physician in 1517, expressed the opinion that sweating sickness could be eliminated through the demolition of the many old buildings, which suffered from poor ventilation - a situation compounded by the filth which lay hidden on the floors beneath:

> The floors are generally strewed with clay, and that covered with rushes which are now and then renewed, but so as not to disturb the foundation, which sometimes remains for twenty years, nursing a collection of spittle, vomits, excrements of dogs and human beings, spilt beer and fishes' bones, and other filth that I need not mention. From this, on any elevation of temperature, there is exhaled a vapour which, in my judgment, is by no means beneficial to the human constitution...
>
> I should have confidence in the island becoming more healthy if the use of rushes could be abolished, and the bedrooms built as to be open to the sky on two or three sides...The vulgar laugh if you complain of their cloudy sky: I can only say that for thirty years past, if I entered a room in which no one had been for some months, I would immediately begin to feel feverish...Then there might be policemen who should have the charge of seeing that the streets were kept free from filth; and they should also look after the neighbourhood of the city.

Other diseases, which rapidly emerged with devastating effect during the Tudor period, included smallpox, measles, typhus (a disease transmitted by lice), 'consumption' (i.e. tuberculosis) and 'agues' or 'fevers' (i.e. malaria). By far the most deadly sickness, however, was that brought about by the **bubonic plague**. This had been endemic in England since the time of the Black Death in 1349 with particularly severe outbreaks experienced in the years 1552, 1558, 1563, 1570, 1574, 1592/3 and

1603. Towns were especially vulnerable. Norwich, for instance, suffered six epidemics between 1579 and 1665, while Bristol lost a sixth of its population on three occasions between 1565 and 1603, including two thousand in the outbreak of 1597. The filthy streets and densely-packed houses of the large cities provided an ideal environment for the black rats on which the infection-bearing fleas bred.

Although bubonic plague was in itself a disease of rats, when the host rat died the infected fleas attacked humans (if another rat could not be found). The disease - indicated by swollen lymph glands (buboes) in the neck, groin and armpits, a high fever, delirium and red blotches all over the skin - was highly infectious. Bath by comparison remained largely immune from threats of this kind within the community. Its main problem was to ensure that a city, which actively encouraged visitors to flock in numbers to sample its healing waters, did not at the same time encourage the importation of plague.

Precautions, however, did not always work. Sir Thomas Seymour, for instance, admitted in 1605 that - as the plague had struck down two people in his house in London - he had forsaken the capital and was living in Bath. It is also interesting to note that, in the 1597 outbreak, almost one-third of those who died in St James's parish were not Bath residents at all, but were either visitors from other towns or simply described as 'strangers'. Sometimes potential visitors to the spa were warned in advance of the risk. In 1557, for instance, Richard Goodrich wrote to Sir William Cecil, advising him to delay his planned visit to Bath which was 'so near Bristol, where the pestilence rages'.

It is most probable that the increased death rate experienced in Bath in 1597 was in fact caused by a minor outbreak of this pestilence. Not only was Bath situated extremely close to the the plague-ridden city of Bristol, the corporation had already shown itself alive to the threat posed by infected visitors. In March 1583, for instance, it had rewarded two watchmen, Oliver and Green, 'for seeing that none should come into the city from Paulton and other places which were infected with the plague'. An even worse outbreak, however, was to occur in Bath in 1604 - immediately after the close of the Tudor period - when seventy-two people are thought to have died from the plague in just four months. Twenty-four houses in all were infected. Victims included eight people each from the homes of Goodwife Moore and John Adye; eight from *The Swan Inn*; five from the home of Dr Richard Bailey; and four from Walter Missam's house.

Furthermore, eight sick people, who had been 'carried from the town' into isolation, died in the specially-built 'pest houses' on Bath Common. Local authorities had been empowered to tackle the spread of such outbreaks through a series of plague orders issued by the privy council from 1518. Parish or town constables were therefore instructed, during periods when the disease was rampant, to count and report daily the number of dead; shut up and mark all infected houses with a blue cross; and arrest beggars, who were always perceived to be carriers. The orders of 1563 stipulated that each infected house was to remain closed for at least forty days with the inhabitants inside, although food was usually purchased for them by a team of volunteers.

(ii) Street Cleanliness

In his letter to Cardinal Wolsey's physician in 1517, Erasmus had highlighted the need to ensure that 'the streets were kept free from filth'. However, although there was a growing awareness in some circles of the importance of **street cleanliness**, little was done in Bath to tackle the problem of accumulated filth until well into the seventeenth century. Even by the end of the Tudor period, the condition of the highways was appalling. Foul-smelling rubbish accumulated on every footpath to rot away slowly in the still and humid air of Bath. The open channel or culvert, which ran down the centre of the main streets, was often blocked by ashes, rubble and other unpleasant debris, while horses, cattle and other animals (often on their way to market) left behind them a trail of manure and urine.

Although the city's revised charter of 1590 had given the corporation powers to make by-laws over such matters as street cleaning, it was not until 1646 that these were taken up. Meanwhile, the council limited its action to crisis management, employing casual labour on an irregular basis to clear up any particular eyesores or to repair badly-rutted sections of the road. Consequently, the chamberlain made payments in 1587 'for cleansing the town wall between the West Gate and the tower' (i.e Gascoyne's Tower); in 1588 'for mending the way at Walcot'; and in 1601 (when rumours of a visit by the queen were rife) for substantial new paving in High Street and Westgate Street.

(iii) Sanitation, Water Supply and Fire

Sanitary arrangements were primitive in the extreme. Few people had privies inside the house or even cesspits in the garden outside. Most were therefore forced to rely on chamber pots, the contents of which were emptied by servants into the drainage channel in the street outside (there to be churned up by passing traffic), flung into the river or thrown over the city wall. Rubbish accumulated on unpleasant dumps (or 'mixons') just outside the gates of the city, providing a particularly unpleasant welcome for visitors arriving at the health resort! The council occasionally stirred itself to deal with such unwanted sights, as in 1575 when William Chapman was paid 2s 4d for his work on 'the place where the dung is laid'.

The result of this lax approach - combined with the problems arising from animal droppings and the mess created by butchers who slaughtered their beasts outside their shops - was an obnoxious stench (aggravated by high levels of humidity) and a polluted river. On the credit side, the council had built 'a common privy' or public toilet in 1575, paying a labourer for 'digging a dyke'(or ditch), constructing a timber frame for the building and tiling the roof. Examples of these public privies found elsewhere suggest that they usually consisted of an oak bench with a row of holes (but with no partitions in between) and a pit below.

Nevertheless, Bath had one vital asset which helped to protect its citizens from the terrible hazards to health which affected most cities at the time - an abundant supply of **fresh water**. Even as early as 1530 John Leland had noticed on a visit that Bath 'is environed on every side with great hills, out of the which come many springs of pure water, that be conveyed by divers ways to serve the city. Insomuch that, lead being made there at hand [i.e. on the Mendips], many houses in the town have pipes of lead to convey water from place to place'. This remarkable situation meant that Bath was never in fact obliged to rely on the polluted waters of the Avon and thus was able to maintain its reputation as a healthy place.

The city drew its water from two springs - the 'upper water' on Beacon Hill, drawn from St Swithin's Well; and the 'lower water' on Beechen Cliff. The water was carried down into the city by a variety of underground lead, stone or wood pipes. People who could not afford the luxury of their own piped supply were able to obtain fresh drinking water from several conduits or fountains erected at points around the city, often decorated with elegant stonework - St Mary's Conduit in the middle of the High Street, just inside the North Gate: the High Cross Conduit, near the Market Hall; Stall's Conduit on Bear Corner at the junction of Cheap Street and Stall Street; St James's Conduit, just outside the South Gate; St Michael's Conduit, just outside the North Gate; Broad Street Conduit in the middle of that street; and Carnwell Conduit in Walcot Street.

Realising the vital importance of ensuring a constant supply of clean water, the council lavished unstinting care on its network of pipes. In 1569, for instance, it paid for a quantity of ' cloth, resin, pitch, tallow and cords' to mend the pipes in Walcot Lane; while in 1575, it spent the considerable sum of £3 10s 3d on a major refurbishment of the conduits. It soon realised the sense of appointing one man to be responsible for checking the system on a regular basis. William Collins, therefore, was paid 3s 4d in 1569 'for keeping the water'.

By 1587, however, it had nominated two men - Hugh Hill and William Forte - to be totally responsible for supervising the pipes along each of the two main supply routes into the city and undertaking repairs as necessary. At first they received somewhat random payments 'for fetching home the water' (3s 4d) or 'for mending a leak on the bridge' (3s 2d). By 1588, however, they were each being paid a regular fee of 13s 4d 'for keeping the water'. They were assisted from time to time by various local workmen, including the bellman of the city who was paid on numerous occasions 'for his pains about the water'.

One other threat to health and safety was the serious **risk of fire** at a time when many of the houses were largely constructed of wood and thatched with straw. Fire-fighting methods, however, were basic in the extreme (the first fire engine or 'water machine' did not make its appearance in Bath until 1694). When disaster struck therefore, the council relied on volunteers to lend a hand by using firehooks to pull down burning timbers; a chain of fire buckets via ladders to extinguish the flames; and ropes to rescue trapped individuals from upper floor rooms. It did its best to ensure that stocks of these essential items were regularly replenished. In 1569, for instance, it paid Bird 2s 0d for mending 'the town crooks'; Chandler 8s 0d for supplying eight additional crooks for the new Market House; and Stybbes 2s 0d 'for the carriage of buckets'. These copper-riveted leather buckets were only manufactured in London - hence the need of a carrier to transport them to Bath.

Local Government: The New Royal Charter, 1590

(i) The Corporation and its Guildhall

The new charter, granted to the city by Queen Elizabeth I in 1590, confirmed for the first time in writing - what in reality had been true for several years - that the mayor and corporation had taken over the powers originally exercised by the bishop and the prior (see Chapter 1). As we have already seen, the men who made up the local council were tough businessmen who, following the dissolution of Bath Priory in 1539, had systematically and ruthlessly extended these powers by seizing control of most of the city's property. To all this newly-acquired authority, the charter of 1590 added total direction of law and order by granting the corporation, for the first time, the right to appoint a coroner and two justices of the peace. Furthermore, the bounds of the city

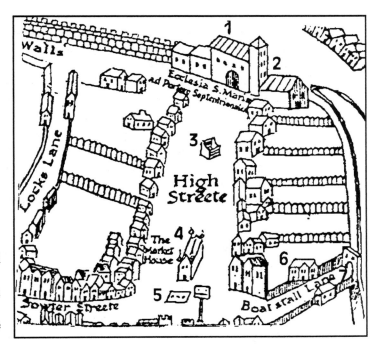

were extended beyond the walls to
include Barton Farm to the north-west
and a large part of Walcot parish, thus
providing space for future expansion.
The year 1590 was therefore a turning
point which launched a gradual
transformation of medieval Bath, a
somewhat stagnant city, into a
bustling new health resort.

The charter conferred the
government of the city on **a 'body
corporate'** consisting of a mayor (who was elected annually and received a stipend of
£16 12s 0d), between four and ten aldermen and up to twenty common councillors. The
new corporation was granted the right to possess a common seal and to elect new
members onto the council for life from among the ranks of the freemen of the city - a
status which could be gained in Bath either by servitude (i.e. serving a seven-year
apprenticeship under a resident freeman of the city) or by purchase (i.e. paying a sum of
not less than five pounds into the coffers of the corporation).

Aldermen and common councillors therefore sat together as a self-perpetuating
oligarchy at meetings of the common council with no great discrimination between
them - but with the vast majority of freemen excluded from all say in elections and
government. Once elected, members of the corporation were obliged to attend all
meetings, except in the case of sickness. Failure to do so would result in an automatic
fine - as William Cocks found to his cost in 1579, when he was fined 3s 4d 'for his
absence at the hall upon an accustomed date'.

The hub of the city's government and the symbol of its authority was the
Guildhall - so called because in medieval times it was the meeting place of the
powerful trade guilds, which had largely declined by the end of the sixteenth century.
Elizabeth Holland has demonstrated that the medieval Guildhall (first mentioned in a
document of 1355 and still in use during the Tudor period) was situated immediately
behind the modern building with access gained from the High Street via a narrow
passage. After improvements made during Queen Elizabeth's reign, visitors could admire
a timber-framed construction with white-washed plaster on its exterior, a tiled roof,
glazed casement windows (including one bay) and a stone floor, which was usually strewn
with rushes.

A meeting hall on the ground floor, with an adjacent kitchen and pantry, was used
for banquets - the mayor sitting on high table, which was set on a dais and covered
(from 1597, at least) with three yards of green carpet. Other improvements included
the installation of oak wainscoting, the provision of cushions to make the bench seating

more comfortable, the erection of the Queen's arms and the construction of a lockable chest for the storage of documents (although, after the loss of the key in 1601, Nicholas Pitcher was paid for breaking open the lock and fitting a replacement!). Quite apart from the meeting hall, the building housed several areas which related directly to the work of the council - including the council chamber itself and the armoury on the first floor (reached by a flight of stairs lit by a lantern); and a bailiffs' court (newly created in 1583).

(ii) The Officials

The corporation, which had the power to return two **'burgesses'** (i.e. MPs) to parliament, was assisted in its routine work by various officials - a chamberlain (who was paid a stipend of £4 0s 0d in 1590), a recorder or legal adviser (£2 0s 0d), a town clerk (£2 0s 0d), two constables, two justices, two bailiffs and two sergeants-at-mace (£1 0s 0d). Apart from the recorder and town clerk, these officers were normally drawn from the members of the council on the basis of one year's spell of duty. Refusal to take office could mean a fine or even imprisonment. The burgesses also received payments from the chamberlain (described as 'burgess money' in the accounts) to cover their expenses while attending parliament. In 1601, for instance, Mr Heath and Mr Sherstone were each granted a sum of £6 6s 0d, representing an allowance of two shillings a day for a period of nine weeks.

The officers of the council played a vital - an often arduous - role in running the city's affairs. The **town clerk**, an attorney by profession, gave legal advice to the corporation. He was also keeper of the city's records, deputy recorder, minuting secretary at council meetings, clerk of the peace and deputy coroner. It was his task to draft documents and petitions, serve writs, attend the county assizes and lobby the government on behalf of the city.

The **recorder**, who was also a person 'learned in the law', was responsible for administering the oath of office to the mayor, presiding at the city's court of Quarter Sessions and sitting as judge at the Court of Record. Although he usually spent much of his time in London (often, in fact, as one of the city's MPs), he was always accorded a warm, official welcome whenever he visited Bath. In 1598, for instance, the corporation accommodated him at the Hart Inn, paying the bill for 'his diet' (8s 6d) and ensuring that his horses were well fed and re-shoed (£1 1s 4d). It was also quite normal for a gift of wine and sugar to be presented.

The two **bailiffs**, who had normally acted as unpaid constables in the previous year, now enjoyed a highly lucrative position - for, in addition to their overall responsibility for controlling the gaol and exercising writs, they were also given the profitable task of managing the markets and fairs. In return for a rent paid to the corporation, they were able to hire out the stalls inside the market for personal profit and charge dues to those country traders who came in with baskets of produce. Their other duties included the task of transporting prisoners to gaol and attending various courts within the city.

The **chamberlain** was the treasurer of the corporation, whose task it was to collect the rents of corporation property, the fines imposed for the renewal of leases and the fee charged whenever a freedom was granted; to pay stipends and wages, settle bills and disburse gifts to distinguished visitors; and to keep detailed and accurate accounts. The most public duty of the two **sergeants-at-mace** was to carry the city's 'maces of gold or silver' before the mayor on ceremonial occasions - maces which had been authorised for the first time by the charter of 1590. In addition, they acted as 'court attorneys' at the Court of Record. Although not trained in law, they were always on hand to offer assistance to both sides in any case (and to receive any resulting fees!).

(iii) The Courts of Law

Under the terms of the charter, the mayor, the recorder and the two justices had the power not only to apprehend felons, thieves and malefactors, but also to make local laws and enforce them through the imposition of fines. They were therefore responsible for the running of several courts within the borough. An ancient medieval court - the **Court Leet** - was held twice a year on the 'Law Days' before the town clerk to investigate such matters as encroachment of property, illegal fences, water supplies, petty larcenies and the use of false weights and measures. After the court had finished its business, a Law Day Dinner was held - traditionally at the chamberlain's expense - for those freemen who had served on the jury. Once the court had met, it was the task of the corporation to collect any fines imposed. In 1596-97, for instance, it gathered in a range of fines for such offences as 'brewing without a licence', 'dressing flesh in Lent' and 'selling ale without a licence' - not to mention the stranger who was fined 3s 4d 'for a bloodshed' or Thomas Welsh who was charged the same amount in 1569 'for abusing Richard Jones'.

The **Court of Quarter Sessions** met four times a year under the presidency of the recorder, aided on the bench by the mayor, the town clerk and the two justices - and assisted by two local juries (a Grand Jury, which decided whether or not there was a case to answer, and a Petty Jury to determine guilt). The court dealt with such matters as the licensing of alehouses, common assault, the maintenance of bastard children, problems

A meeting of the Court of Record, presided over by the mayor, to hear a personal dispute over such matters as trespass or property. The plaintiff, who pleads for redress of his grievance, is shown on his knees; while the defendant is shown standing and in the process of being rebuked by the mayor. A contemporary woodcut. (Author's collection)

over apprenticeships and illegal trading within the city. The **Court of Record** met every Monday throughout the year before the mayor, the recorder, the two justices and the town clerk to hear personal suits arising in the borough over matters of debt, contract, trespass and property. A jury was sworn in to hear such cases. The **Court of Pie Powder** met under a bailiff to try offenders (such as pickpockets) during times of the ancient city fairs.

Although many matters were therefore tried by courts within the city, the corporation was under obligation to refer all serious cases of felony (including murder, larceny, rape and burglary) to the **County Assizes**, which met twice yearly in Taunton, Chard, Wells or Bridgwater. Prisoners from Bath were escorted to one of the county gaols by the bailiffs and their officers to await trial - and the bailiffs were then able to relay back to the corporation any new assize orders, issued on government instructions, in relation to such matters as the implementation of the poor law by local magistrates. Bathonians certainly did find themselves at the mercy of these courts. In 1600-01, for instance, the bailiffs escorted 'a prisoner to gaol that counterfeited passports' [.ie. special licences to travel in England]; arranged a writ and an arrest warrant against Thomas Phelps; organised action against Dytcher for fraudulent conduct over 'Mother Humphreys's money'; and conducted witnesses to give evidence against Everett.

Serious offenders, of course, could well find themselves imprisoned in the Tower of London - as did David Glover of Bath in November 1552 for making 'lewd prophecies'. Nevertheless, according to instructions received by the Mayor of Bath from the privy council a few weeks after he was confined, Glover was clearly treated with more than a degree of leniency. The mayor was therefore required to deliver to London as much of the prisoner's own personal property as he should request in his letter 'for his relief during his imprisonment'. William Garland, a yeoman from Bath, was probably even more relieved in 1562 when he received a royal pardon, in spite of the fact that he had been indicted for murder following an 'inquisition' in Bath. Although he had killed David Hugh in Lyncombe after a violent argument a year earlier, the crown accepted that it was done in self defence.

(iv) Maintaining Law and Order

Before the days of professional police forces, the corporation was also directly responsible for the security of the city, its buildings and its inhabitants. Supervising the operation were two **constables**, whose task it was to organise the small team of minor peace-keeping officials - namely, the bellman and the local parish constables. Working closely with the magistrates, these two officers had overall responsibility for apprehending criminals, dealing with beggars and containing public disturbances. They carried painted staves of office and, although unsalaried, had expectations of election to the profitable office of bailiff in the following year (see above).

The gates were locked at night and the streets patrolled between dawn and dusk by a **bellman** [later, by the seventeenth century, accompanied by two watchmen], who was required to call out the time and raise the alarm on sight of either fire or felon. Although he was also expected 'to attend Mr Mayor in the Guildhall', as and when required, his annual stipend only amounted to ten shillings in 1587. Nevertheless, Nicholas Baker (who was bellman in 1598) was able to supplement his income by working for the council in other ways, including work on the network of water pipes and repairs undertaken at both the King's Bath and the almshouses. He was provided with a distinctive coat, which had a smart red lining.

Suspected felons and drunkards, who were arrested during the night, were usually secured in the small wooden 'cage' or lockup, which stood near the North Gate. A new one was constructed in 1580 and thereafter maintained in good condition. Its frequent use to contain the rowdy youth of the city is illustrated by the fact that major repairs were required in 1593, 1596 and 1601. There was also a **dungeon** in the basement of the North Gate, which could be used for detaining people on a temporary basis. Its door was repaired by the corporation in 1600 - a clear indication that it was still in active use.

Convicted criminals or debtors would be housed in the city prison, which was situated in the tower of the disused church of St Mary just inside the North Gate; while those convicted of other offences would be put into the stocks, the pillory or the ducking stool. The **gaoler**, a private contractor, was appointed by the bailiffs to keep the prison clean, detain prisoners in secure but humane conditions, supervise visits by friends and respond to the orders of the courts. Although he received no salary, he could make a living by charging prisoners authorised fees on both their admission and their release - as well as by accepting tips for special privileges granted.

The bellman with his lantern on patrol at night. His companion is carrying a ladder for use in the case of fire. Line drawing by Mark Withers.

The city **pillory** and city **stocks** both stood outside the Guildhall and are clearly shown on John Speed's map of Bath published in 1610. They were kept in constant repair throughout the century (a new pillory was constructed in 1579) and were used, according to the law, for the punishment of certain prescribed offences, including sex crimes. A second stocks - which was repaired in 1588 - stood 'by the bathside' of the King's Bath for the punishment of those guilty of improper behaviour. The **ducking or cucking stool**, which stood permanently by the river at the end of Boatstall Lane, was employed to humiliate 'scolds' (i.e. unruly women or unfaithful wives) by giving them a good ducking in the water. The culprit was fastened by six iron loops into an arm chair, which was suspended from long wooden beam and then lowered into the water. The device was maintained in good condition by the corporation and was subjected to an important adjustment in 1581, when the chamberlain paid a carpenter for 'cutting the cucking stool shorter'.

(v) Control of the Market

Under the terms of the 1590 charter, the Mayor of Bath was designated as both the coroner and the **clerk-of-the-market**, which was held twice a week on Wednesday and Saturday (although much of the active, daily control had been delegated to the bailiffs, and the supervisors of fish, flesh and leather). An important task was to ensure that quality was always maintained in all foodstuffs and that customers were not cheated through the use of false measures. Authorised brass weights were therefore regularly obtained from London. In 1573, for instance, the city chamberlain purchased 57lbs of weights, four brass measures and a number of special weights 'to weigh bread'; while in 1588, when a new set of weights was bought, Nicholas Pitcher was paid for making some 'iron letters to mark and size the weights'. Offenders were firmly punished for fraudulent practice. No fewer than seven people, for instance, were fined in 1597 for 'engrossing up butter and cheese'.

The new charter also gave the mayor the right to hold an **Assize of Bread** whenever it was deemed necessary. Although in Bath the price of each type of loaf remained constant, the Assize of Bread enabled the mayor to adjust its weight according to the prevailing price of corn in the Bristol market. The revised, authorised weight of each type of bread was then announced to the bakers, and spot-checks were undertaken to ensure that loaves were not sold underweight.

From medieval times, the twice-weekly market had been held in the large open area at the southern end of the High Street on a site marked by a High Cross - a traditional practice in most towns and cities of the period. The cross itself, carved in stone, was usually no more than a small ornament crowning an impressive open-sided structure, which provided a shelter from the rain. The fact that eleven loads of stones were carried away on its demolition by the corporation in 1573 is an indication that it had been a substantial structure. In about 1552, a more permanent home was established through the building of a **market house**, which stood in the middle of the street (see map). A clue to the dating of this is provided by an entry in the churchwardens'

New Fish Street, London - the site of a flourishing fish market in Tudor times. In this busy street scene, women can be seen carrying their shopping, including items bought from the fish stalls which have been set up outside the houses. A fish market also existed in Bath with stalls erected around the Market House. From Hugh Alley's Caveat for the City of London, *1598.*
By permission of the Folger Shakespeare Library.

accounts for St Michael's Church: (1551-52) '40s. 0d given by the consent of the parish towards the building of the market house'.

This consisted of a two-storey construction (probably timber-framed) with a tiled, pitched roof. We know from the chamberlain's accounts (which are only available in Bath from 1569) that improvements to the building continued to be made for the remainder of the Tudor period. A good deal of re-tiling, for instance, was undertaken in 1569; the windows were glazed by Mr Forte in 1573; and a substantial refurbishment took place in 1601, including the provision of new lead gutters and a new casement window. Market stalls were rented out to traders - including 'Green the pewterer' in 1587 and no fewer than five butchers in 1588 - at sums ranging from 1s 4d to 5s 0d.

This nineteenth-century line drawing of the High Cross at Malmesbury gives a good idea of what the High Cross in Bath would have been like - a substantial stone structure with a small crowning ornament to represent the cross. This was the focal point for the twice-weekly market. From M.R. James: Abbeys, *1925. (Author's collection)*

(vi) Methods of Communication

One of the important tasks faced by the corporation was the need to maintain communication in London with the government and the city's own members of parliament - and in Somerset with the bishop and the lord lieutenant. Although some instructions from the monarch to local authorities were relayed via the bailiffs at the county assizes, more pressing matters were brought to the mayor's attention by royal pursuivants in the form of **proclamations**. These related to a whole range of matters, including the wearing of excess apparel (1580), the carrying of daggers (1580), the suppressing of guns and crossbows (1601), the transportation of money to Ireland (1601), the suppression of rogues (1594), the seditious rumours and words uttered against Her Majesty (1581), the treasonable activities of the Earl of Essex (1601), shipping and piracy (1602), the Jesuits (1588), the price of wine (1580), vagrant soldiers (1590) and the sowing of woad (1594).

Although the first postal service for general use was not established by royal proclamation until 1635, a system for the delivery of royal messages was first established in the sixteenth century. This was based on a network of 'postmasters' throughout the country, who were normally innkeepers based at appropriate distances along the main routes. Having paid a fee of £20 to gain the appointment, the postmasters were granted the monopoly of both providing royal messengers with fresh horses for the next stage of their journey and hiring out horses for independent travellers. The term 'riding post' therefore meant fast travel by means of a relay system of hired horses - whether or not letters were being carried. Royal correspondence was actually carried in a leather bag known as a 'maile' - from the French word *malle* - hence the expression **royal mail**.

By 1574, official communications from the queen or her ministers to the Corporation of Bath (or vice versa) travelled from London along 'the Bristol Road' via Marlborough, Chippenham and Marshfield, where letters for local delivery were unloaded. In view of the fact that Bath was not a 'stage' along the route, the postmaster in Marshfield was responsible for sending a messenger on foot (known as a 'footpost') with the delivery to Bath - a journey which could take up to three hours.

  The corporation itself, of course, also needed to send messages and documents to other people by reliable means, which usually meant employing **private messengers** to travel on horse or foot. Footposts were often far more reliable than other methods of communication. A fit man, using a combination of walking and running over a long distance across rough ground, could often beat a horse, whose speed and stamina would badly flag as the miles increased. It is a fact that Thomas Lynne, the Bristol footpost in Elizabeth's reign, carried letters to London and back for fifteen shillings, averaging thirty miles a day - twice the speed of an ordinary goods carrier.

  In 1587/88, when the corporation bought in a new stock of 'red wax', paper and 'points' [or quill pens] for use in its official correspondence, it paid John Macey 'for carrying a letter to answer Mr Attorney'; Thomas Gregory 'for carrying a letter to Mr Ashe [the city's recorder]'; and Anthony Cavell 'for carrying the subsidy books to the Lord Bishop and to Sir John Horner [the county sheriff]'. On other occasions, horse riders were used to convey messages in 1569 to such places as Bridgwater, Ilchester, Chew, Mells or London.

  Quite apart from submitting tax returns for the city, the corporation was also caught up in an increasing amount of **bureaucracy**, which resulted from various pieces of legislation during Queen Elizabeth's reign. For instance, the mayor was regularly required to submit certificates to the government concerning the observance of Lent. In the same way, following the Statute of Artificers in 1563, the mayor and justices were required to fix annually the standard wage for each occupation according to local conditions and prices - and then to submit details to the chancery in London. In 1580, therefore, the city chamberlain spent 2s 6d 'for making the certificate for flesh' and 2s 0d for a similar certificate 'for labourers' wages'.

(vii) Management of Corporation Property

By the end of the sixteenth century, the corporation was responsible for something like four-fifths of the property in Bath, either as the owner of the freehold in its own right or as trustee for the lands belonging to St John's Hospital, the property contained in the endowment of King Edward's School or the assets previously attached to the city's churches. Furthermore, the new charter granted the corporation for the first time the right to purchase additional lands under the yearly value in rent of twenty pounds. One of its most important tasks, therefore, centred on the management of property, including the granting of leases and the collection of rents. Normally a lease would be granted for a maximum of three lives (i.e. the lifetimes of three named individuals in the contract - with a ceiling of 99 years, 'if the lives live so long').

  The tenant, having paid a 'fine' or fee for the lease, together with the clerical costs of the 'seal' on the contract, would then be expected to pay no more than a modest annual rent. In 1598, for instance, there were eleven fines paid for leases ranging from two pounds to twenty pounds, although it was possible for the less affluent to pay in instalments (Thomas Howell paying 'part of his fine', which amounted to £4

10s 0d). Seals cost a standard charge of 6s 8d. The tenant, however, would also be expected to pay a further fine whenever an amendment was made to the original lease. For instance, when the first named 'life' in the lease died and the second one succeeded to the property, a 'heriot' was paid - as Widow Ireland did in 1589 at a cost of four shillings. In the same year William Quayle was charged 6s 8d for 'altering a name in his lease'. It was even more expensive, however, to make substantial changes to the actual nature a lease, Richard Bowden paying twenty pounds in 1601 for the privilege.

(viii) Finance

The Bath chamberlain's accounts show clearly the main sources of **income**. In 1601/02, for instance, £112 18s 0d was raised from annual rents for the corporation's property - an increase from the £101 7s 11d collected in 1572/73, reflecting no doubt the additional property acquired by the corporation during the intervening years; and £300 7s 8d from 'casual receipts', which mostly consisted of fines or fees for the granting of freedoms and the renewal or amendment of leases. This sum also included the sale of unwanted materials - in 1569, for instance, 'candles left at the Guildhall', 'an old chimney', 'a plank', 'an iron bar', 'old boards and rafters' and 'eighteen vessels', not to mention 'the hire of a dozen vessels to Swainswick'; in 1587, 'the brazen cock that was in the conduit at the end of the market house; and in 1601, 'the 193 pounds weight of lead which was at the gutter over the kitchen by the hall'.

The casual receipts also included payments made for the cost of a certificate and seal when an apprentice qualified to become a freeman. In 1569, for instance, nine freedoms were granted, costing the recipients fees ranging between 3s 4d and 20s 0d. The sum could, however, be paid in instalments, William Emery settling his debt by paying 6s 8d 'for the rest of his freedom'. Sometimes the guild itself would pay part or all of an impoverished apprentice's fee. Thus in 1573 Robert Stephens and James Stowell, 'masters of the occupation of tailors' paid ten shillings towards Robert Storey's freedom; while William Stephens and Nicholas Salter, 'masters of the occupation of shoemakers', paid the whole twenty shillings for Thomas Levett. By 1573, in addition to the shoemakers and tailors, there were in Bath companies of clothiers, weavers, carpenters, cordwainers, tilers, bakers, barbers, grocers and drapers.

Once elected, the new freeman qualified for a number of privileges. These traditionally included the exclusive right to open shops inside the city; an invitation to attend the annual merrymaking on the Wednesday in Whitsun week, when the corporation provided beer, bread and cheese in the Guildhall; and the right to graze their animals on the common land (see Chapter 1). In 1570, however, the corporation had taken a controversial decision by agreeing to forfeit the freemen's right of common on the enclosed grounds of the Barton estate to Peter Bewshin (the sub-tenant of the Barton) in return for an annual rent of forty shillings. [Their right to graze animals at specified times on both Kingsmead meadow and the open field stubble after harvest was unaffected by this agreement.]

The decision, however, was to cause an increasing amount of ill feeling among the majority of the freemen (who, of course, were not members of the corporation). In particular, they were aggrieved that the rental went straight into the corporation's coffers without regard to their individual rights of common and that their traditional area for grazing had been substantially reduced. In 1591, a group of citizens brought a suit to the court of chancery against one particular alderman 'for taking from them the

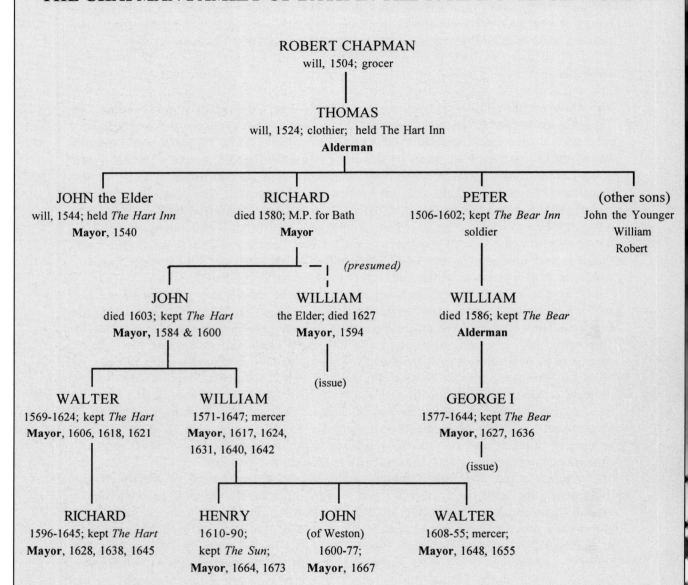

THE CHAPMAN FAMILY OF BATH IN THE 16TH & 17TH CENTURIES

ROBERT CHAPMAN
will, 1504; grocer

THOMAS
will, 1524; clothier; held The Hart Inn
Alderman

JOHN the Elder
will, 1544; held *The Hart Inn*
Mayor, 1540

RICHARD
died 1580; M.P. for Bath
Mayor

PETER
1506-1602; kept *The Bear Inn*
soldier

(other sons)
John the Younger
William
Robert

(presumed)

JOHN
died 1603; kept *The Hart*
Mayor, 1584 & 1600

WILLIAM
the Elder; died 1627
Mayor, 1594

WILLIAM
died 1586; kept *The Bear*
Alderman

(issue)

WALTER
1569-1624; kept *The Hart*
Mayor, 1606, 1618, 1621

WILLIAM
1571-1647; mercer
Mayor, 1617, 1624,
1631, 1640, 1642

GEORGE I
1577-1644; kept *The Bear*
Mayor, 1627, 1636

(issue)

RICHARD
1596-1645; kept *The Hart*
Mayor, 1628, 1638, 1645

HENRY
1610-90;
kept *The Sun*;
Mayor, 1664, 1673

JOHN
(of Weston)
1600-77;
Mayor, 1667

WALTER
1608-55; mercer;
Mayor, 1648, 1655

A small section of the Chapman Genealogy, researched and compiled by Elizabeth Holland, which demonstrates the powerful influence of this family on Bath Corporation throughout the Tudor and Stuart periods. It also helps to explain the continuity of the council's policy as son succeeded father in membership of that body.

most part of their common and converting the same to his private use'. Disputes like this rumbled on until 1619, when a judgment was made setting aside a hundred acres of the West Field for the exclusive use of the freemen in lieu of their general rights of common. This area, which now consists of Victoria Park and the approach golf course, became known as Bath Common (see John Wroughton: *Stuart Bath* for details of subsequent developments in the seventeenth century).

The **expenditure** of the corporation was made up of 'stipends and out rents' (which included the salaries and wages paid to the corporation's officials, including the school master; the annual distributions to the poor at Christmas and Lent; and a rent of £10 paid to the monarch for the school's endowment property); 'gifts and rewards' (which covered the entertainment of visiting judges etc and the presentation of wine and sugar made to important dignitaries); and 'general payments' (which consisted of bills for fabric repairs, work on the roads, gifts to individual paupers, the mending of water pipes, travel expenses for council officers, improvements to the baths, additions to the armoury etc).

During the twenty years between 1569 and 1589, the corporation usually managed to show a small credit balance or a small deficit in its accounts - although the latter was much heavier in 1569, when a new row of houses was being built; in 1580-81, when major repairs were undertaken on the water supply; and in 1587, when many rents remained unpaid. By 1590, however, the corporation's finances were in a much stronger position with increased revenue and a comfortable annual surplus being regularly recorded.

Life in the Health Resort: the Transformation of the Spa

> Allured by the fame of its beauty and for the sake of health, many persons resort to this city and so much are they struck with its grandeur, it elegance and its beauty...Add to this the perennial flow of heated springs marvellously supplied for the benefit of man...What can be more wonderful or blessed than this provision by which all men, high and low, rich and poor, receive cure for all their maladies.
>
> Thomas Chaundler: *Libellus de Laudibus Civitatum* (1452)

(i) The Baths in the Early Sixteenth Century

There is little doubt that the city's hot water baths were known and admired throughout the medieval period. An Italian, who visited Bath some years after Chaundler had penned that glowing description, wrote home to praise the healing properties of those 'springs of hot water' which were 'wholesome and salutary for various disorders'. Polydore Vergil (the archdeacon of Wells, who had been commissioned by Henry VII to write the History of England) admired the baths 'whose waters bubble and boil in a warm place'; where local boys not only swim for pleasure, but also for profit 'bringing up with their teeth silver coins thrown in for fun by onlookers'. John Leland, who twice visited the city during the 1530s and 1540s, gave a detailed description of the three main baths - the Cross Bath, the Hot Bath and the King's Bath - which 'were much frequented', he said, 'of people diseased with leprosy, pox, scabs and great aches'.

By the early sixteenth century, therefore, the baths were undoubtedly used by people living in the vicinity of Bath and by casual visitors to the city. Nevertheless, as Peter Davenport has shown, there is no evidence to suggest that the Priory had been exploiting the spa either from a commercial angle (by advertising its health benefits) or from a religious point of view (by claiming miraculous cures for bathers). The monks, of course, were perfectly happy to enjoy the waters themselves, for it is highly probable that there were two baths (known as the Prior's Bath and the Abbot's Bath) within the Priory complex, fed by water piped into the precinct.

They did little, however, to promulgate its virtue far and wide. Indeed, although Dr William Turner had 'heard tell' of 'a natural bath' within the city, it was not until his appointment as Dean of Wells in 1550 that he was able to discover for himself that the waters were 'a very excellent treasure, but unworthily esteemed and judged of all'. Their very existence, he wrote, was virtually unknown by diseased people living in the northern and eastern parts of England - thanks to the envy or ignorance of their physicians. Turner therefore immediately set about the task of rectifying the situation by promoting the spa with enormous energy and commitment (see below).

(ii) The Sudden Growth in Demand

It was not really until the reign of Queen Elizabeth I (1559-1603) that the city's baths were developed on a more commercial basis. Several factors combined to make this possible. There was, in the first place, a sudden interest in health benefits to be gained from visiting hot water springs. Numerous writers and physicians began to extol the merits of these spas in general and Bath in particular, including Dr Turner, 'the father of English physic', who wrote *A Book of the Nature and Properties...of the Baths in England* in 1568 and an enlarged version *The Baths of Bath in England* in 1568; John Jones, physician, who published *The Bathes of Bathe Ayde* in 1572; and William Smith, traveller, whose *Description of England* in 1558 listed the city's baths as one of the seven wonders of England.

These men were writing just at the very moment when society was becoming more civilised and members of the upper classes were looking for new leisure pursuits. Their search was aided by Queen Elizabeth, who - anxious to retain the goodwill of English Catholics in the face of an ever-increasing threat of Spanish invasion - relaxed the prohibition that Henry VIII had imposed on holy wells (fearing, as he did, that these

This contemporary print, entitled Street Cries, *illustrates more of the ordinary basket traders and workers who would have been a familiar sight around the markets and streets of Bath in Tudor times. By courtesy of the Pepys Library, Magdalene College, Cambridge.*

merely encouraged superstitious beliefs in miraculous cures). Members of the Catholic nobility, who had therefore been forced to visit continental spas during the period of the ban, readily seized the chance to explore those in England. This process was speeded up by the fact that wars were now raging on the continent, which made visits there increasingly difficult.

Queen Elizabeth made one other vital contribution to the growth of a prosperous health resort by visiting Bath in 1574 with the whole of her privy council (see Chapter 4). Although she did not personally bathe in the waters, her courtiers undoubtedly took serious note of the civilised pleasures on offer. Some of them in fact made a quick return to explore for themselves, including the Lord Chancellor (the Earl of Sussex), who was given authority in 1578 to borrow four carts 'to carry his stuff to the baths and back again to the court'. In 1590, Lord Burleigh wrote to the queen from Bath apologising for his non-attendance at court. He explained that he was in the middle of his cure and could not break off the treatment without causing harm and delay to his recovery.

Courtiers who had visited Bath were quick to recommend the treatment to their friends - as Sir Walter Raleigh did to Lord Cobham in 1601: 'I will presently return to the Bath with you', he wrote in an attempt to pressurise his lordship even further. Such visits soon became highly fashionable and the source of general gossip at court. 'Lord North droops and is going to the Bath' wrote one observer in 1610. Indeed, most of the leading members of Elizabeth's court made the journey to this emerging social rendezvous at some time or other - including the Duke of Norfolk and the Earls of Salisbury, Leicester, Lincoln, Cumberland, Northumberland, Sussex, Warwick and Worcester. Each distinguished guest was welcomed most royally by the mayor and corporation at the North Gate of the city to the peel of church bells - and then presented with official gifts in appreciation of their presence in the city.

Army officers, too, joined the throng in an attempt to gain a cure for their wounds. In 1593, for instance, Captain John Buck was given special licence 'to repair to the baths' on full pay for two months. He had apparently 'received a very dangerous hurt' while on service in the Low Countries - but the operation, which had been performed by a surgeon there, had only made matters worse, resulting in 'continual pain and ache in his shoulder and arm'. Similarly Captain Foulkes, who had suffered 'sickness and hurts' abroad, had been granted 'a passport' to visit Bath for two months during the spring of 1593, but had been so sick during his stay that he had been unable to bathe. He was now granted a further two months in the autumn and the attendance of two servants.

By 1602, this rapid rise in health tourism had become so substantial that the mayor (Thomas Power) was forced to write a hurried letter to the Court of Requests seeking to excuse the city's most prominent baker (John Sachfield) from attendance. He pleaded that Sachfield's services were urgently needed to bake bread for the large influx of noblemen and other visitors to the resort. Indeed, the baker had already been forced to buy in extra stocks of grain from the market at Warminster to make good the shortfall in Bath.

(iii) The Corporation takes Control

The sudden growth of this new market coincided with dramatic changes (both political and economic) which were taking place within the city of Bath. The dissolution of Bath

Priory in 1539 had enabled the corporation not only to complete its seizure of local political power from the prior (see Chapters 1 and 2), but also to take control of much of the Priory's property within the city. The corporation was now anxious to use this new power to bring about a revival in the local economy, which had been in a state of crisis following the decline of the cloth industry (see Chapter 2).

It was hardly surprising, therefore, that it rapidly spotted the new opportunity presented by the quickening interest in health spas. Many members of the corporation were themselves shopkeepers, innkeepers and lodging house owners, whose trade would stand to benefit considerably from any influx of visitors - just as the broader community would benefit from a boost to employment. It was therefore crucial that its own control over the hot water baths was firmly established. This task, however, was to prove more difficult than it seemed.

The story of what happened is complex in the extreme and firmly entangled in legal niceties. The main points, however, are clear enough. Until the dissolution of Bath Priory in 1539, control of the baths had been exclusively in the hands of the prior - after which they reverted to the control of the crown. However, as part of his 'redundancy' settlement in 1539, Prior Holloway was granted the lease of a house in Stall Street together with the rights to all the profits from the baths. On Holloway's death in 1547, Richard Frampton (former crown bailiff) secured a lease from the crown for the same property and immediately assumed (rightly or wrongly) the rights to the baths as an appurtenance of the house.

Shortly afterwards, Frampton assigned his lease to a local physician, **Humphrey Cotton**, who quickly and wisely gained a special grant from the crown confirming his control over the baths. The letters patent of 1550 praised Cotton's 'long study in the art of physic' through which he had 'found how to cure and heal any our subjects, being diseased, of diverse infirmities...and kinds of gout by virtue of the waters of our baths commonly called the wells or baths of Bath Town'. It then went on to grant him the management and profits of the baths 'for life' in return for a payment to the crown of four pence a day - on condition that one of the baths should be reserved without charge for the use of the poor.

Two years later, however, the situation became even more complicated when Edward VI granted the Priory's former property in Bath, which had included the hot water baths, as an endowment for the new grammar school - with the corporation as trustee! (see Chapter 3). A struggle for the possession of the baths now became inevitable. Believing that Cotton had no legal right to the baths and that he had merely assumed unauthorised control through his occupancy of the house in Stall Street, the corporation launched a policy of harassment to secure his eviction.

So serious did this become that Cotton was forced to lodge a complaint before the Court of Requests against John Davis (the mayor), Edward Ludwell, Richard Chapman and other members of the corporation. In it he alleged that they had been continual 'menacers', interfering with the operation of his work and treating him 'as never poor man was evil treated before'. Finally, 'still persevering in their hateful mind', they had taken the keys of the baths from him 'by force of arms', refusing him entry to the baths - to the utter ruin of himself, his wife and his nine children. Furthermore, he had now lost his considerable three-year investment on the cleaning, repair and improvement of the baths.

The complaint was eventually heard in January 1554 by the privy council's commission of enquiry. In its report, the commission ruled that Cotton was to surrender

IN PRAISE OF THE BATHS OF BATH

Dr William Turner was a leading physician who, after visiting the spas on the continent, wrote the first definitive work on the virtue of hot water baths. A scholarly and religious man, he not only published a three-volume work on the healing qualities of herbs, but also became - later in life - the Dean of Wells.

In *The Baths of Bath in England* (1568), he listed eighty-six diseases or health problems which, he stated, could be cured by a visit to the baths. These included:

the premature birth of babies
constipation
trembling of the heart
foulness of the skin
diabetes causing 'too much water'
sciatica
the madness called melancholia
dullness of smelling
diseases of the nostrils
barrenness of man or woman
piles
worms in the belly
members that are made numb with cold

shortness of breath
deafness or dullness of hearing
stones in the bladder
hardness of any place in the body
breaking of bones
leprosy upon the skin
French pox
dullness of the eyesight
gout
the trembling of any member
tingling in the ears
infertility
forgetfulness

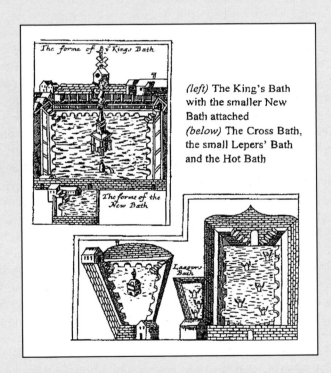

(left) The King's Bath with the smaller New Bath attached
(below) The Cross Bath, the small Lepers' Bath and the Hot Bath

These delightful drawings from John Speed's map of 1610 show the five main baths (new or refurbished) which were in operation by the end of the sixteenth century. Notice the recesses where bathers could sit and the slips which led down into the baths. (Author's collection)

his claim to the baths (and certain other properties, which were also in dispute) to the mayor and corporation; but that he was to receive in compensation the sum of ninety pounds. Whatever the merits of its legal case or its commendable plan to use the baths in order to boost the local economy, the corporation had again resorted to tactics of a most dubious nature in order to secure its aim - as it had done over its acquisition of church property and the school's endowment.

Having taken control of the baths, the corporation was quick to appoint a '**keeper of the baths**' to be responsible for their management. As with most civic offices, the post was farmed out to individuals at a rent in the clear knowledge that the office holder would be able to make a handsome profit out of the sizeable tips received from wealthy clientele. From the outset, it became normal practice to offer the post to the sergeants-at-arms (see above for their other duties). In 1569, therefore, Henry Mace, town sergeant, paid 59s 8d 'for the baths'. By 1573, with the rapid increase in visitors, the job was divided with Thomas Burr, town sergeant, paying 20s 0d 'for the King's Bath' and John White 39s 0d for the other baths.

Their duties were to be in attendance during the two sessions of bathing each day; to ensure that the doors were locked at night; and supervise the 'guides' who cleaned the baths and assisted the bathers in and out of the water. Apart from receiving annual payments from the keepers, the corporation itself made very little profit as such from the baths. The only other source of income came from the rents paid by the seven or eight favoured individuals who were permitted to have their own private doors from their own houses into the King's Bath at a charge of five shillings a year.

(iv) The Baths in the Late Sixteenth Century

The baths over which the corporation gained control in 1554 were not in the very best of condition. It is true that - according to John Leland and William Harrison - the basic structure of the three main baths remained intact. **The Cross Bath**, which was named after the cross standing in its middle, was 'very temperate and pleasant, having eleven or twelve arches of stone in the sides thereof, for men to stand under when rain does ought annoy them'. **The Hot Bath** (or Common Bath, as people referred to it at the time) was smaller with only seven arches. It was appropriately named, 'for at the first coming into it, men think that it would scald their flesh and loose it from the bone; but after a season...it is more tolerable and easy to be borne'. **The King's Bath** was much more impressive in both size and splendour. Surrounded by a high stone wall, it had thirty-two arches 'for men and women to stand in separately'. It was used mainly by 'the gentry', who conducted themselves in a decent manner - unlike the situation found in the baths and hot houses' on the continent, which apparently were 'little better than brothels'.

However, in spite of the fact that all three baths were clearly operational in 1554, the facilities on offer were basic in the extreme and hardly suitable to act as the centrepiece of a fashionable health resort. It was Dr William Turner who highlighted **their deficiencies** in a scathing attack in 1562. He not only lambasted the complacency of physicians for shamefully neglecting to send their patients there, but also - in particular - the utter meanness of rich men who, knowing that the baths were already profitable, would 'not bestow one penny upon improvements'. He noted in passing that although they were quite willing to spend vast sums on 'cockfightings, tennisplays, parks, banquetings, pageants and plays', not one of these rich men had spent a single groat on these marvellous baths over the previous twenty years.

Turner then went on to draw up an urgent list of **suggested improvements**. First of all, the baths needed to be properly cleaned at 8.00pm every evening with the old water completely drained away and the bath 'full of fresh and wholesome water' by the next morning - a system which clearly did not exist in 1562. Indeed, according to William Harrison, the baths were simply closed twice a day so that - with the waters boiling 'very fervently' - they could 'purge themselves from all such filth as the diseased do leave'. Secondly, Turner recommended that, although the baths could be left open to the atmosphere under normal conditions 'so that the vapours might go out', in really bad weather each bath should have a temporary cover to protect the bathers.

Thirdly, there should be some areas within the complex which offered privacy to those bathers who 'would not be gladly seen in the baths'. He suggested that a gallery should be constructed over the baths, which could house a number of 'artificial baths' so that 'those honest people...may bathe themselves in vessels of wood made for that purpose'. Fourthly, separate baths should be created both for those with 'infectious or horrible diseases' and for women. He vehemently condemned the fact that no partition was provided between men and women as they bathed - a situation which forced them 'to go together like unreasonable beasts to the destruction of both body and soul of very many'. Finally, he recommended a special bath for horses so that those with diseases in the legs and joints 'might stand in the bath almost to the belly'.

Turner's well-reasoned attack quickly paid dividends. Stung into action both by his criticism and by economic necessity, the corporation set in motion a programme of improvements during the last quarter of the century - funded in part by donations from those 'rich men', who had been so fiercely condemned. In 1576, **the New Bath** was opened exclusively for women. Adjacent to the King's Bath, which supplied its water, this smaller bath with just eight seats was later styled the Queen's Bath after a visit in 1613 by Anne of Denmark, wife of James I. Turner would undoubtedly have been pleased by the fact that the corporation had provided its two justices with 'purses' so that they could organise a house-to-house collection in aid of the new bath.

The Lepers' Bath (or Poor Folks' Bath) was situated in Nowhere Lane next to the refurbished Hot Bath, from which it drew its water. Founded by Dr John de Feckenham in 1576 'for the benefit of people diseased with leprosy, pox, scabs and great aches', it was very small in size and was linked to the adjacent Lepers' Hospital. This had also been built through de Feckenham's generosity in the same year to provide accommodation for seven people with serious skin diseases. **The Horse Bath**, which stood outside the South Gate and was fed by the overflow from the King's Bath, followed soon afterwards in 1598.

Meanwhile, the King's Bath had been embellished in 1578 through the provision of an elaborate structure over the central hot water inlet. This consisted of a pinnacled tower with recessed seats for bathers in an area known as 'the Kitchen' (in view of the intense heat which rose from the spring). It also contained a drinking fountain, which enabled people to drink pure water from the spring itself rather than the polluted water of the bath (which had been the previous practice). Further improvements were made between 1598 and 1601, including the installation and painting of a new clock; the painting of the queen's arms and 'the lion and the vane upon the fountain'; the installation of twelve metal rings in the walls of the bath as grips for bathers made unsteady by the flow of the water; and masonry repairs on the steps and the slips (or passage ways) leading into the bath.

Finally, the Cross Bath was also given a face-lift. During a major refurbishment in 1593-94, a sluice was installed to make possible the daily draining and cleansing of the bath; three dressing rooms constructed for the comfort of bathers; and a new cross erected in a structure which incorporated four additional seats covered by a dome.

Even by 1577, when William Harrison wrote his *Description of England*, the improvements were already most striking. 'What cost of late hath been bestowed on these baths by divers of the nobility, gentry, communality and clergy, it lies not in me to declare; yet, as I hear, they are not only very much repaired and garnished...but also better ordered, cleanlier kept and more friendly provision made for such poverty as daily repairs thither'. Although great strides had been made in the transformation of the old baths into a civilised spa, some of Turner's recommendations were proving more difficult to achieve.

The corporation did in fact try its best to deal with the problem of the exposure of bathers during periods of inclement weather, but with limited success. Although it had authorised the **erection of covers** as early as 1569, it was forced to pay workmen in 1588 'for taking down the covering of the Hot Bath' (presumably because they were either ineffective or unwieldy). A further experiment was tried in 1621, when covers were installed at the Cross Bath - covers which (according to one observer) were capable of being removed 'in a quarter of an hour as occasion may serve'. Alas, these were to suffer the same fate in 1631, when orders were given for their removal.

Nor did the corporation enjoy any lasting success either with the total **segregation of sexes** or the control of immoral and indecent behaviour. Although it is true that those women who preferred could now bathe in a bath of their own, the practice of mixed nude bathing had a long tradition in Bath. As early as 1449, for instance, Bishop Beckington had been horrified at the unruly and unseemly activities he had witnessed. 'The heavenly gift of warm and healing waters...is turned into an abuse by the shamelessness and uncleanness of the people of that city'. Bathers, he complained, who had put on drawers or smocks 'to cover their privy parts', soon found that the locals 'barbarously and shamelessly strip them of the same garments and reveal them to the gaze of the bystanders'.

The situation did not improve. Dr John Jones, in 1572, pleaded for the total separation of the sexes 'so that they may not see and embrace each other, it being not only so indecent, but also a thing most uncivil and barbarous'. Complaints along these lines had clearly reached the ears of the privy council in London. In 1573, therefore, the council wrote a stern letter to the mayor insisting that the instructions, which had already been made 'for the ordering of the baths', be strictly enforced. In spite of all these efforts, however, the problem was to continue throughout the seventeenth century (see *Stuart Bath: Life in the Forgotten City*).

(v) A Visit to the Spa

Patients who wished to visit Bath's new health resort were forced, first of all, to endure a highly uncomfortable and **hazardous journey** by horse or coach along roads which were badly rutted and often infested with highway robbers. The approach into Bath itself via steep descents was particularly difficult. According to Fynes Moryson, writing about his travels in England, coaches were very rare in the middle of the sixteenth century. Most people therefore travelled by horse (which was very costly), changing their mounts every ten miles or so at the post horse stations along the route.

Even by 1605, when Moryson commenced his travels, coaches could only be hired in London - that is, if you could persuade a highly reluctant coachman to venture across England where 'the ways far from London are so dirty'. The alternative was to travel in a covered wagon of a goods carrier - 'but this kind of journeying is so tedious', he complained, with early starts and late arrivals at the inns. Wealthier visitors would normally bring with them several carts in which to carry curtains for the bed, plate for the table, fuel for the fire and clothes for the duration of their stay - not to mention several casks of their own brew of ale. The Earl of Sussex, as we have seen, brought four carts with him in 1579; while in 1613 Anne of Denmark required twenty.

Having arrived at the resort, there was a good **choice of accommodation**. An observer had noticed that, after the queen's visit in 1574, the city had 'wonderfully beautified itself in fine houses for victualling and lodging'. Quite apart from the several inns, there were numerous private lodging houses, some of which were run by local physicians - including Abbey House, the Prior's former dwelling, which was leased by Dr John Sherwood; and the house now known as Abbey Church House which, from 1591, was occupied by Dr Robert Baker. Sherwood's house was particularly well placed for visits to the King's Bath - an important factor, because most people preferred to change in their lodgings rather than risk the sub-standard changing facilities at the baths.

Medical opinion at the time was unanimous in urging the **need for proper preparation** before visiting the city - in consultation with the patient's own doctor at home. Dr William Turner even urged people to avoid making the journey at all 'unless a learned physician despairs of healing your sickness'. Once the decision had been taken to visit Bath, it was important to pray for forgiveness, because sickness was regarded as 'a symptom of sin'. 'If God has smitten you with any diseases', wrote Turner, 'before you go to the bath, you must confess your sins and show repentance'. It was then important to choose the very best time of year for a visit, avoiding cold, windy or rainy weather. Early summer (April to May) or early autumn (September to October) were regarded as being ideal - certainly not July and August.

In August 1552, Richard Goodrich wrote to Sir William Cecil advising him that it would be extremely unwise to rush to Bath immediately, as he intended. Not only had he

This contemporary print, entitled Street Cries, *illustrates more of the ordinary basket traders and workers who would have been a familiar sight around the markets and streets of Bath in Tudor times. By courtesy of the Pepys Library, Magdalene College, Cambridge.*

made no preparations for lodging and 'diet' (including his special drink made with 'slow-dried malt'), this was quite the worse time to visit the city, 'being so dangerous for fevers and so near Bristol, where the pestilence rages'. 'The benefit of your legs', he argued, 'is not to be sought with so great a hazard of your whole health'. His advice was to defer until the spring of the following year, when conditions would be better.

Having eventually arrived at Bath, the patient was then urged to take **local medical advice**, because each bath boasted different qualities and therefore specialised in treating specific complaints. The local doctor would also be able to prescribe a full course of treatment to include - in addition to bathing - massage, poultices, cordials and ointments. First of all, however, it was important to rest for one or two days to get over the effects of the journey and 'to clear the body from superfluities' (i.e. through movement of the bowels).

The best time for a visit to the baths was 'an hour after sun rising', immediately after a half-hour walk in the fresh air. A second visit was permissible in the evening at least seven hours after mid-day dinner. Patients were recommended to bathe on an empty stomach and to stay in the water between one and two hours. There should be no eating or drinking during that period, although some physicians did permit their weaker clients to take into the bath either two spoonfuls of raisins or a few soaked prunes with a little water and wine. On leaving the water, the bather was to wrap up well and return to his lodgings, where he should sweat for a while in a warm bed. During the whole period of his treatment the patient, who was given a strict diet, was to avoid all over-indulgence: 'You must rise from the table with some appetite, so that you could eat more if you would'. Furthermore, he was 'to keep himself chaste from all women - and so must he for a month after'.

Turner also recommended other **specialised forms of treatment**. 'Bucketing' could be highly effective for those with catarrh or head colds. 'A bucket should be held over their heads with a hole in it the bigness of a man's little finger, about four feet above their heads' - so that 'the water may come down with great might' upon the affected parts. Other physicians suggested 'two men alternately pouring water from buckets with a quick movement upon the patient's head' - with between twenty and thirty buckets used initially in total. Secondly, Turner believed that the 'clay or mud of the bath' could be beneficial 'for any swollen or hardened parts'. In between bathings, therefore, the doctor would plaster the affected parts, allowing it to be hardened by either the sun or a fire in the room - following which 'the foulness of the clay could be washed away by 'the water in the bath'.

Thirdly, he considered that breathing in the vapour or 'hot breath that rises up from the bath' could bring considerable benefits to certain ailments. Finally, if he weather proved to be highly inclement, he recommended a course of private bathing at home, making use of the spring water 'in a bathing vessel' in the patient's own bedchamber. Indeed, he thought that it would be a good idea to create, within the bathing complex itself, a good number of small baths or bath tubs, which could be individually covered and partitioned. All-in-all, the course of treatment at the baths was to last a minimum of three or four weeks.

Quite apart from the merits of bathing, it had long been believed that **drinking the waters** could help purge the body. However, it was Dr John Jones who was the first physician in Bath to advocate drinking the local spa water in his book, *The Booke of Bathes Ayde*, published in 1572: 'About an hour after sun rising...drink the water out of the spring...So much of the water as shall not be grievous to the stomach may be drunk'.

This action, he believed, would not only quench the thirst, but also purge the body by bringing relief to the problem of constipation. By the seventeenth century, Bath spring water had become highly fashionable and was being marketed in bottles. In 1625, for instance, Lady Manchester was prescribed 'a pottle of bath water out of the spring of the King's Bath'; while Queen Elizabeth herself had become something of an addict. Sadly, however, she ordered water from Buxton, not Bath!

*****

As the Tudor Age drew to its close in 1603, the citizens of Bath could rejoice at the striking transformation that had taken place. Although many outward symbols of its medieval heritage were still intact and rightly prized (including its sturdy outer defences and its priceless water supply), the city's appearance and atmosphere had been noticeably modernised with the arrival of a new church, a new school, a new row of houses, a new market house, a new royal charter, a newly-reformed religion and a newly-furbished spa. The old Priory, which had dominated life for centuries, had finally disappeared; while political power had been placed firmly in the hands of local people. The economy, too, was being skilfully adapted to changing circumstances - for while agriculture remained important, the cloth industry (on which the city's affluence had been built in the middle ages) was gradually giving way to health tourism with the rise of a new leisure resort.

This modernisation, however, came at a cost to local people. A city that had previously been largely self-sufficient, concentrating its efforts on the production of food, cloth and other goods, now found itself catering for a consumer society of affluent visitors - a task which required different skills and attitudes. The management of this transition was to prove painful for some - particularly those spinners and weavers who found themselves impoverished and unemployed. Furthermore, the sense of community and harmony, which had been created within the small medieval parishes; the colour which had been brought into drab lives through the drama of church ritual; the continuity with the past, which had been established through the cult of the dead; the fun, which had been generated through processions, festivals and feasts - much of this had been swept away as the Reformation had taken root.

Queen Elizabeth had in fact done her best to create a number of new festivals to fill the void (as Philippa Gregory has shown). Her accession day (17 November) was raised to the status of an annual feast-day to be celebrated nationally with church services, performances by players, bell ringing and local festivities. Similarly, St George's Day continued to be celebrated on 23 April (even though all other saints' days had been abolished) - as did the anniversary of the defeat of the Spanish Armada (9 August) and, later, the anniversary of the discovery of the Gunpowder Plot (5 November). It was not enough. The rise of Puritanism in the early Stuart period was to bring about in north Somerset a tightening of moral standards, the suppression of many popular sports and entertainments and the growth of bitter factions, which badly damaged the city's old-fashioned neighbourliness. In Bath, as elsewhere, 'Merry England' was in a state of terminal decline.

SOURCES USED IN CHAPTER 6

1. Printed Material

Bettey, J.H: 'Life & Litigation in Bath and its Environs in the 16th Century' (in *Bath History*, vol. 6, 1996)

Chappell, Helen: 'A Medieval Christmas' (in *Heritage*, January 2005)

Chaundler, Thomas: *Libellus de Laudibus Civitatum* (1542)

Davenport, Peter: *Medieval Bath Uncovered* (2002)

Exwood, Maurice & Lehmann, H.L. (eds.): *The Journal of William Schellinks' Travels in England, 1661-63* (Camden Society, 5th Series, vol. 1, 1993)

Fawcett, Trevor & Bird, Stephen: *Bath: A History and Guide* (1994)

Gregory, Philippa: 'Reinventing Elizabeth' (in *BBC History*, November 2005)

Harrison, William: *Description of England*, 1577 (ed. F.J. Furnivall, 1877 edtn.)

Hentzer, Paul: *A Journey into England in 1598*, ed. Horace Walpole (Aungervyle Society Reprints, 1881)

Holland, Elizabeth: 'The Earliest Bath Guildhall' (in *Bath History*, vol. 2, 1988)

Hutton, Ronald: *The Stations of the Sun: A History of the Ritual Year in Britain* (1996)

James, P.R: *The Baths of Bath in the 16th and Early 17th Centuries* (1938)

James, P.R: *Documents of the City of Bath*, pt. 2 (1942 transcript, BRO)

Jenkins, E.S. (ed.): *Registers of St Michael, Bath, 1569-1760* (1988)

Jewers, Arthur (ed.): *Registers of the Abbey Church of SS Peter & Paul, Bath, 1569-1800*, vol. 2 (1901)

Jones, John: *The Booke of Bathes Ayde* (1572)

King, A.J, & Watts, B.H: *The Municipal Records of Bath, 1189-1604* (1885)

Osborn, James M. (ed.): *The Autobiography of Thomas Whythorne*, c. 1576 (1961 edtn.)

Picard, Liza: *Elizabeth's London: Everyday Life in Elizabethan London* (2003)

Razzell, P.(ed.): *The Journals of Two Travellers in Elizabethan and Early Stuart Times* (1998) - regarding the travels of Thomas Platter

Shickle, C.W: *Ancient Deeds Belonging to the Corporation of Bath, 13th to 16th Centuries* (1921)

Shickle, C.W. (ed.): *Registers of St James, Bath, 1569-1685,* vol. 1 (1903)

Sim, Alison: *Pleasures and Pastimes in Tudor England* (1999)

Smith, Lucy T. (ed.): *The Itinerary of John Leland, 1535-1543* (1907 edtn.)

Southern, Antonia: 'More than Child's Play' (in *BBC History Magazine*, December 2004)

Stokes, James (ed): *Records of Early English Drama: Somerset, vol. 1, The Records* (1996)

Stubbes, Philip: *Anatomy of Abuses in England*, 1583 (1877-79 edtn., pt. 1, ed. Frederick J Furnivall)

Symons, Katharine: *The Grammar School of King Edward VI, Bath and its Ancient Foundation* (1934)

Turner, William: *A Book of the Nature and Properties of the Baths in England as of Other Baths in Germany and Italy* (1562)

Turner, William: *A Book of the Baths of Bath in England* (1568)

Wilson, F.P: *The Plague in Shakespeare's England* (1927)

Wilson, Francesca: *Strange Island: Britain through Foreign Eyes, 1395-1940* (1955)

Wroughton, John: *A Community at War: The Civil War in Bath & North Somerset, 1642-1650* (1992)

Wroughton, John: *Stuart Bath: Life in the Forgotten City* (2004)

2. Documentary Material:

Bath Record Office: Bath Chamberlain's Accounts, 1569-1603

Inquisition as to Flesh Eaters, 1572 (BRO, no. 32)

National Archives: Calendar of Patent Rolls, 1550 (pestilence in Bristol); 1562 (the Garland case)

Acts of the Privy Council, 1552 (the Glover case); 1573, 1578, 1591 (complaint by the freemen) ,1593

Calendar of State Papers Domestic, 1547-53, 1590, 1595-97, 1598-1601, 1576

For a fuller account of the water supply, public health and the effects of plague, typhus and smallpox in Bath, see John Wroughton: *Stuart Bath: Life in the Forgotten City, 1603-1714.*

Index